D1453427

To talk of many things

Published in our
centenary year
≈ **2004** ≈
MANCHESTER
UNIVERSITY
PRESS

'The time has come,' the Walrus said,
   'To talk of many things:
Of shoes – and ships – and sealing wax –
   Of cabbages – and kings –
And why the sea is boiling hot –
   And whether pigs have wings.'

(Lewis Carroll (1832–98),
Through the Looking Glass, 1872)

To talk of many things

AN AUTOBIOGRAPHY

Dame Kathleen Ollerenshaw

Manchester University Press

Manchester and New York

distributed exclusively in the USA by Palgrave

Published by Manchester University Press
Oxford Road, Manchester M13 9NR, UK
and Room 400, 175 Fifth Avenue, New York, NY 10010, USA
www.manchesteruniversitypress.co.uk

Distributed exclusively in the USA by
Palgrave, 175 Fifth Avenue, New York,
NY 10010, USA

Distributed exclusively in Canada by
UBC Press, University of British Columbia, 2029 West Mall,
Vancouver, BC, Canada V6T 1Z2

British Library Cataloguing-in-Publication Data
A catalogue record for this book is available from the British Library

Library of Congress Cataloging-in-Publication Data applied for

ISBN 0 7190 6987 4 *hardback*

EAN 978 0 7190 6987 1

First published 2004

13 12 11 10 09 08 07 06 05 04   10 9 8 7 6 5 4 3 2 1

Typeset
by Northern Phototypesetting Co. Ltd, Bolton
Printed in Great Britain
by Biddles Ltd, King's Lynn

To my mother – who would have been amazed

Author's publications

'Old Schools in England and Wales in 1954', *Education* (Journal of the Association of Education Committees), Vol. 106, No. 2248 (September 21 1955), 475–82

'Education for Girls' (Conservative Political Centre, June 1958)

Education for Girls (London: Faber & Faber, 1961)

The Girls' Schools (London: Faber & Faber, 1967)

'Returning to Teaching' (Department of Educational Research, University of Lancaster, 1972–73)

The Lord Mayor's Party (children's book, illustrated by the author) (Manchester: E. J. Morton, 1976)

'Form and Pattern', *Proceedings of the Royal Institution of Great Britain*, Vol. 53 (1981), 1–24

'Manchester Memoirs' (Manchester Literary and Philosophical Society, 1981–82)

'Magic Squares of Order Four' (with Sir Hermann Bondi, KCB FRS), *Philosophical Transactions of the Royal Society*, A 306 (1982), 223–532

'On "most perfect" or "complete" 8 x 8 pandiagonal magic squares', *Proceedings of the Royal Society*, A 407 (1986), 250–81

First Citizen (London: Hart-Davis, MacGibbon, 1977)

'Starting with a CCD Image Camera', in Patrick Moore (ed.), *1996 Year Book of Astronomy* (London: Macmillan Reference Books, 1995)

Most-Perfect Pandiagonal Magic Squares – their Construction and Enumeration (with Professor David Brée) (The Institute of Mathematics and its Applications, 1998)

Numerous papers in the Bulletin of the Institute of Mathematics and its Applications, 1965 onward, including:

'Pythagorean Triads, "Mathematics Today"', *Institute of Mathematics and its Applications*, Vol. 40, No. 2 (April 2004)

Contents

List of illustrations

Illustrations appear between pages 112–13 and 160–1

Acknowledgements

This book was a long time in preparation and has passed through many transmogrifications. It began in 1999 at the instigation of Christopher Potter, editor of the publishing company Fourth Estate (now part of HarperCollins), in the aftermath of the hugely successful trend-setting book *Longitude* by Dava Sobel. This was followed by the equally successful *Fermat's Last Theorem* by Simon Singh, *Galileo's Daughter*, also by Dava Sobel, and several others telling of sensational successes in mathematics. The hope was that there might be a similar story about magic squares, in which for a special class of squares I had recently found, with a collaborator, a notable new result. I soon realised that this was not a proposition. A new definitive popular book about magic squares is certainly overdue (the last was written in 1917), but the project was not for me. Such a history, if it is to be worth while and authoritative, would require years of research and travel, mainly in the Far East, and would need the energy, professional expertise – and time – of someone younger than I am, with sufficient years ahead to withstand the enormous worldwide correspondence with a plethora of amateurs and students after publication.

On my confession of inadequacy, Christopher came up with the suggestion that I should write a story of my life seen from the point of view of a mathematician. This was much more promising and the autobiography began. It took time. Without his interest and occasional praise I would have shut down completely. I was, however, greatly helped at this stage by the recently retired Principal and Vice-Chancellor of the University of Manchester Institute of Science and Technology, Professor Harold Hankins, who read my original draft and made most encouraging suggestions. I began to see for myself that a truthful autobiography would not meet the criteria of most publishers. I had experienced no childhood abuse, no hardship; I was happy both at home and at school despite being deaf – and privileged, perhaps sometimes because of this handicap. When, on approaching forty, the first effective hearing aids became available, my life dramatically changed. Largely by chance, I became involved in public service, centred at first mainly in Manchester where I have always lived, but expanding to national and international commitments to mathematics and to education, especially higher education. The story soon got out-of-hand in length – and was 'too jumpy', covering too many diverse fields for most potential readers.

Although I can be a ruthless 'trimmer' of my own screeds, it seemed almost impossible to decide, without assistance, what to cut out and what to leave in, although the requirement of drastic cuts was plain. A miracle occurred. I am fortunate in having a neighbour living across the road from me, Colin Vickerman, who retired a few years ago from the post of chief executive of the Joint Matriculation Board, which had its headquarters in Manchester. In the New Year of 2003, he remarked casually that he would be willing to read what I had written if this would help. This offer I eagerly accepted. It grew into a partnership of invaluable worth to me. Bit-by-bit Colin read every word of every draft chapter and suggested what could be eliminated or modified. Although some points led to discussion and re-writing, I do not recall that there was any suggestion for amendment that I did not instantly agree with and implement. We developed a technique for communication – by written scribbles and exchange of hand-annotated corrected drafts pushed through each other's letter box almost every day (sometime twice a day) for the better part of a year, Saturdays and Sundays not excluded. Between us we have worn a groove across the tarmac of our suburban road. This involved no wasted time in chat or cups of coffee, and could be fitted into whatever else we had to be doing. I shall never be able to express my full gratitude to Colin – and to Eleanor, his wife, who somehow put up with this without complaint, often making her own suggestions from her extensive experience as a graduate teacher of history. Both contribute actively to the local community and are prolific readers. In the final stages of proofreading, when deteriorating sight made the work increasingly difficult for me, Colin's incredibly generous help and enthusiasm became a crucial factor in bringing the project to eventual fruition.

My first draft was reduced by more than a third and the contents much improved as a consequence of many discussions, but when a satisfactory draft was first arrived at, the central problem remained – there was no assured method of publication. Here, I am grateful to Nicholas Conran, a professional musician and conductor, and his wife Jenny. They have a holiday cottage near my own in the Lake District and read both the original and the revised drafts, insisting that it 'must be published'. But where and by whom? I was reluctant to arrange private publication.

Again with Colin's help, and with the intervention of the Vice-Chancellor of Manchester University, Professor Sir Martin Harris, together with that of the chairman of the management board of Manchester University Press, Mrs Margaret Kenyon (the distinguished retired headmistress of Withington Girls' School, who is, as am I, an Honorary Fellow of Somerville College, Oxford), Manchester University Press were approached. Fortuitously, MUP agreed to publish such an appropriate volume in their centenary year'. I am grateful to the staff of MUP for the professional help and guidance they have given me in bringing the book to completion and for the design of the dust cover. I am also extremely grateful to Martin Hargreaves, a professional indexer accustomed to working with MUP, for offering to create the index without charge in recognition of the work I had done over the years for Manchester. The index he designed and constructed has met all my demands and highest hopes.

I owe my thanks to all those who read individual chapters at various stages where these referred to their activities in the past; to Professor Ian Stewart FRS who kindly read those sections that deal specifically with mathematics; to Sir John Manduell and Michael Kennedy for checking details in the chapter about the foundation and early days of the Royal Northern College of Music; to John's successor as Director of the RNCM, Professor Edward Gregson; and to Sir Patrick Moore FRS for his preface. To Kevin Kilburn, twice president of the Manchester Astronomical Society, and to Ray Grover, a member of the Society, I owe thanks for their help over several years. My thanks are also due to

Ray Grover for his computer reproduction of my arms and motto and for other pictures.

In particular, I owe a big debt to Bernard Lawson, who was lord mayor's secretary when I was Lord Mayor of Manchester in 1975–76, living for the year, together with my family, in the town hall. Bernard and his wife, Ann, became and have remained staunch friends. His exceptional knowledge of civic affairs over the past thirty years has been invaluable, and his enthusiasm for the book, never doubting eventual publication even when my morale was at its lowest, has been an inestimable source of encouragement.

To the many stalwart friends and mentors of my own and earlier generations and to others who have now gone their way ahead of me, especially to the beloved members of my own family for whom I mourn and to whom I owe so much, I extend in fondest memory my enduring devotion and gratitude.

Kathleen Ollerenshaw
April 2004

Foreword
Sir Patrick Moore CBE FRS FRAS

When Dame Kathleen asked me to write a foreword for her autobiography I was deeply honoured. I have been privileged to know her for many years, and I well know that she is indeed a most remarkable person, who has made notable contributions in many fields of activity during a long life. In her main interest, mathematics, she recently received international acclaim for devising a method of construction and enumeration for an infinite class of magic squares. She has been active in civic and national affairs for over fifty years, particularly in the field of higher education and the creation of the new universities. She was Lord Mayor of Manchester in 1975–76 and is an Honorary Freeman of the City. There can be few people, if any, who have had such a varied career. Moreover, all this has been accomplished despite personal tragedies. She has outlived not only her husband, but also their daughter and their son. She has battled with, and overcome, deafness since early childhood, in no way allowing this handicap to restrict her activities.

Dame Kathleen has countless friends and admirers, and I very much doubt whether she has ever had enemies. Her autobiography is timely, because she has much to relate. Her career is far from over; as her book comes out, the most suitable thing we can say is: 'Thanks for everything – and keep going for a long time yet.'

Patrick Moore

CHAPTER 1

Passion for numbers

It began with Peter Rabbit. This was the first book that I was able, aged about 4 or 5, to read for myself. I told my mother proudly that Peter's jacket had four brass buttons and I drew them for her. This must have been the first sign of what has proved to be a life-long passion for numbers and for the patterns in which whole numbers can be arranged. I could count to a hundred long before I could read fluently and was always counting. If we can count to a hundred, then why not further and further? This brought me quickly to very large numbers. Once I knew my two-times table, multiplying successively by two, which someone showed me how to do, gave strings of numbers with more and more digits that would not fit into one line on a piece of paper. Soon these numbers were written in rows and columns as multiplication tables and they became familiar friends.

Both my father and my mother had been born and brought up in Northamptonshire; my mother the eldest of eleven – my father the seventh child in a family of twelve children. They married on 15 January 1908 and, after a honeymoon in Wengen, Switzerland (I still treasure the large carved wooden brown bear they bought), came to Manchester where I have had my home all my life. They rented an Edwardian yellow-brick semi-detached house that still stands exactly as then (now occupied by university students), No.1 Parkgate Avenue – a small cul-de-sac fifty yards from Palatine Road in Withington, about four miles from the centre of Manchester. I was very fond of this house. It has a good staircase and hall, two entertaining rooms and a kitchen with scullery on the ground floor, three bedrooms and a bathroom on the first floor, a two-roomed attic, a cellar and a small garden.

There were only two of us. Mother had seen enough of large families – never enough money or time. My sister Betty was born on 27 October

1908 – at 3 o'clock, in time for an afternoon nap. I was born in the same front bedroom four years later on 1 October 1912 at 7 o'clock in the morning. The previous afternoon mother and father had been walking home from the shops; mother dragging behind. Father, not an uncaring man but typical of his era, grew impatient: 'Come on, Mary, just put one foot in front of the other. I want my tea.' All babies were born at home, brought into the world by the family doctor assisted maybe by a midwife. Fathers were firmly banished to a downstairs room, anxiously awaiting the sound of the first cry. Father said that when he was brought into the bedroom to see this newborn second child, I looked at him wide-eyed as if to say I was ready for an immediate day's work. Today this would be described as 'hitting the ground running'. I have always been an early-riser, which was lucky, because mother used to say that if we were not out of bed and properly dressed by 7.30 each day at the latest then we would end up in the workhouse. This had real meaning, because the workhouse buildings in all their stark Victorian reality (later converted into our local hospital) were near where we lived. Nowadays I go to bed late as well, burning the candle at both ends. It doesn't seem to do me any harm and it gives more precious hours to the day.

Betty, being four years older, was always one educational stage ahead. There were no nursery schools and I had mainly to amuse myself: with pencil and paper; with dominoes and playing cards; making patterns with bits of coloured paper and using a box of cowrie shells for counters. I spent a lot of time with my mother in the kitchen, stamping out circles in pastry; making little animals from dough; arranging rock cakes (mother's speciality) or jam tarts on the baking plates. The significance of these arrangements in the context of the mathematics of 'closest packing' was certainly not known to either of us, but I liked counting the rows and twisting the little bits of pastry left over into rosettes. I played outdoors on my own, bouncing a ball against the wall of the house or playing hopscotch, adding up scores to try to improve on last time. I became expert with a skipping rope, always counting, trying to break my own record of how many skips before tripping.

I was 5 in 1917 when the First World War was at its grim worst and I learnt to knit. I began to knit a 'scarf for the soldiers'. The wool kept wrapping itself around the needles, making extra stitches at each new row and the scarf grew wider and wider. The wool soon ran out. Mother gave me money to walk to the shops to buy more wool – by myself aged 5, the best part of a mile along a busy main road. When I got there the lady behind the counter asked me 'What ply?' I did not know what ply meant. Colour was easy: there was only one – khaki. I told her that I was knitting a scarf for the soldiers, but she refused to sell me any wool unless I knew what ply it was to be. I ran all the way home trying not to cry. The scarf was never finished. Wild horses wouldn't have dragged me back there ever again. I pass the shop, now a greengrocers, almost every day and never forget the stinging rebuff.

In one context or another, ply and twists and spirals came to fascinate me. The 'count' in spinning was a main concern when I was in my first paid job in cotton research. Ply turns up in rope; in electric flex and cables; in the double helix and DNA; in the ornamental stems of Georgian drinking glasses; and, by extension, in spiral staircases; in the tool called an augur that bores holes in wood; in nature all over the place, and, as a surface, in the Archimedes screws that lift sludge at the City of Manchester's sewage disposal works. The ideas associated with ply have been a strand in the golden threads of mathematics that have enriched my life.

There were few toys, but Betty and I each had a boy doll we greatly loved. I called my doll – guess what? – Peter. He had a red jersey, not a blue jacket like his namesake Peter Rabbit. Betty called her doll SonJohn in one word. This name came from the nursery rhyme:

> Diddle, diddle, dumpling, my son John,
> Went to bed with his trousers on.
> One shoe off and one shoe on,
> Hey, diddle, dumpling, my son John.

I thought this a lovely jingle. SonJohn had a smart blue suit and a tie made for him by one of mother's sisters. Both Peter and SonJohn had cloth faces. SonJohn's face eventually wore out with too much loving. Peter could say 'Mamma' when he was tipped up. Sadly, when about 10 years old, I was persuaded to send Peter away to a deprived child whose needs were greater than mine. In a tough, grown-up do-good-ing mood, I packed him in a shoe box, wrapped it in brown paper and took him to the local post office. The counter lady took the parcel, weighed it, took my money, and hurled Peter to the back with other parcels. He went 'Mamma' as he fell. I burst into tears and begged to have my parcel back. Just as it had been with the wool some five years earlier, the counter lady was adamant: 'Once a parcel is accepted there can be no retrieving it.'

Although we had few toys, we had nice clothes and, father being in the shoe trade, good shoes. Slippers had buttons, black boot buttons, said to be like my eyes. They were difficult to do up and were always flying off. In winter, legs would be encased in brown leather gaiters, also buttoned laboriously using a button hook. They hurt behind the knees and I hated them. Both Betty and I had our hair done in plaits. Mother was never very clever about these plaits – she didn't have the patience.

Betty married in 1933. She and her husband, Roger Wood, set up home in Prestbury about fifteen miles away in Cheshire where they brought up three children. This was close enough for day visits, but not so far away that we ever stayed in one or the other's house overnight. Roger died in 1992; Betty eleven years later in July 2003 aged 94. There are seven grandchildren.

My passion for numbers didn't seem to come from anywhere. Neither mother nor father showed any special interest, although father sometimes noticed and was impressed. With my dominoes, I showed father that we could see that 2×3 is the same as 3×2 by the pattern of six dots. On Armistice Day, 11 November 1918, father came to fetch me, then in my first term at school. I remarked that it was 11 o'clock on the eleventh day of the eleventh month and he thought this was rather bright. He bought me a small Union Flag as we passed a stationer's shop and I waved it excitedly all the way home.

Mother, being the eldest child, had been expected to look after the many siblings and never went to school. She could add up efficiently but never mastered 'take away' or 'carrying' from pence to shillings columns if this meant dividing by twelve. When doing the weekly household accounts she wrote down all expenditure in a ruled cash book and put the pounds (if any remained in her purse at the end of the week) and the spare coins at the bottom of their respective columns, adding them in. The grand total then had to come to the round sum of money father had given her for the week's housekeeping. One week mother was very put out: the pennies column would not add up correctly – there was one penny too many. I suggested that it would come out right if she gave me the penny. She did, and we were both happy.

One day, on arriving home from the shops with my mother, we found outside our gate a house-for-sale board. Although it was only rented, it was for me 'my house'. There had been no warning and I never forgot the sense of shock. My mother, typically, took instant action. Next morning, she walked to the local (now closed) Midland railway station in Didsbury and went by train to Kettering, where she tackled my father's father, Grandpa Timpson, asking him to buy us a house of our own. This he promptly agreed to do. We moved in 1919, when I was 6 years old, to 11 Elm Road, Didsbury.

I was thrilled, aged 6, with living at 11 Elm Road. Men with large heavy brooms swept the pavements once a week. A milk cart with a churn weighing it down at the back came by every day and we ran out with a jug and the appropriate coins. We bought new bread each day, also from a passing horse-drawn cart. On the opposite pavement was a lamp-post. I stood at dusk at our half-landing window and watched for the lamp-lighter, who came with a long pole and switched on the gas jet which then lit the mantel. He came back at dawn to switch it off. I had to be lifted to post letters in the pillar-box at the corner of the road; the same original red Victorian pillar box as I use today.

This house in Elm Road (there were no elm trees, each house had a large lime tree near the gate) was my home from which my husband, Robert, and I were married on 6 September 1939 at the outbreak of the Second World War. This was where our two children spent their childhood. When, in 1946, Robert was finally demobilised from active war service my parents moved to a smaller house around the corner in Pine Road, leaving us in Elm Road. In 1952 we followed them around the corner, into a house we built alongside in their garden. This is where I still live. There have been many changes, many sad times, but much joy too in the fifty years since then. I have wonderful neighbours and many friends nearby. Walls are lined with my most-loved books accumulated over the years. I hope never to have to live anywhere else.

CHAPTER 2

Families

My paternal grandfather, William Timpson, was born in 1829 in Rothwell, a small town near Kettering in Northamptonshire with a reputation for silk weaving and boot-and-shoe manufacture. He was the sixth and youngest child. At the age of 8 he was already helping to make leather boots. Times were hard. His eldest brother, Charles, had walked the 150 miles from Rothwell to the city of Manchester to find work. There was a link between silk weaving and the boot-and-shoe trade. High boots had become the fashion of upper class ladies in the middle of the nineteenth Century. These high boots required strong, thin laces. Silk, with its long fibres, was the ideal raw material for their manufacture. A group of Huguenots from northern France had found refuge over a century before in Macclesfield, a flourishing town fifteen miles south of Manchester. My father's Uncle Charles found work selling boot laces. At the age of 11, William was sent to join his brother Charles. There was no direct rail link between Kettering and Manchester and he was misdirected in Derby. His sandwiches long since eaten and with no money, he was found, alone and weeping, sitting on a station platform in Sheffield. He had a label round his neck giving his intended destination and an elderly gentleman took him to Manchester and delivered him at his brother's address.

William worked for his brother, went to night school and became a member of the local non-conformist church, attending their Bible classes. Manchester was famed for its public libraries and the young William made full use of them, becoming in due course a well-read man. When aged 15, after a quarrel with his brother, he went back to Rothwell to learn shoe-making, at which he became very skilled. However, he soon realised that, whereas it took him a full week to make a good pair of shoes, it took only a few minutes to sell them; and so, at the age of 16, he returned to Manchester with a brother-in-law and in 1865 they opened a boot-and-shoe shop near the centre of the city.

Leather boots were taking over from the clogs of the Lancashire mill workers, but the boots were expected to last indefinitely, as had the clogs. The two young men sold sturdy leather boots made in Northampton-shire that could be repaired repeatedly and continue in use for a work-ing life-time. In 1870 William struck out on his own. William Timpson shops always maintained a strong line in boot and shoe repair and a chain of repair outlets was established in 1903. As the business expanded, premises were acquired for a large warehouse within a few hundred yards of Manchester Cathedral.

Grandpa Timpson was a generous man. It was he in 1919 who so readily paid for our house in Elm Road, Didsbury, when the house my parents rented in Withington was put up for sale. He set great store on caring for employees. As an illustration of this tradition, unusual for its time, when a warehouse hand, caught with a stolen pair of child's boots, was about to be dismissed, Grandpa sent for him. The wrong-doer told him that he had seven children and they could not go to school because they had no shoes (a common occurrence). My grandfather took him along the rows of shelves and gave him boots for each child, telling him never to steal again, but when he needed help to come and ask. Grandpa Timpson showed generosity to anyone in genuine need. He set up a register of men who had lost a foot in war or accident (there were many) and arranged that all such amputees should be supplied with their single shoes without payment. A friend of mine, who lost a leg at sea when his ship was sunk by enemy action in 1942, was supplied with his single shoes by William Timpsons throughout the rest of his life.

Grandpa married Elizabeth Farey, a first cousin, in 1872 and they had eight children: five daughters followed by three sons, the second of whom was my father, named Charles after his uncle. They lived first over their shop in Oldham Street and then moved to Withington in south Manchester. All five daughters were born in Manchester. Grandpa inherited from an uncle a boot-and-shoe factory in Rowsley and, partly to escape the fume-filled air of Manchester which was seriously affect-ing his health, the family moved to Kettering where the three sons were born. There my grandmother, pregnant with a ninth child, died aged 41. Grandpa married again and had four more children. He was a good-looking man with auburn hair which I inherited. By the time I knew him this had turned a soft and silky white. This he wore in a quiff and he favoured a pointed goatee beard. He died aged 80 in 1929.

There was a history of deafness in both the Timpson and the Farey families. When Grandpa first went back to live in Kettering, he was elected as a Liberal to the town council, but had to resign because of his poor hearing. This was inherited by all their children, other than my father who escaped it and had good hearing all his life. Unfortunately, I was a throw-back and inherited this deafness, although it was not apparent until I was at school. One of my father's sisters, Nellie, was almost stone deaf and I still remember how, with some reluctance, we had to shout to her through a large horn that she held to an ear.

Father was born in Kettering in 1881. He lost his right eye in a fire-work accident at the age of 9 and was badly bullied at his day school where the boys ran after him shouting 'little one-eye, little one-eye'. To get him away from this, he was sent to a boarding school in Buxton where the headmaster had created a kinder environment. He left school at 17 and, given no choice about his future, he went automatically into the family business, joining his older brother, Will, in the warehouse in Manchester where he worked until retirement. Betty and I understood about the glass eye and got used to it. He had to go to Germany when a replacement was needed, because before the First World War only there could good glass eyes be made. He had a habit of putting the eye in a tooth-mug at night and leaving it in water on the bathroom window-sill. It scared me and eventually mother persuaded him to leave it in a cupboard where no-one would come across it unexpectedly.

Father was a taciturn and gentle man, strongly influenced by my mother who was always forceful. His main interests were playing golf (not particularly well), watching football (Manchester City, not United which was then only a local club) and glueing himself to the cricket at the Lancashire Cricket Club ground in Old Trafford. He took no part in running the household or in our upbringing, content to leave every-thing to mother. I don't think he ever saw either Betty or me in a bath, even as babies (that was women's work) and I don't think that I ever sat on his lap (it was not expected). The closeness came much later when I was fully grown-up.

If I ever wanted to know something – in history or about world affairs – I would ask father and he always had a worthwhile answer. But if I asked how to spell some word, he would give a 10-minute discourse on the word's derivation, so I soon learnt to go to a dictionary instead. It would never have occurred to either Betty or me to ask father about anything personal (it was not that kind of relationship). We always went to mother for sympathy and the physical love of a goodnight kiss. I never remember father reading to us even when we were little, or playing with us, but then neither did mother; we did our own reading. I do, however, remember father giving me my first grown-up book. We were in a bookshop in Ambleside on our usual Whitsun holiday in the Lake District. I must have been about 12. Father bought me a copy of *Lorna Doone*. I was never more surprised and thrilled with any gift.

Father had no ear for music. We all went routinely every Sunday morning to church (a large Wesleyan edifice with a gallery next to the Manchester Royal Infirmary). Mother liked listening to a good preacher even if the favoured non-conformist chapel was some distance from home. All too often, father, having stayed silent during the first verse of a hymn while he picked up the tune, at the second verse that we had been instructed to leave to the choir, suddenly joined in loudly, wildly off key. This was a dreadful embarrassment. Years later, mother found her own solution. She said that she preferred to go to somewhere nearer home. From then on, father went to chapel alone and we attended the local non-conformist chapel around the corner from Elm Road. It was not until much later, when I was engaged to marry Robert whose home was at the opposite side of Didsbury and near St James's Church, that I began attending Church of England services.

Father was kind, tolerant, considerate and wise in his judgements of people. He became a much-respected magistrate and president of the local Liberal Party Association. The sight of his left eye remained excellent throughout his life and he wore spectacles only to disguise the disfigurement of the artificial right eye. He had excellent hair, which he never lost, even in old age. His main fault from our point of view was that he was an atrocious car-driver. It was a miracle that we escaped a nasty accident in the days before I was old enough to take over the driving. He died in 1967, aged 86, having outlived mother by thirteen years.

Mother, Mary Elizabeth Stops, was born on 20 January 1880, the eldest of the eleven children of Thomas Spincks Stops, who owned a farm in Tiffield near Towcester about twelve miles from Northampton. Towcester was and still is known for its racecourse. Tiffield was used as the winter headquarters of the once-famous Fossett's Circus, and the family always had a soft spot for circuses as a consequence.

All the Stops children were born at home in Tiffield – four girls and seven boys. All except mother, who died aged 74, were long-lived. Westley, the fourth sibling, after a day sightseeing, sat down in his armchair saying he was rather tired – and died. He was 104. The youngest sibling, Vera, blind and being cared for in a home, celebrated her 105th birthday on 29 March 2004 and died a fortnight later. Only one, William, did not marry, but they seemed to have had enough of large families and themselves had only two or three children. Nonetheless, I had twenty first 'Stops' cousins. In September 2003, Uncle Westley's daughter, Angela, organised a family party at her home in Leicestershire to celebrate her fiftieth wedding anniversary. It was a beautiful September Sunday – English countryside at its best. Among sixty or more guests, ten of us were first cousins, the offspring of six of the Stops siblings; all with an unmistakable family resemblance.

The seventh sibling, Alfred, fell from grace by putting a girl from the village in the family way. Grandpa and Granny Stops were so fiercely upset by this that Alfred was thrown out of the family home and his name was never to be mentioned. It is perhaps not a good idea to probe too far into family genealogy: one can find aspects that are best forgotten. There were rumours and a family likeness to my grandfather showed itself retrospectively. Father became interested and he drove mother and me to the village of Amersham in Buckinghamshire. In the Church register he traced the information he was seeking. It was apparent that a generation earlier, the son of a local aristocratic family had also stepped out of line, having a son whose mother was quietly 'married off' to an employee, George Stops. The cost of the boy's education was met by the family of his natural father and he did well, married and had fourteen children of whom twelve survived into adulthood – one of these my grandfather. Maybe it was this that caused so great a reaction about Alfred. In 1950, my mother held a 70th birthday celebration luncheon party at the Midland Hotel in Manchester to which she invited all her siblings. This was the first time that Alfred was accepted back by them all. Only the youngest brother Neville and George who was in Australia were unable to come.

William, the only one who never married, was often on the dole but was looked after by two of his brothers. He was one of the two or three hundred unemployed but fit men recruited to hang on to ropes at the launch of the inaugural flight of the great airship R101 in Bedfordshire in October 1930. It took off safely, but the hydrogen-filled craft crashed and exploded in flames in Beauvais, France, killing all those on board.

The family all had to work hard. Their world was based on the countryside, on horses, on farming in difficult conditions, without subsidies, only self-help and 'making do'. Mother measured our minor domestic mishaps in terms of farming finances: 'That's only a calf lost'. The real disaster had been to lose the bull – then no-one had a new coat – or foot-and-mouth disease when all cattle, including the bull, were confined to their own field. There were no vaccines and no national slaughter policy.

The girls' education was for the most part only what the law demanded, but they grew up to be excellent, even obsessive, housewives. Elementary education had been compulsory since 1870. When the school attendance officer was in the area Grandpa Stops hired a governess temporarily to teach the girls who were still at home and sack her when the inspector had moved on elsewhere. Mother had to stay at home to help with the succession of ten younger siblings. When she was 18 one of her aunts persuaded Grandpa to allow her to go to a college for a year. Later, in her mid-twenties, longing to get away from the confines of Tiffield, she went as a home help to look after the step-children in my father's family in nearby Kettering. Here she met my father, Charles. She was almost 28 years old when they married in 1908.

I took special delight in the dairy at Tiffield. It was large and cool, down a few steps opposite the kitchen. Cream was whisked from the top of the new milk. The girls had to help turn the wheel of the big wooden churn making butter. Cheeses were stacked on shelves around the walls. One or two hams hung from hooks in the kitchen where there was a huge range. The family sat down together each day at the large table in the dining room. The kitchen garden was a fairyland, with rows of raspberry canes, strawberries, runner beans and peas, plum trees, pear and apple trees. There were farm dogs, in particular a large friendly white English sheep dog who would allow me to play with her all day. When a pig was to be killed in the yard, Betty and I were taken out for a long walk so as not to hear the terrifying squeal of air escaping from its slit throat. Although forbidden, I did watch from a window a bull servicing a cow in the yard, with a number of farmhands shouting and pulling on ropes. I wondered what it was all about, but was never told.

Granny Stops, Elizabeth (Bessie) Ann, born in 1854, was a skilled needlewoman and made clothes for all the family. Her hobby, when she could find the time, was tatting – that is, making lace. I was fascinated by this and remember it, even though I was then only very young. Stored away somewhere in a box is still a white linen table-cloth edged with Granny's elaborate and exciting cotton lace. Granny played the piano well and for many years regularly played the harmonium in the small (Baptist) chapel in Tiffield. She died of cancer aged 64 in 1918. Burdened by child-bearing and caring for babies nearly all her married life, she had longed for the freedom enjoyed by her sister, Polly, whom my mother adored. Aunt Polly was married to a successful Sheffield businessman. She was always dressed in the height of fashion and was my mother's role model. It was Aunt Polly who had insisted that mother should go to a finishing school at 18 and persuaded Grandpa Stops to let her take the job as a mother's help with the Timpson family in Kettering.

Grandpa Stops had a beard that would be fashionable today. Although he was a formidable man and probably too strict with his own children, he must have softened when it came to his first grandchildren, Betty and me. I loved him dearly and I would sit cuddled in his lap stroking his beard. Perhaps, in some ways, I gave more outward affection to my grandfather than I did when little to my own father who had no knack with children. Grandpa died before I was 7, after the end of the First World War. He is buried, together with Granny Stops, in Tiffield Church yard.

Mother reacted against the chore of making the Stops family's clothes. As a result she never touched a needle if she could help it. As I grew up, the ordinary sewing and mending to meet the lesser needs of our smaller family were left to me. My sister Betty, never handy with a needle, spent all her spare time with her head buried in a book. I never got to lace-making, but it was from this that I developed my taste for intricate embroidery, always in miniature: pictures and small tapestries, cushions, chair covers and so on, usually with detailed and symmetrical patterns and squares. During the war, I took to making Robert's army uniform shoulder badges in gold thread under the guidance of the Royal School of Needlework.

Although none of my close relatives had any special interest in mathematics, there was great sympathy towards me and even a certain pride that I was good at it. Perhaps, ironically, the only one who never really understood was my mother. In some ways this was sad, because I was so very close and devoted to her. She would say, 'Why are you doing those sums again, you haven't shelled the peas'. I would then meekly go to the kitchen to shell the peas. It took such a long time, but I systematically chose the fattest pods first to build an encouraging pile of peas until I got to the last thin limp pods and popped the peas into my mouth. Mother regarded anything to do with science or technology as beyond her; even the telephone, although communicating by telephone with her sisters became her greatest joy. Radio was a mystery that she never got used to. We had our first television set only two years before she died and it meant nothing to her. We never mentioned sex (the subject would have been altogether taboo), but if she became aware that a couple had so much as contemplated sleeping together before their wedding night, they were barred completely from entry to our house. Sex before, or without, marriage was an unforgivable sin. Not until I was myself grown up did I know that this was the cause of the unexplained estrangement of her brother Alfred.

Mother had exemplars. She was invited as the wife of a local Liberal Party member to a function at Broomcroft, the home of E.D. Simon, the Member of Parliament for the constituency in which we lived, and his wife, Sheena, whom thirty years later I came to know well as a member of the Manchester education committee. The Simons were flour millers and that was industry. So they could hint (politely) that the Timpsons, being 'in trade' were mere shopkeepers, socially inferior. Mother was always prepared to pick up ideas and learn. All the floors at Broomcroft were of beautiful parquet hardwood and covered with valuable oriental mats. Mother came home and vowed that she would never again buy a carpet. The drawing-room at No.11 Elm Road had our first parquet floor with a patterned parquet border. Gradually every floor in the house, including the stairs, was laid with hard wood (strips, for economy, not tile-blocks).

Mother became a member of the Manchester Antiquarian Society, which father thought a great joke, but she really learnt about antique furniture. As soon as I was 17 and could drive the family car, I would take mother down into Staffordshire or over to Harrogate where we found astonishing bargains. We never spent too much – mother, although always generous about helping others, was careful about money. On one occasion, when I was driving her to Northampton to visit one of her sisters, she shouted to me to stop. There, outside a small roadside store, was a half-moon mahogany table. We bought it for £25 and somehow managed to get it into the back of the car. It is still in my possession. She had a good eye for such treasures and we had many adventures together – father 'having kittens' when we went off on these jaunts. She also had strong ideas about burials and was an original member and shareholder in the society that built, by private subscription, the first crematorium in Manchester, not far from where we lived. She called herself a 'Life Member' which amused us. This carried the right to be cremated when the time came without charge. When she died over sixty years later I insisted that this agreement should be honoured, which it was, although by then the 'old' crematorium had been taken over by the city.

Mother was always thinking up improvements. She was never happier than when providing work for the local joiner and plumber. We were rarely free from decorators – she could not tolerate the dirty walls caused by Manchester's fogs. The rooms of the entire house were painted every spring – the black-and-white outside had to last for three years. I was brought up on the smell of fresh paint – and loved it. Towels and other linen were washed every day – in the bathroom basin or the kitchen sink. There was a free-standing iron mangle in the cellar with two heavy wooden rollers turned with a handle at the side. It was usually my job to take the wet washing down the outside cellar steps, do the mangling and hang it out on the line in the garden. When it rained we rushed out to bring in the wet washing and hang it on the ceiling rack in the kitchen.

Mother was an obsessive spring-cleaner, tidying cupboards, drawers and wardrobes, never hoarding anything. So much so that it risked turning the rest of us the other way: hiding treasured belongings from her. She packed parcels and sent things off to someone or other before we had time to stop her, even books or clothes we still wanted. When, aged 74, she learnt that she had an inoperable cancer, she set about organising from her bed the distribution of all her disposable possessions to her sisters and other relatives and to people who had worked for her. When she died, she felt her job was completed and she left nothing for Betty and me to do, except to look after father and the house itself.

Father was devoted to my mother and became totally dependent on her. After she died his mind went (it had probably begun to deteriorate before that, but mother covered up). He never again mentioned her name; it was as though she had not existed. He simply transferred his dependence to me. Perhaps he thought I was mother: I was very like her in my ways and talked in much the same voice. Until the end of the Second World War I had lived under the same roof as my parents (Robert being away on active service for our first seven years of marriage) and then almost next door. Happily, Robert was very fond of both my mother and father and they of him. Over the next thirteen years, with help and with my sister (still living only a half-hour drive away) having father on Sundays, we were able to care for him in his own house, taking him with us to our cottage in the Lake District when on holiday. Our greatest fear was that he would set the house and himself alight. He remained an inveterate smoker. In old age he could not flick out the matches he insisted on using. Fortunately the tough hard-wood floors merely scorched. We did at least manage to impose a strict rule that there was to be no smoking in bed. At the end, in 1967, he died peacefully aged 85.

CHAPTER 3

To school: the onset of deafness

Mother was determined that Betty and I should have the best education available. One of her idols was C.P. Scott, editor of the Liberal newspaper the *Manchester Guardian* (as it then was). His children went to Ladybarn House School, then in Withington, just over a mile away from where we lived. What was right for Scott's children must be best for us. It was a Montessori school taking children at 6 years old. There was a kindergarten for children aged 5, mornings only, and I was there for the summer term before my 6th birthday. The kindergarten occupied a large front first-floor room with a bay window and an open coal fire surrounded by a high brass fender with a latticed screen that I found fascinating.

Robert, my husband to be and the elder of two brothers, was born four months before me and lived in a house about half-way between our house and the school. He started in the lowest class of the main school at the same time as I did in September 1918, two months before the end of the First World War. My route to school took me past his house and we walked there together. One day on the way to school I picked up what I thought was a chrysalis. Proudly I showed it to Robert and he launched into a long dissertation about caterpillars and butterflies, only for us to find when we got to school that it was only a date stone. I have a snapshot taken on 17 June 1919 at his 7th birthday party. He has his arm around my shoulder as if I was the only girl in the world. When, a few months later, we moved house to Elm Road, Didsbury, I still walked to school each morning – now a full two miles – my route still taking me past Robert's house. Also *en route* lived Marghanita Laski, daughter of the eminent lawyer Neville. She was two years younger than I was. I was entrusted with escorting her to school across the main roads. While still very young she was a fantastically fast speed reader and I admired this tremendously. She took the lead role in a production of Carroll's *Alice's Adventures in Wonderland*, with shoulder-length hair and an 'Alice band', the image of the Tenniel illustrations. I marvelled that she learnt the whole part word-perfectly almost overnight. We met again when she arrived at Somerville College, Oxford in my third undergraduate year there; by then her phenomenal literary talents, clear when she was only a child, were all the more evident.

Most boys moved on from Ladybarn House School at about age nine to preparatory schools before going to public school at 13. We girls tended to stay on until 11 or 12 or even 13. A special virtue at Ladybarn was that each main subject was taught by a teacher with expertise in that subject – not by a 'class teacher' who taught across the board for a whole year as was customary in most state elementary schools. We were never taught mathematics other than by someone competent and experienced. Staff were chosen to meet this policy. The form mistress for the lowest class, Miss Ratalick, was a gifted teacher, not only of arithmetic but of mathematics more generally. We learnt Latin (from nine years old) and French; and we parsed English sentences in books ruled in columns headed 'noun', 'adjective', 'verb' and so on, but no-one managed to teach me how to spell. I have no visual memory (it has to be logic). I have never overcome this weakness but I did learn that it is impolite, indeed thoroughly bad manners, to make spelling mistakes when someone else has to read what is written – for this wastes their time. Even now, I never travel without a small dictionary in my baggage for fear of being caught unable to spell some word I need.

While having the midday meal at Ladybarn, we played mind games. Our plates were white with Greek frieze stencil borders. When a plate was put on the table, we competed to be first to find the join in the stencil. Afterwards we had to spend half-an-hour sitting still 'to allow our food to digest properly'. We sat at tables in the hall window recesses and played chess, draughts, halma and other board games. Chess was wonderful. I acquired a pocket chess set to use at home, although there was rarely anyone to play against as neither mother nor father played chess and Betty preferred to read.

Although there were plenty of playmates once I was at school full time, I still had to amuse myself when at home, at weekends and during school holidays. There were a lot of absences from school with children's maladies or being in quarantine for them. There was whooping cough, chicken pox, mumps, measles and (almost every Spring term) influenza. In addition there were the usual coughs, colds, sore throats, earaches and tummy upsets. There were no quick cures, but to have the disease gave some measure of immunity. Vaccination against smallpox was compulsory. It tended to leave a nasty permanent scar on the upper arm. We might have a sore arm for a week and wore rather proudly a red tape around the arm to warn people not to bump into it. Almost all childhood illnesses involved three or four days in bed, and there was no television or radio, or even a gramophone, let alone computer games. There was, however, much to keep a girl occupied at home besides helping in the house – playing cards, solitaire, jigsaw puzzles, embroidering, knitting and, above all, reading. We grew out of Beatrix Potter although knowing them all by heart, but there were Hans Andersen's Fairy Tales, and Lewis Carroll's *Alice* and later on, *The Railway Children*, *Tom Brown's Schooldays* and other classics. Whenever Betty or I was stuck ill in bed a stream of books was borrowed from the local public library. Most important, we had the eight volumes of Arthur Mee's *Children's Encyclopaedia*. As well as interesting articles and pictures, they contained a host of games, puzzles and 'things to make and do'.

There was a succession of visitors at home apart from aunts, uncles and their young children staying for weekends. Mother liked to give hospitality to young people. When I was about ten years old, some friends asked if she would keep an eye on a son who was training at Metropolitan Vickers engineering works in Trafford Park. He visited us regularly for Sunday lunch, sometimes bringing a fellow apprentice. He began to set me mathematical puzzles, challenging me to have the answers by the next Sunday. I found this irresistible. Other visitors provided challenges and I always had ready my own questions. For example, why does water running out of a wash basin always go round in a spiral in the same direction however hard one tries to prevent this? I would be impatient for answers which no-one at school seemed to be able to give.

When I was nine, a new headmistress was appointed to Ladybarn, Miss Jenkin-Jones (Miss Jones for short). We never knew her first name; all women teachers were 'Miss'. In the state system if a woman teacher married she automatically had to leave teaching, a requirement that was not reversed until 1946. Miss Jones had read mathematics at Girton College, Cambridge, without being given a full degree as these were still denied to women. She was tall with straight hair brushed back into an untidy bun. Her rather shiny face never knew make-up. Although she was strict and sometimes almost fierce, she was always kind to me. She took a special interest in this girl who so eagerly grabbed at every mathematical challenge. In the next four years Miss Jones fed my passion for numbers. She introduced me to the classic *Flatland* by 'A Square', Edwin Abbott, first published in 1874, which gave me my first understanding of dimensions beyond the two and three dimensions of the natural world. She insisted on exactitude, formal proofs, and total accuracy at all times – with checks. She emphasised the need for 'proof' and the difference between conjecture and logical mathematical proof. This didn't turn us all into mathematicians, but no-one who started school at Ladybarn House, including Robert, had difficulty in passing their mathematics exams at the secondary school stage. Later I averred that I owed my scholarship to Oxford in 1931 to the mathematics I had learnt at Ladybarn before the age of 13.

Across the road we had a small field where we played lacrosse in winter, cricket in summer, and held a much-looked-forward-to sports day each July to which parents were invited. I was a good runner from an early age and enjoyed this, usually winning the hundred yards race that was handicapped in order to give everyone a chance of winning. Paired for the three-legged race with another girl of my size, we became unbeatable over two or three years.

We did not go to the swimming baths from school, but were expected to learn to swim during the holidays. The city of Manchester, always go-ahead, had built public swimming baths in 1911 in Withington just around the corner from where I was born. They are still in use. Mother took Betty and me every week in summer until we were old enough to go on our own. There are twin pools, then with two separate entrances: one with 'Male' in the terracotta above it; the other with 'Female'. The charge was 3d (old pennies) on Mondays and Thursdays, clean water days; 2d on Tuesdays and Fridays; one penny on Wednesdays and Saturdays when the water was plainly dirty. Needless to say, mother only allowed us to go swimming on Mondays or Thursdays. The baths were closed on Sundays. We were taught to swim (breaststroke only) by an instructor who waded backwards holding our chins out of the water, our plaits pushed under a rubber cap with a thick chin strap that hurt. There were three wooden diving spring-boards jutting over the water at the deep 6ft end, which were not removed for the next forty years or so until it was decided that indiscriminate diving was a danger to other swimmers.

Deafness strikes

In August 1921, after a wet and cold summer holiday at Trearddur Bay in Anglesey, the great blow fell. I caught a severe cold which presumably today would be diagnosed as a viral infection, and it brought on sensori-neural deafness. Added to this, increasingly as I grew older, was the family-inherited genetic *otosclerosis* for which there was then no cure or treatment. It was decided I should learn lip-reading. The specialist teacher of the deaf at the University of Manchester was the renowned Professor Alexander Ewing. He forbade his pupils to learn sign language. He held that it inhibited lip-reading, which requires total concentration. More importantly, sign language allows communication only with those who also know sign language, whereas lip-reading makes possible communication with anybody who speaks clearly.

The onset of this deafness had a profound effect, although I was probably somewhat deaf before that disastrous holiday. This may have accounted for my early preference for playing with numbers rather than words, which I may never have heard accurately. What is certain is that mathematics and the passion for numbers came into its own and inten-sified as I progressed through school, partly because I could not hear properly. This was the one subject in which I was at no disadvantage. Nearly all mathematics equations and diagrams are found in books or are shown on a blackboard as the teacher speaks. Answers are written down. Learning mathematics is rarely as dependent on the spoken word as are most lessons and lectures in other subjects. The mathematics became my life-line as well as an increasing source of joy.

I became Professor Ewing's star pupil. He had not had such a young pupil before. He demonstrated to me that it is impossible to tell the difference by lip-reading alone between a 'p' and a 'b' and how to make allowances for this. I was encouraged to practise with a mirror in order to learn from watching my own mouth as I said selected words. I went to him about once a week for at least three years.

Lip-reading is tiring, and there is an enormous difference in capability between when one is in good form and when over-tired. Mother saw to it that I was never tired, and we were in bed early and had lots of sleep. At boarding school the regular hours were a great boon. I was able to get by with lip-reading throughout formal education including university and a first job. Music is a different problem – but there are ways in which it can still be greatly enjoyed.

Ladybarn House School's link with Montessori and Switzerland brought us Dalcroze eurythmics – movement to music. I found I could excel at this – and I was rewarded by being given a leading role in exhibitions and displays. I could sense the beat of the music and clearly understood somewhat mathematically how to combine or change from one time scale to another. I gained a lot of pleasure and satisfaction from this.

It was particularly fortunate that I was at a school like Ladybarn House when this deafness first became apparent The relatively small school where every teacher knew every pupil; the small classes (never more than twenty even in the lowest forms and fewer after the boys had moved on); the specialist teaching of mathematics – all were hugely advantageous. Had I been in a large school, I would have been lost. Indeed, within the state system the only provision then would have been in a 'special school', with very little chance of ever having been taught mathematics at the level I received. As it was, I had the best possible opportunities, and, while I was still at school, the deafness probably added to these rather than hindered because staff gave me special attention.

I was never allowed any specific privileges because of being deaf, either at school or at home. I was expected to take part in every activity, whether I could hear properly or not, and to obey the same rules as everyone else. But sometimes I did get things badly wrong. In 1922 I came home from school one day and asked my mother what a 'listening insect' was. One of the girls in my class had been given a 'listening-in' set and had been boasting about it. She invited several of us to her house specially to listen-in. We took turns to put on the heavy earphones to listen to the new 2LO London Calling *Children's Hour*. I was too deaf to hear a thing, however much we fiddled with the cat's whisker. The disappointment was so great that it was difficult to hold back the tears. Later, at home, I tried to make a receiver myself, but it never worked.

Ladybarn House School was an excellent preparatory school, but there was no physics and no chemistry. By 13, it was high time for me to move on. My sister, Betty, was already at boarding school in St Andrews and I was eager to follow her. I left Ladybarn at the end of the Spring term 1926, after eight happy years.

CHAPTER 4

Boarding school – St Andrews

Both Betty and I (and our daughters a generation later) had our secondary education at St Leonards School, St Andrews. This came about again largely because of my mother's admiration for C.P. Scott. His wife had been there and this had great influence with my mother. Father did not object. He was delighted to have the excuse to go regularly to St Andrews for the golf. St Andrews is an historic city, its fine houses in South Street built of stone purloined from the old cathedral ruins. The school grounds, lined with trees and bordered by ancient walls, are overlooked by the tower of St Rule; white cliffs in the distance to the East.

My first day at St Leonards was 6 May 1926 during the General Strike. Betty was in her last term there. After months of looking forward to going to St Andrews, I was determined to be there on the first day of term. We had just acquired our first family car, a four-door Fiat saloon. At my insistence we set off for St Andrews in the car, our two school trunks strapped on the carrier grid at the back. It is 275 miles by road from Manchester to St Andrews and father was an appallingly bad driver. Charitably, we put it down to his having only the one eye. Mother sat nervously beside him. Betty and I were in the back and I was navigating with the AA route map. I always loved maps. The journey at a maximum speed of about 40 miles an hour (faster downhill) took over eight hours. AA patrol men in yellow-piped jackets and hard peak caps were on motorbikes with side-cars full of jacks and other rescue gear. They saluted cars with membership badges and there was a secret code. If they did not salute, the myth was that it was a warning that there were police lurking behind the next hedge waiting to pop out and catch drivers exceeding the speed limit. This alone was thought to be worth the membership fee. We had many break downs and often needed AA help, the chief fault being dirt in the petrol clogging the slow-running jet. Father, though clueless, was happy with his head under the bonnet, but mother, Betty and I standing out in the cold would be less than sanguine.

As it turned out few other girls, at least those from England, made it for the first day of term. At the morning assembly, my place was at the end of the row of the lowest class. I was thrilled to be there at all, proud to be part of this famous school at whatever level.

For the first time I was among people I had not previously known, without the protection of a small school where everyone knew everyone and that of the family at home. There were between thirty-five and forty girls in each boarding house, and ten houses including one for day-girls. We recognised that we were in privileged education. Our return for this was that we were expected to give all we could to others less fortunate than ourselves. This was the ethos drummed into us so forcefully that it remained for the rest of our lives. We behaved well 'for the sake of the House'; 'for the sake of the School'; 'for the sake of the community' and, ultimately, 'for the sake of our country.' Most of us, later on, became committed to voluntary public service in one form or another. Working hard and seeking distinction in academic subjects or other activities was one way of improving our opportunities to do good for others, not to be regarded as an aim in itself.

As well as 'setting' on general ability there was 'streaming', that is, 'cross-setting', for mathematics and for languages. I started the new school year the next September in the top 'stream' of the Lower Fifth, streams being decided on grounds of general academic ability. For mathematics and languages the whole year group was re-arranged according to special aptitude or attainment into 'sets'. I was in the top set for mathematics and the lowest set for French. For my first two full years at St Leonards, concentration on subjects other than mathematics was essential if I was to hold my own with my contemporaries. The mathematical grounding from Ladybarn House was sufficient to take me through School Certificate (which I took early at fifteen) but I was behind others of my age in arts subjects. There was Shakespeare to read and learn – and history and geography – and French. German was optional. We were weak on biology and nature study, and I never caught up with these until long after I had left school.

I have one particular regret. Although most of the specialist teachers at St Leonards knew about my deafness, the head of the science side, a fierce lady, showed no sympathy for me if I didn't respond exactly as she thought I should. There was no allowance for my not having heard properly and I became scared by her. When it came to choosing subjects for our School Certificate (the equivalent of today's GCSE), I asked to exclude physics and chemistry. So it happened, merely on the flimsy basis that I was afraid of the science mistress, that I never even got started with physics or chemistry and dropped both completely at the age of 14. I have regretted this ever since.

Teasing was never countenanced and good discipline was taken for granted; but, looking back, it was the quality of the teaching staff that gave St Leonards such high standards, in particular of the house-mistresses who were themselves academics of distinction and subject teachers in school. We were never allowed in the dormitories during the day-time, except briefly to change clothes for games or into our own non-uniform dresses for the evening. We were not permitted to write letters to people other than relatives – or to those whose names and addresses were not made known to the house-mistress. We had no easy way of posting our own letters; they were put out on a ledge for posting. There was no telephoning, even to our parents, unless in real emergency and by permission. Romance was not encouraged. Robert wrote to me from time to time from school at Oundle and I managed to sneak letters out to him in reply, but that was it. The great seal of our long-standing romance was that, when he entered his sixth form and decided that he wanted to follow his father into the medical profession, he carefully packed and sent me his slide-rule. He felt he wouldn't be needing mathematics and I would make better use of it. This slide-rule was of a superior design: large, with a powerful cursor. He had made a leather case for it and I counted this as the mark of true love. I did not use the slide-rule often; the work I was doing was better done using logarithms. There were still fifty more years to go before desk and hand calculators became readily available and logarithm tables were set aside.

My happiness at St Leonards was perhaps partly because I was good at games and in sport being deaf does not matter. We had played lacrosse and child-level cricket at Ladybarn. Here at St Leonards there was more opportunity. The magnificent playing fields (not surprising when we had the same quality of turf as at the renowned St Andrews golf courses) meant that we had ideal conditions. Apart from days of pouring rain, snow or a thick Scottish haar, the pitches could always be played on: hockey one winter term, lacrosse the other; cricket in summer. I gained school colours in the two winter games, and, although I had 'half-colours' for cricket, I came rather to dislike this particular sport – the ball was so hard and fielding it hurt. We also had two fives courts – a game at which I excelled, depending as it does on angles and tactics. At tennis I was outclassed by girls who had tennis courts at home. There was also a well-equipped gymnasium and this was a special pleasure. I had no fear of heights and revelled in rope climbing and tricks on adjacent ropes. Vaulting on the horse did not come easily at first, but it was all a matter of knack. Once mastered, performance can be steadily improved. All this came in useful when, later, I had the opportunity to go rock climbing in Austria and in the Süd-Tirol Dolomites.

We played golf too if we wished, but not until the sixth form as it took so long away from the school on weekdays. On Saturdays the crowds, even then, were too great. There was no golf on the public courses on Sundays. We were not allowed on the hallowed Royal and Ancient Old Course, but there were two other courses. At an Open Championship (then in term time) we were allowed time off to follow competitors. It was possible to follow from one hole to the next for all eighteen holes except perhaps in the final rounds. There were no stands, no vast crowds with booked seats (and no television). We had golf lessons from Willie Auchterlonie who had won the Open in 1893 when he was 21. In 1930 he was caddying for Bobby Jones, who that year won both the British and the US Open championships. The tradition was that when the winner picks his ball from the 18th hole, he tosses it to his caddy to keep as a memento. Auchterlonie passed Jones's ball to us schoolgirls to hold before putting it into his pocket.

Normally mild-tempered, I had never thrown a tantrum in my life, but just once I did fly into an almost hysterical rage, stamping my foot and bursting into tears. During my School Certificate year the head of mathematics was away ill for a long time. I had covered at Ladybarn House all the work required, so instead of going to 'further mathematics' lessons, I spent the time on other subjects and this was not noticed. When it came to the exams, the mathematics seemed very easy. I waltzed through every paper with loads of time to spare for checking answers. I gained maximum marks in every paper, indeed more than the maximum as I answered every question, not merely a choice. On arrival back at school for the autumn term, happy to have obtained the required number of credits to satisfy any university entry requirements and so not saddled with retakes, the future course had to be discussed. To my dismay my house-mistress, Miss Tunnicliffe, told me that, as I hadn't been in the proper mathematics group in the previous year and had done no applied mathematics, to do higher mathematics in the sixth form would not be possible. Worse, it was pointed out that there was no future employment for a girl in mathematics other than in teaching and, as being deaf ruled out teaching, I should choose some other subject. I went berserk. How could anything so terrible be suggested? From before I was 6 years old my best subject had been mathematics and I never wanted to work at anything else . . . and now this was to be denied me. I heard myself saying that it was mathematics and only mathematics that I wanted to do, that the year before was all a mistake, and that if mathematics was barred then I would write to my parents and demand to be allowed to leave school immediately. Miss Tunnicliffe was stunned by the vehemence of my protest. A compromise was reached: I was allowed to join the mathematics sixth form 'for the first half of the term'. I was back in my element. Nothing more was ever heard again about my not specialising in mathematics. The strength of my emotion had surprised everyone – even me.

One of the joys of St Leonards was the time given to reading. The advantage of boarding school is that no time is wasted in commuting between home and school. Every Sunday a full hour was set aside before supper, at least in the winter terms, for what we nicknamed 'Stale'. I suppose to contrast with modern novels, we were required to spend this hour reading approved books available in the house library. Most of us had read Dickens at home, but there was Walter Scott to be read, Bernard Shaw and H.G.Wells; dozens of classics to choose from. Once stuck into a good book and over the first resistance, all reluctance disappeared and we read voraciously in every spare moment even if, like me, we were not natural bookworms. Miss Tunnicliffe was a brilliant raconteur. She read aloud to us every weekday evening in what was called the 'drawing-room' while we sat on the large comfortable sofa and arm chairs in front of a glowing coal fire. We knitted for charity or did embroidery work, while she read *Jane Eyre.* Her reading was magical and we never wanted her to stop. She would have been a sure choice for a *Book at Bedtime* had such programmes existed.

Not only did Miss Tunnicliffe lead us into a love of good literature, but she made sure that I read the lives of the great mathematicians. She bought for me a newly published first edition (1929) of H.W.Turnbull's *The Great Mathematicians.* Professor Turnbull was Regius Professor of Mathematics in the University of St Andrews. If anything was to turn me on for ever this was it – a pearl of a book.

I had two splendid teachers of mathematics in my sixth form. The senior of the two, Miss Herman, who taught me applied mathematics, was the daughter of a renowned aspiring Wranglers' coach at Cambridge. The junior, Miss Coley, was in her first post, fresh from Girton College Cambridge. It is typical of the time that I did not know the first names of either of them. Miss Coley taught the pure mathematics that I enjoyed most. She had lovely golden hair and I thought her beautiful, but any sign of a 'crush' would have been quickly stubbed out. I met her several years later when she had moved on to be head of mathematics at Cheltenham Ladies' College, her hair just as lovely as ever. She never married.

With these two first-rate teachers, a stimulating battle developed. There was a system of 'Excellents'. This entailed having three successive weeks of 'prep' marked 'V.G.'. Very good in mathematics meant challenging problems solved with style and absolutely without fault. If one could achieve three successive Excellents (which meant nine successive weeks out of a twelve-week term) they accumulated into a 'Signing Excellent'. This was the highest recognition obtainable in any subject. It was announced at morning assembly and the recipient went to the headmistress's study for congratulations and to 'sign' in a special red leather-bound book. I was on the way to two concurrent Signing Excellents: one with Miss Herman in applied mathematics, the other with Miss Coley in pure. They set me harder and harder problems to solve each week. This was precisely the kind of challenge I liked best. I became determined not to be beaten. I brought in every ounce of effort I could muster. It worked and a record of two Signing Excellents was achieved. It was the greatest possible fun and I must have learnt more mathematics in those nine or ten weeks than at any time at school before.

It was at St Leonards, probably because it was a boarding school, that I discovered and developed as a positive habit the powers of what I call 'subliminal learning'. We kept very regular hours and were never tired or stressed at school. Lights out at 9 p.m., even when in the sixth form. Out of bed at 7 a.m. The accepted wisdom is that one should relax before going to bed, emptying the mind of problems. As far as mathematics is concerned I could not agree less. We looked forward to 'drawing-room' each evening, but I usually cheated and stole ten minutes back at my desk before bathtime. I would make certain to sort out in my head, as late as possible, what problems needed to be solved the next day and what might be usefully committed to memory. Before falling asleep, I 'drew' with my finger any relevant geometrical figure or algebraic equation on the partitioning of the dormitory cubicle that formed a bedside wall. The result would be miraculous. Without fail, on waking in the morning, the details, the logical argument required or the facts that I needed to recall were clearly imprinted in my mind and, because of the clarity, any required solution would often be clearly 'written' on the partition. For this to work, it is essential to make sure to wake at least five or ten minutes before the prescribed time for getting out of bed, giving one-self time to go over what has been resolved while asleep. This became honed to a fine art, without my ever telling anyone, and I have used the technique deliberately ever since. It works equally well in a train sleeper, in aircraft or on any long journey.

Sixth-formers were obliged to keep up general education even if not offering other than specialist subjects for examinations. I still continued with French at a rather elementary level. There was an inspired teacher of history, Miss Ketelby, a lecturer in the University, who could set any historical subject alight with insight and realism, bringing judgements of past events into their historical context. We read and acted out

Shakespeare's histories, tragedies and comedies. We were expected to scan main articles in a leading newspaper each day and be able to make sensible comments about world affairs. The weekday evening meal in our houses was formal, Miss Tunnicliffe sitting at the head of the 'top table', and conversation had to be of general interest. There was little opportunity for gossip and we didn't indulge in it. I do not remember ever seeing a glossy magazine among the common-room papers provided every day. The mealtime conversations turned out to be good training for my two years as a wartime don at Somerville, where any kind of 'shop' or personal chat at dinner at the High Table was absolutely barred and the basic defence was to prepare by reading *The Times* correspondence or a major leader each day.

Two current techniques in education I was spared. The headmistress during my school years, Miss McCutcheon, was a considerable scholar and a fine educationist. She was a shrewd judge of a girl's ability and potential. IQs (intelligence quotients) were emerging in the late 1920s as a new 'infallible' educational tool. St Leonards was invited to take part in tests of their efficacy. Each of us, from the sixth form downward, sat an experimental graded test. When Miss McCutcheon studied the completed papers she was so disillusioned that she refused to disclose the results. In her opinion they gave totally false assessments: the real potential scholars got poor marks, whereas the mediocre did comparatively well. The problem was the multiple-choice questions. Although suitable maybe for some purposes, they did not bring out the best in, for example, an aspiring mathematician more used to analysis and deeper thinking. For my part I was paralysed by them, and still am, being reduced to trying to guess what the questioner wants, rather than to endorse any one of the half-truths (or inanities) of the alternative answers proffered.

The second more recent education measure is by 'continuous assessment'. This may suit a majority of pupils, but it would have sunk me without trace. My performance in class was generally poor. When I couldn't hear properly, I tended to 'switch off' as I can do all too easily. Except when the subject was mathematics, I let my mind wander. What a teacher might be saying could pass comfortably from one side of my head to the other without making any contact in the middle. When it came to a formal examination I was on my toes, fully alert and at my very best, doing far and away better in an examination than in ordinary class work. I seemed to need the focus, the challenge and, above all, the excitement. I was always at my best when facing a formidable challenge. I remember Miss Tunnicliffe once saying to me before some important examination, 'Don't get excited – keep cool and calm' and I, knowing myself, and knowing that I needed to be 'teed up' and really enjoying myself if I were to give my best, told her so. She could see, and found out by experience, that I was right about this. Like a racehorse trained for an event and looking forward to it, it has to be an 'occasion'. I worked hard, did any necessary revision to a strict self-imposed timetable, using my own ways of learning, and was raring to go when the time came. I would have lost badly if judged only or principally on week-by-week attainments or mid-term tests. This is no disadvantage in real life – anyway not in public life – where success largely depends on giving a good performance under pressure. All of the essential background work completed beforehand goes unnoticed.

Only four of us specialised in mathematics after School Certificate. It was not a usual girls' subject. By the time I was in the Upper Sixth there were just two of us, and my colleague eventually turned to medicine as a career. It was a disadvantage to have no competitors, but a great advantage in that it meant there was no longer any problem about hearing the lessons. These became almost individual tuition and I could use the lip-reading of ordinary conversation. In July 1930, aged 17, as soon as I had taken Higher Certificate, I left school. It was suggested that I should try for a place at Oxford or Cambridge. The school offered to arrange the invigilation if I came back to St Andrews for the required fortnight for the examinations in March of the following year. This I did.

There was one more significant school-based commitment in 1930. We had heard much about efforts to secure permanent peace in Europe. My contemporaries and I had all as children experienced something of the deprivations and tragedies of the First World War. We did not need to be convinced of the value of the League of Nations. The public schools and other leading secondary schools in the United Kingdom were asked to send representatives to Geneva in August 1930 to attend a conference in the League of Nations Headquarters building to discuss disarmament. I was in a group of six girls from St Leonards selected to attend. Importantly as it later turned out to be, I was asked to write the report on our visit for the School Gazette. Although I couldn't hear the speeches, I had the sense to pick up all the available literature. I took a lot of trouble and wrote a rather splendid report. By the happiest of chances, this stood me in good stead at interview in Oxford six months later.

In 1950, twenty years after I had left school, I was invited to be a member of the School's governing body and went up to St Andrews regularly for the next twenty-five years. There was then a gap when I went only occasionally. In 1981 I was invited to become President, a position that I relinquished only in the summer of 2003. The school gave much to me. I like to think that, as expected of us, I have in return passed on many of its gifts to others.

CHAPTER 5

A year on ice

The immediate target on leaving school in July 1930 was the university entrance examinations for Oxford and Cambridge at the beginning of the following March. As I didn't believe there was much chance of my gaining a place, I didn't take it all that seriously. Cambridge had special attractions as first choice because of its reputation for excellence in mathematics, led by the legend of Isaac Newton. Also, both of my mathematics teachers at St Leonards, Miss Herman and Miss Coley, had been at Cambridge as had Miss Jenkin-Jones who had first inspired me at Ladybarn House. Oxford had a different appeal: Robert was already at Magdalen College, having gone up to Oxford directly from Oundle – and Oxford had an ice-rink! It seems astonishing now that any consideration as bizarre as a skating rink should have come into it. Meanwhile, having left school, I wanted to have a nice time and I spent most weekdays at the ice-rink up the Cheetham Hill Road in North Manchester, where I proceeded to gain medals for figure skating and ice-dancing, none of which depended on hearing.

One day it dawned on me that something more had to be done. I could hardly spend six months doing no mathematics at all, especially as I had never really covered the full school syllabus taken for granted at a boys' grammar school. Compared with Manchester Grammar I was at least a full year behind. I contacted Manchester University, got on the tramcar and barged into the presence of the then head of mathematics, Professor Louis Mordell, explaining my predicament. Instead of sending me packing, he introduced me to J.M. Child, who had come to Manchester from Cambridge in a non-teaching post and was writing his definitive book *The Higher Algebra*. Child had never taught a woman student, but for a modest fee he seemed glad to share his mathematical skills for an hour a week. He had a shock of grey hair and seemed to my eyes to be very old. His large table was stacked with papers; his room a dismal basement down the main staircase from the university quadrangle. It would not have occurred to him to get up from his chair to greet me or to say good-day – he just waved a hand for me to sit beside him and we got on with the mathematics, he showing me excitedly his latest discoveries. Neither of us gave a thought to the real purpose: to help me prepare for university entrance examinations. Child told me stories of the great mathematicians and of living mathematicians at Cambridge: how two professors, chatting, said that no-one really understands a mathematical problem unless he can explain it to the first man he meets in the street who is willing to listen. This isn't strictly true: some mathematical ideas are very abstruse, but it is an excellent precept for any young mathematician to try to adhere to. Child wrote everything in the masculine. To him women in mathematics were an irrelevance – perhaps that was why we got on so well.

Two aspects of higher algebra – and geometry – I found particularly attractive. One was 'cross-ratios'. They have to do with the ratios of lengths of sections of a straight line drawn across a fanned-out 'pencil' of lines that meet in a point. The other was 'projective geometry' – how one shape or configuration in two or more dimensions can often be projected into another that may be easier to deal with. This device of transforming one problem into another for the purposes of simplifying proof can be most useful.

Child's erudite *Higher Algebra* was far above school level. His work was captivating both in its contents and its clarity. It was a great experience and an opportunity to pick up a lot of pure mathematics not normally taught to students. The disadvantage was that we did not touch on any of the rest of the syllabus I should have been studying. There is much that I never knew that I ought to know, but have not had the opportunity or self-discipline to learn on my own. I owe a great deal to J.M. Child. It would be nice to be able to think that he could know now that he is thus remembered.

There was another gaping hole to be filled. For Oxford, in addition to any main specialist subject, two other papers had to be taken – an

English essay paper and a foreign language translation. I could get by with translating a piece of French prose, but writing an essay could scupper me. I was really bad at it; so I enrolled at the famous coaching establishment known as 'Grimes', situated in a row of houses opposite the present Manchester University students' union on Oxford Road. Many Mancunians in the University seemed to have resorted to this crammer at some time for special short-term coaching. I went there for once-a-fortnight tuition in essay writing. They found me hopeless. We fell back on the strategy for proving Euclid's geometry theorems, learned while at Ladybarn House: 'given', 'to prove', 'what do we already know' (that is 'construction'), 'argument' and 'conclusion', QED. There is one additional technique: 'find the most interesting statement, wherever it may have occurred, extract it and place it as the first paragraph.' With this plan, one can usually tackle any compulsory essay reasonably adequately.

During this year I developed my ice-skating. One of its attractions was that it was in no way dependent on hearing, provided I could get the beat of the loud music for ice-dancing. Preparing for tests or competitions meant taking a tram at 7 o'clock in the morning from the terminus in West Didsbury and changing trams opposite the town hall in Albert Square to be at the ice-rink by 8 a.m. in order to have clean ice before the general public swarmed in at 10 a.m.. The charge for half-an-hour of this privilege was 2s 6d (about 12p) – a lot of money. I took the standard school-figure tests in rapid succession and quickly became proficient in ice-dancing. It seemed to come naturally. I found there is a way of learning how to achieve difficult turns on the ice (such as 'back outside loops') in the mind by the techniques of the subliminal learning that I used for mathematics problem-solving previously described. It requires a clear idea of what one needs to do and to have had opportunity to find out what *not* to do, such as leaning the wrong way at a critical stage in a turn. Then, away from the ice, I could switch off the active brain, go into a trance and 'feel' the action. This can be done lying in bed – or in church – anywhere where the mind is free to roam undisturbed. After doing this several – even many – times, at the next session at the ice-rink it was possible to go straight onto the ice and make the turn perfectly. Achieved once on the ice, it was merely a matter of practice to gain certainty, accuracy and confidence. The same technique can work for skiing, learning from a book to make the most of a short holiday on real snow slopes. Learning to ride a bicycle is much the same – once the knack is acquired, it is never forgotten. There is perhaps a parallel with fusing a pair of images in a stereoscope in order to 'see' a three-dimensional image. Some people never manage this.

March came all too soon and I went back to St Andrews to sit the Cambridge and the Oxford entrance examinations, held within a single week. I must have been at my best as I was invited to interviews at both universities. My two erstwhile mathematics mistresses, Miss Herman and Miss Coley, waited outside the examination-room door at the end of each session to find out how I had got on. One memory is vivid. There had been a long algebra-geometry paper set by Oxford. With the recent experiences with J.M. Child, I found one question not only easy, but ridiculously so. This had to do with hyperbolas, intended to test skills in analytical geometry. Thanks to Child the answer 'fell out' in a few lines of argument. I told my two former teachers, rather nervously, afraid that I had been too daring and maybe wrong. I remember to this day their looks of amazement. I have always thought that this answer in particular clinched the happy result I was to have at Oxford.

At the interview in Cambridge I came unstuck. No one knew I was deaf. I was not able to lip-read my key interviewer and made the fatal mistake when leaving the room of telling someone that I had not heard a word that had been said. An exhibition was offered me at Newnham reluctantly, because it was considered that deafness would be too much of a handicap to overcome. The prejudice against the deaf was considerable, as opposed to that against the blind for whom there is a natural sympathy. There is more understanding nowadays and help for all handicaps. Then, the deaf were classed as either stupid or inattentive or even just rude when we did not respond politely to (unheard) greetings or questions.

At Oxford a few days later there was better luck. I was more careful and cunning, and they never found out about the deafness until I came back six months later in October. Then they had to know, for my personal safety, apart from other practicalities. In addition to the individual interviews with college dons, it had been decided at Somerville that, for the first time, the top twenty applicants who were in the running for one of the awards (six open scholarships and six exhibitions), should be interviewed by all the dons collectively. This 'don-rag', as it was later nick-named, became a standard pattern in subsequent years. Previously, decisions were based mainly on the enthusiasms of the subject examiners. Non-scientific dons had no yardsticks for judging mathematics.

Two of us who were offering mathematics were selected for this ordeal. My competitor's surname began with 'C', Joyce Cawley, and she went in first. Thirty-five years later we met again: she was headmistress of a large girls' school in Whalley Range, Manchester, and I was the chairman of the Manchester education committee. Joyce was full of confidence. I didn't think that I had a chance, particularly as it would be almost impossible to hide the deafness when sitting at the end of a large table in front of a dozen or so formidable ladies, led by Miss Margery Fry, the then principal. But this time the gods were with me. The first question, conventional enough, was 'where had I spent my summer holiday?' Not only had I attended the Disarmament Conference Symposium arranged for school sixth-formers in Geneva, but I had written this up for the school magazine as I have related. All the facts and correct names were at the tip of my tongue. There could not conceivably have been a greater piece of good fortune. This sufficed. No more questions of consequence were asked. I did not have to 'hear' anything. A few days after my return home, I received a telegram informing me of the award of an open scholarship. I was stunned. I dashed to our telephone to ring Robert, just a mile away at his home in Didsbury. He could not believe it – we would be together again, now at university. The scholarship, means tested, amounted to £50, enough only for essential books, but the kudos it brought was immense. St Leonards School, although accustomed to academic successes, awarded the school a day's holiday in acknowledgement.

Robert was reading for a degree in physiology in preparation for going into medicine like his father. He wore spectacles and was always hopeless at games. He made up for this by becoming a first-class shot, representing Oundle, and later the University, at Bisley. He also gave a lot of spare time to the Corps of army cadets. At school he had risen to being sergeant major, strutting in the approved manner in front of the school band, tossing the mace in command. At Oxford, although not accustomed to handling horses, he became a gunner with all the risky excitement of riding one of the six horses with a field gun in tow. During his first year, he also took up rowing and succeeded in gaining a place in the Magdalen second boat. I was not due to come up to Somerville until that October (1931). He suggested that his parents should come to the May 'Eights Week' and bring me with them – which they did.

I was entranced by the whole event. Every afternoon we went to the Magdalen Barge, moored with others on the banks of the Isis alongside Christ Church Meadows. The weather that week was glorious: a heat wave, blue skies, white puffy clouds, green grass and the majestic river. We women wore long flowery dresses, wide hats, gloves and high-heeled shoes. Fathers were in white flannel suits and Panama hats. This was equal to anything Ascot or Henley could offer. The excitement centred on the races – the long lines of boats, each battling to bump the boat immediately ahead so as to move up in the starting order the next day. I do not remember whether the Magdalen second boat did well, but that didn't matter; it was just as exciting, bump or bumped.

I spent the summer with my parents and on holiday. In the second week of October 1931, aged 19 on the first day of the month, I arrived at Somerville to start my three years as an undergraduate.

CHAPTER 6

Oxford

The first task on arrival at university is to meet one's tutor and arrange the academic programme. Somerville had no mathematics tutor and there were only two of us in my year reading mathematics. The tutor responsible for all the women mathematics undergraduates, Dr Dorothea Wrinch, whom I had met at interview six months before, was based in St Hilda's College, but she had gone to America on a sabbatical leave which in fact lasted two years and I never met her again. The two of us from Somerville were sent to a young don in Balliol College. I enjoyed my once-a-week tutorials, his first-floor room overlooking St Giles, but I do not remember learning much, although we must have covered the first-year syllabus. I was probably too busy occupying myself with everything else. I should, I suppose, have asked for more guidance, but it didn't occur to me to do so. It was assumed that undergraduates were able to manage their own affairs efficiently, but there were too many diversions outside the mathematics. Looking back, I threw away the academic opportunities that were available, unaware of the guidance I needed.

As an undergraduate I never lived outside Somerville itself. As a scholar I could have a choice of available rooms in college. I chose a room on the top floor of the original building. It has a fine view over the main quadrangle and I occupied it for two years until moving for my final year to a larger room overlooking the then newly built front quad. During my first two years, on this third floor, apart from my room the only others formed a suite occupied by one of the dons. It was all very civilised and completely different from a school dormitory. There was however the problem of being deaf. I could never have heard a fire alarm or other bell and there were no individual internal telephones. In practice, all it meant was exercising a maximum amount of self-discipline about watching the clock, never missing an appointment or being late – particularly for meals. Although we could boil a kettle and make tea, there was no means of preparing anything to eat. If we wanted to entertain a guest, this was done formally downstairs in the junior common room. Indeed, we were not allowed to have male guests in our room at any time. We could visit men in their colleges only by special invitation and then had to have written permission with times stated. I took all this on the chin, accepting restrictions as normal.

Robert, now in his second year, was already installed in digs just outside Magdalen College, a ten-minute bicycle-ride from Somerville. For my birthday he gave me a set of records with excerpts from 'Die Meistersinger'. I owned a wind-up gramophone. Sitting close up to it, I played these records over and over. Miss Lascelles, the don who occupied the suite adjoining my room, must have been driven mad, though I don't remember any complaints. Perhaps I took care only to play them when she was out. I came to know every note. If I want to sing in the bath or on long solo car drives, it is something from these records that I choose.

I cycled to Magdalen to visit Robert fairly often. He was reading physiology and this required a lot of work in the science laboratories during afternoons. He was still rowing and, being an excellent shot, he spent a lot of time on the university ranges and on his duties with the Gunners of the Officers' Training Corps. I went with him to Bisley twice as a visitor and became quite good at target shooting with a light rifle. I never managed to fire a full-size rifle without it bruising my shoulder. Between us we won a whole array of engraved silver drinking beakers and crested teaspoons that are still used and treasured.

In my first term Robert invited me to go with him to a dance at St Hilda's College. I think we both knew this would be the occasion when he would 'pop the question'. And he did. On Saturday evening, 14 November 1931, in bright moonlight among the cabbages of St Hilda's kitchen garden, Robert asked me to marry him. The reply was a firm 'Yes' and we had our first real kiss, despite having been devoted friends since we were both aged six. We went back to the hall and the undergraduate jazz band, the Oxontrixts, in which Robert a little later became the double-bass player. He wrote to his mother telling her about our commitment to marriage. The next day she drove to Oxford from Manchester, alarmed by his letter, fearing that we were about to dash off immediately and marry. This would have put an end to all the family expectations of his becoming a distinguished surgeon like his father. Both of us had far too much to do (and too much common sense) to have had any such idea. What we certainly did not imagine was that we would have to wait so long. Throughout the years that followed, until Robert died in 1986 aged 74, we always celebrated this special day, 14 November, rather than our actual wedding day of 6 September 1939 in the first week of the war.

Becoming engaged to be married in my first term at Oxford undoubtedly diminished any incentives to apply myself to study. I envisaged a life as Robert's wife, he a practising surgeon, myself playing the traditional role of the supporting wife and, hopefully, mother. No-one, and certainly not our parents, put it to me that life doesn't always work out to plan, and in 1931 another world war was unthinkable. The only parental anxiety was that we might be careless enough to have a baby (there was no pill) which would have meant immediate marriage and the ruin of any prospects for Robert's planned career.

A second diversion was being too good at sport. I had played hockey, lacrosse, cricket and fives for St Leonards and was the winner there of the annual 100 yards flat race. I made the choice to play hockey, gained my 'Blue' playing Cambridge in my first year and was elected captain in the two following years. I allowed this to take up far too much of my time. The only good thing that came out of it was the friendship of John Wolfenden. He was then a young don at Magdalen College and played goal in the men's English hockey eleven. We organised 'mixed' hockey matches, a more lethal game (for the women) being hard to imagine.

After a few weeks at Oxford the Principal of Somerville, Miss Helen Darbishire, a Wordsworth expert, became aware that no-one on the college staff knew anything about me or how I was getting on. She decided that I should write an English essay once a fortnight and take it to her for discussion. We struggled nobly with this for a while, but eventually gave up. We were on different wavelengths with her English literature and my mathematics. It seemed more fruitful just to have the discussion and the social chats and do without the essay. This face-to-face contact grew into a lasting friendship, but it didn't fill the gap caused by my not having a normal college tutor in my own subject.

I went to every prescribed lecture, whether I could hear or not, rain or shine. All the mathematics lectures were given in the college to which the lecturer belonged. By always attending, I gained the respect and sometimes the help of other undergraduates and was often able to return this by helping them with their maths assignments. I took care to find out which of the lecturers were to be our examiners (and so the question-setters) and made sure that their lectures were never missed. Two I came to know really well: T.W. Chaundy at Christ Church and W.L. Ferrar at Hertford. Theo Chaundy, who ten years later was my supervisor for a DPhil, was a don (called 'Student') of Christ Church. He gave his lectures in the Great Hall, surrounded by portraits of founders, including Henry VIII and Cardinal Wolsey. He deliberately lectured far above the heads of his first-year audience, until (lecture-going being voluntary and with no signing-in) he had reduced his attendees to a handful of four or five. Then, and only then, he reckoned it was time to begin to teach. I could not hear a word he said but, as usual, continued to attend hoping matters might improve. Astonishingly, they did. Chaundy noticed this woman still there on a front bench. When he learnt that the reason was because I could not hear, it tickled his sense of humour: from then on he lectured to me almost as an individual. This was great and I stayed the course.

W.L. Ferrar was very different: a distinguished algebraist, he was also Hertford's bursar. He had a dreadful habit of starting every sentence with a long-drawn-out 'Er . . . r . . . rr'. Despite this, his lectures were masterly expositions of higher algebra. As this had become my special interest through J.M. Child in Manchester the previous year, I was on familiar ground. When I came to my third undergraduate year, I asked if he could be my tutor. This was agreed and a lasting friendship was formed. It was with his help that I was able to return to Oxford as a wartime don in 1944.

Both Chaundy and Ferrar called themselves 'Mr' and wore ordinary black graduate gowns even on ceremonial occasions. They were so well known and respected that no other attire was needed. After the war the undergraduate population swelled and they became less well known by the new generation of staff and students. At an important university function a young woman undergraduate introduced Ferrar to her parents as 'the bursar of Hertford'. That tore it. He was one of the most distinguished algebraists in the country. Both he and Theo Chaundy were persuaded to apply for an Oxford Doctorate of Science, which they were both automatically awarded on the strength of their published books alone. This gave them entitlement to the scarlet and white silk gowns and no more mis-introductions.

A highlight of my undergraduate years was attending a public lecture by Albert Einstein. The hall was packed. Squeezed into a back row, I could neither hear nor understand a single word – he lectured in German – but I had seen this famous mathematician in person. I probably did not realise at the time just how great a genius he was. As a pure mathematician I had got nowhere near studying relativity, but I was most deeply impressed – his large head and intensity bringing so much power into the room that it could almost be felt. Another great event that sticks in my mind was John Gielgud playing Richard in *Richard of Bordeaux* in an OUDS (Oxford University Dramatic Society) production in the Playhouse. Later I saw Gielgud in many roles, but it was this first time I watched him, at Oxford in 1932, that remains in my mind.

The mathematics degree course was theoretically a four-year course, but, as so many bright boys from leading grammar schools had covered the first-year syllabus before coming up to university, a fashion had grown of doing the first two-year 'Prelims' in one year, reducing the four-year course to three years. This put me at a disadvantage, but I did not want to be at Oxford for more than three years and planned accordingly. Robert would complete his normal three years by the end of 1933, so I wanted to be back at home in Manchester where he would be doing his clinical work to qualify as a doctor.

Incredibly, I spent six weeks of my penultimate term knitting a sweater for him. It had an intricate cable pattern depicting the Magdalen College Arms. Knitting, with my final examinations only a couple of months away! I must have been out of my mind and with no tutor in college or anyone else to tell me not to be so stupid. Just two weeks before my finals in June 1934, I received a telegram from Robert telling me that he had failed the physiology part of his Royal College of Surgeons 'Prelims'. He would have to wait a year before taking it again. This came as a big shock to me. Robert had never failed an exam before and I had thought his successes automatic.

Suddenly I realised that, in the final reckoning, one must depend on oneself alone and one's own efforts. I had been fooling around, coasting for the better part of three years and there were only two weeks before my finals. I got hold of the University Regulations and read the syllabus and what I was supposed to have covered for finals in mathematics – something that had never been brought to my notice. I weighed up what I thought I knew, and what I certainly did not know and was far too late to learn. Then I set about revising like mad what I thought I knew. I probably taught myself more in that last fortnight than I had learnt in a lackadaisical way over the past year. The old techniques of subliminal learning worked again. By the time I set out for the Examination Schools building in the High Street, dressed as required in formal black and white, I was in top form, able to give better than my previous best, despite the despicably late start at serious learning. There were four or five papers – but in each there were up to eleven questions with answers expected for not more than four. I selected in a flash the four that looked most promising and concentrated on these with confidence. No one needed to know that I probably didn't even understand what the other seven were about. It worked – but what a narrow squeak. Having been scared rigid only a fortnight before, I was now elated – on a veritable high.

I thoroughly enjoyed my undergraduate years at Oxford, but I did not make the best use of my time academically. I spent too much time playing hockey and going with Robert to dances when he was playing in his jazz band. I have vivid memories of his transporting his double-bass to and fro in the back of a small Morris 8 while I tried to squeeze into the passenger seat. As things turned out, I had a second chance, returning during the war to Somerville as a temporary wartime don and gaining my DPhil. The links made as an undergraduate with Theo Chaundy and W.L. Ferrar fortunately remained as strong and valuable as they had been ten years before.

CHAPTER 7

Broome House

From November 1931 when Robert and I became engaged to be married, his parents came closely into my life. Tragically, in less than two years Robert's mother, Florence Eleanor, died. She was born in 1884, one of four daughters of a Canadian Senator, Robert Watson. She met Robert's father, also Robert but always known as Bob, when she and one of her sisters were attending an art college in Brussels. They fell so completely in love that they married there secretly. A formal wedding ceremony (with parental approval) was held a year later on 17 June 1911 in Manchester Cathedral. They settled in Withington only a few minutes' walk from Parkgate Avenue where my parents had begun married life three years before. 'My' Robert, the elder of two brothers, was born in 1912 on their first wedding anniversary. He was always teased that he had been born on his parents' wedding day. He was inevitably always called 'Bobby' within his family, but after his father had died I preferred and adopted the full 'Robert'.

Robert's mother was vivacious, full of laughter and fun, a great entertainer, the house kept busy with guests and visiting relatives from Canada. Father Bob, as I came to call him, was a successful orthopaedic surgeon. He had volunteered for military service immediately on the outbreak of the First World War and spent most of the war on the Western Front. His gruesome experiences gave him an utter horror of war and for the next twenty years he clung stubbornly to the belief that it could never happen in Europe again.

With their two sons, Robert and Gerry, they moved in 1922 from Withington to Broome House in Didsbury. Everyone in Didsbury knew Florence Eleanor. She made Broome House available for frequent charity concerts, whist drives and tea parties. She was a genius with flower arrangements. Every Friday morning the gardener brought in huge bundles of flowers and cuttings and she arranged displays to adorn the spacious music room. She had a gift for finding exactly the right piece of furniture in some sale to fit an empty niche in this big house. Once she returned from a sale and asked Father Bob what 100 bottles of champagne should be worth. He had a fit. An attractive bureau was on sale, but as part of a 'job-lot' that included the champagne (and a chamber pot). The buyer had to take all or nothing and she wanted the bureau. Cellar space was found for the champagne and for a long time we had champagne with every Sunday lunch.

Florence Eleanor liked her food and as the years went by she became very oversized, but this did not seem to worry her. When she gave a dinner party it was on a grand scale. She was very superstitious and would not think of allowing thirteen to sit at table. One evening at about 7.15 the telephone rang at my home. Fourteen were expected to dinner at Broome House, but one guest had failed to turn up. Would I get into evening dress and come immediately to make the number at table fourteen? A taxi would be at my door within five minutes. It was at this dinner party with Cook (as she was called) at her limit, every pan in the kitchen in use, that one of the guests (the local GP's wife, another formidable character) asked if she could have, of all things, instead of the proffered wine, a glass of warm milk. We laughed about that for many years.

In January 1933, this all came to a sudden end. Florence Eleanor, then just 49 years old, contracted a streptococcal infection in the throat when working at a fundraising Christmas Fair at Pendlebury Children's Hospital in Salford, where Father Bob was by then the senior orthopaedic surgeon. Robert was at home for the Christmas vacation. Antibiotics were not discovered until some years later and there was no effective treatment. On a Sunday morning, just eight days after she fell ill, she began to choke. Father Bob, knowing that only an immediate tracheotomy could save her, sent Robert to find the sharpest knife in the kitchen. Together they operated, but in vain. It was too late. I was in Margate on the South coast, taking part in an inter-county hockey festival and returned home on the first available train.

Robert had adored his mother. When thirteen years later our daughter was born, we naturally named her Florence, after the paternal grandmother she had never known. Florence Mary Watson Ollerenshaw, to give our daughter's name in full, was almost uncannily like her grandmother both in looks and character.

After Robert's mother's death, I became even closer to his father. He was only 51, handsome, rather portly, not always in good health. He was the elder son of George Ollerenshaw, who ran a successful grocery business near Preston in Lancashire. At about the age of 12, Father Bob gained entry to Manchester Grammar School, then in its old building near the Cathedral, and he travelled to and from school each day by train. He went on to Manchester University and Manchester Medical School, his father determined that he should not remain in trade. He tended to be lazy about his studies, preferring to play billiards, for which he had great flair, but he was challenged by a friend into gaining his Fellowship of the Royal College of Surgeons. So great was his skill at billiards that his father, having moved the family to a large house in Glossop in Derbyshire, added a billiard room in order to keep him away from the public billiard halls. The main attraction of Broome House for Father Bob, years later, was that it has a billiard room (as well as the large music room).

When in the 1930s Father Bob, Robert, Gerry and I visited fairgrounds, we chose the largest shooting booth with the best-looking prizes, had a few shots ourselves with little or no success and then went through the motions of persuading Father Bob to have a try. With assumed reluctance, he proceeded to demolish every target in turn with his first shot. He accepted the first prize offered and then another, but after that the owner paid him to go away and never come back.

When widowed in 1933, Father Bob was an established concert-goer with a prominent public life in Manchester. I had still another eighteen months to complete at Oxford, but after the end of June 1934 I was back living at home in Didsbury and Robert (by then at Manchester Medical School) was living with his father at home at Broome House. A prospective daughter-in-law, I provided the companionship that Father Bob needed. He had two season tickets at the Free Trade Hall for Hallé concerts and took me with him as his regular guest over all the years until the Hall was gutted in the German fire-bomb raids of December 1940. We then went to make-shift halls where the concerts continued. He was one of the six prominent Manchester citizens who invited John Barbirolli to come to Manchester from America in 1942, during the worst years of the war.

It was through Father Bob that I gained my deep-felt pleasure in music. He was tolerant of my deafness and helped me to appreciate concerts by playing pieces in advance on the gramophone at top volume. He had a large range of miniature scores and I could follow these and always heard the beat. The pre-war Hallé programmes printed the first bars of the principal themes and this helped. Visiting conductors were welcomed to Broome House, where I filled the role of hostess. Father Bob was not himself an instrumentalist, although he took lessons on the bassoon. But he had a good bass voice and as a young man took part in amateur productions, particularly of Gilbert and Sullivan operas. He was a useful pianist (he frequently accompanied Gerry, Robert's younger brother, who was a gifted flautist) and we had a lot of fun playing four-handed piano duets (badly) with scores borrowed from the Henry Watson Music Library, then housed in Manchester's Central Library. He took me to London for four days to hear *The Ring* (and to go to Wimbledon Tennis Championships during the day) and on another occasion to Glyndebourne. It was his passion for music and opera that led him to accept the invitation to share a villa in St Gilgen am Wölfgangsee in the Salzgammergut which gave us easy access to the Salzburg Music Festival.

Father Bob, Robert, Gerry and I went together to St Gilgen, near Salzburg in Austria for our summer holidays from 1933 until 1939. Looking back now, it seems strange to realise that in the 1930s, throughout the Second World War, and until Father Bob died in 1948, I saw far more of him than I ever saw of Robert himself. Before the war Robert was busy gaining his medical qualifications and obsessively occupied in his spare time with the Territorial Army. In effect, from 1933 to 1948 I had two homes: my own in Elm Road with my parents, where I always slept, and Broome House where I spent some part of almost every day when at home in Manchester.

CHAPTER 8

Austrian interlude

Soon after Robert's mother died in January 1933, Father Bob received an invitation from a long-term friend of the family, Ellie Kaufman, who had lived in Manchester with her husband, a Swiss businessman, during and for some years after the First World War. Ellie had recently been widowed and had returned to the family home in Vienna where her sister, Mimi Weinberger lived. For many years the two families had rented a villa in St Gilgen am Wölfgangsee near Salzburg and they needed help with the rent. She suggested that Father Bob, together with Robert, his brother Gerry and me, should spend August in St Gilgen sharing the villa (and the cost).

The invitation was accepted instantly and sustained, with many vicissitudes, each year up to and including August 1939. We drove there by various routes in the old reliable soft-top Buick. It had a small enamel Union Flag on the side door that from time to time played a significant role.

The Salzburg Festival offered the prospect of opera and music at their best in superb surroundings. Father Bob immediately booked seats for the Festival and for two other operas on the route of our journey: Bayreuth for Wagner's *Die Meistersinger von Nürnberg* and Munich for Strauss's *Elektra*. The Wagner theatre in Bayreuth, like Glyndebourne in Sussex, is set in extensive grounds. We sat on the lawn having supper during the interval. The stage was built with a back that could be removed in part to give a clear view through to the woodlands behind the theatre. In the last act of *Die Meistersinger*, as the villagers gathered to listen to the prize-song competitors, the young apprentices poured down the stage street leading from the woods into the bedecked square with dramatic effect.

Elektra evokes different memories. On the drive south from Bayreuth to Munich on a hot afternoon with the soft roof of the car folded back, a wasp became trapped down the inside of my cotton dress. I was stung dozens of times before I could get it out, the wasp soaring away unharmed, which didn't seem fair. My whole midriff was a flaming mass of stings and I was in torment all through the opera that evening.

'Rätz Villa' was a large single-storey house, its outer walls faced with traditional wood shingles, set back from the road leading round the western end of the lake, in an unkempt field running down to the water's edge and a dilapidated jetty. The views up the Wolfgangsee and over to Schafberg, the mountain on the lake's northern side, were magnificent in all weathers. For sightseers there was a mountain railway from St Wolfgang to a station near the top of Schafberg. I preferred the 4-hour walk up the steeper slopes directly from St Gilgen to the summit. My favourite walk was to the top of the smaller mountain, Zwölferhorn, to the south. A sign-board indicated that it was a two-hour walk, but I was in good trim and several times followed the path by myself to arrive at the summit in under an hour. From the top there were splendid views across the surrounding mountains of the Salzkammergut.

Our Viennese friends brought with them their elderly mother – a redoubtable old lady although almost bedridden. They also brought their cook and we had memorable meals. In particular she made äpfel-strudel that, fresh from the oven, was scrumptious. She allowed us into the kitchen to watch her stretching the dough over her thick white arms to form the wafer-thin pastry sheet into which the prepared mix of cooked apple, berries, soaked dried fruit, nuts and cinnamon was folded.

Within days of first arriving at St Gilgen, Robert and Gerry had persuaded their father to hire a sailing boat for us. It was a wretched craft, but before a week was out we were taking part in a local regatta. Gerry, then 17 and with all the right talents and enthusiasm, took the helm. Robert and I were content to be crew. We trailed in a poor last, but it had whetted our appetites. Father Bob was a great one for keeping the British flag flying high and, when we returned to St Gilgen the following August, he bought a worthy boat, a Zwanziger (20 square meters of sail), with a centre-board that was drawn up with a rope by the helms-man into a casing in the centre of the boat when running before the wind. We named her *Ferret* and equipped ourselves with sweaters with the name across our chests. While at Rätz Villa, Ferret was moored at night to the jetty. One calm evening, when Robert and I had stepped out of the boat onto the jetty, we watched Gerry drop the mainsail, preparing to lash it to the boom. We had forgotten to let down the centre-board and had neglected to secure the boom. To our astonishment and almost paralysed with laughter, we saw the boom slowly, as it were deliberately, swing outward with Gerry perched at its end. As the centre-board was up there was nothing to prevent the boat tipping over and Gerry was dunked in the water, mad with rage and humiliation.

It was not safe to take *Ferret* out single-handed. For the constant tacking needed when sailing into the wind two people were essential, three better. Storms blew up almost without warning. We capsized more than once – unpleasant and scary, involving a lot of hard work. By regulation, all the sailing boats had to have buoyancy tanks, so there was no real risk of sinking, but recovery was difficult nonetheless. On one occasion when we were in the centre of the lake Robert was at the helm, Gerry and I side-by-side hanging out at full stretch to windward to keep the boat from going over without losing speed. I saw that Gerry's rope was beginning to fray near the point where it was attached to the centre-board casing. The fraying increased strand-by-strand with terrifying speed until the last two strands snapped with a loud bang. It happened too quickly for me to give Gerry any warning. His legs flew in the air as he somersaulted backward. I caught sight of him spiralling down beneath the surface of the water. He said later that he had thought he would never stop going down and down. I yelled to Robert and we hauled in, went about and aimed for the spot, now far back, trying to follow our own wake. I sprawled over the bow hoping to catch sight of Gerry surfacing. Mercifully I did, but he was only about a foot away, almost directly beneath us and gasping for breath. Had we crashed into him that would have been that. We had to come about again and have another try, by then more in control. Neither Robert nor I were experienced. I don't know who was the most frightened: Gerry in the water or Robert and I in the boat. We never dared tell Father Bob or anyone else about it. If we had, it might have been the end of our sailing.

Most evenings at sundown we went to the St Gilgen village square, the Mozartplatz, with its fountain and the little statue of the young Mozart playing his violin. We sat on the bench outside the general grocers, eating pickled gherkins straight from the barrel and swilling lager. The theatrical effect was heightened one summer by having Marlene Dietrich and her partner of the time, Douglas Fairbanks (Senior) sharing our bench. 'Zum Weissen Rössl am Wolfgangsee' from *White Horse Inn* was the current catch-tune. St Wolfgang itself and the Weissen Rössl are at the other, eastern, end of the lake and are most favoured by tourists. St Gilgen, at the sharp, Salzburg end, was more choice to our minds. Few tourists came to St Gilgen – there was only one hotel – and certainly no English other than ourselves. On Saturday evenings we went to a popular inn in St Gilgen; with the harmonicas and tubas and country dancing, the noise was so great it did not matter that my hearing wasn't all that good.

At least twice a week we drove to Salzburg. We came to know it well. The Festival performances were always outstanding and I remember a particularly notable performance of *Faust*. Robert acquired a fine head of Mephistopheles carved from a block of wood that still has pride of place above my desk at home.

St Gilgen has an attractive church with an onion dome. The markers of the graves in the church yard are of metal. One day I watched a skilled craftsman beating a piece of sheet metal into the image of the Madonna cradling the child in her arms. He asked me to pose for him. He hammered the metal on a leather-covered 'form' holding it over a simple blow lamp to soften it where needed. When he was shaping the Madonna's nose he accidentally made a hole through the over-stretched metal. He thought nothing of it, but just moved the metal sheet slightly and remodelled the head at a different angle. He worked fast. At one stage the metal sheet slipped and burnt his finger very badly. I was horrified but, again, he seemed to think nothing of it, bandaging the finger with a dirty handkerchief and continuing as if there was nothing amiss. He said that it happened so often that he had lost all sensation in the fingers of that hand and could carry on without worrying about it. In less than half-an-hour the work was finished. I would have been proud to have it for my own grave.

After three successive August holidays at Rätz Villa, a larger and much more attractive villa came up for sale and Father Bob chipped in with a third of the purchase price together with Ellie's and Mimi's one-third each. Tonder Villa still stands: a two-storey house on the edge of the lake near the centre of St Gilgen. Its thick timbers were painted black and the wattle walls white with a red-tiled overhanging gabled roof. The front elevation was built into the lake on piles and there was a rather rickety deck over the water. We now moored *Ferret* to a buoy about 20 yards out into the lake. This meant we needed a dinghy. Father Bob, his generous behind silhouetted against the water, was a familiar sight, becoming more and more impatient as he pulled on the cord to kick-start the fractious outboard motor. He liked to take us out to *Ferret* and then bring the dinghy back so that he could mooch around in it on his own while we were sailing. We became regular participants in local races – mostly on a friendly level, although it became noticeable that the friendliness of our rivalry was diminishing as the influence of Hitler over the border became each year more evident.

These were August holidays, when we did our best to keep free from political anxieties and evidence of the developing power of Adolf Hitler. But we had a taste of this in 1934 on our second journey to St Gilgen. In 1933 Marshall Hindenburg, the veteran of the First World War and a very old man, resigned the Chancellorship of Germany in favour of Hitler. He retained the Presidency, but died in 1934. That August we went first to Oberammergau and the Passion Play. Our route south along the Rhine and through the Black Forest took us to Ulm. We had not realized that there would be demonstrations of military and Nazi political strength that day to mark the death of Hindenburg. We were caught up in a huge parade of young men in combat uniform and berets marching three abreast. Robert, ever the keen photographer, wanted to make a ciné-film. He had adapted a gun stock to mount his heavy camera and gave it to me to hold while he moved away to look for a good vantage point. I found myself stuck in a doorway, alone, holding this gun stock, separated from the others as the troops passed by, eyes turning to glare at me. This went on for an hour. I don't know who was the more scared of what might happen: Robert and Gerry on the far side of the road or I in the doorway. Father Bob, stuck in a car park, was thoroughly alarmed and very angry with us. But Robert had his pictures and none of us were arrested.

When I first came down from Oxford in the summer of 1933, I did not look for a full-time job. I went to Pitman's and learnt touch typing, filled in for my sister in a secretarial job while she was having her first baby, was selected to play hockey for Lancashire County and for the North of England, which occupied most weekends, and spent a lot of time at the ice-rink, as well as keeping Father Bob company in the evenings at concerts and at Broome House. In the new year of 1936, I decided it was time I learnt how to ski and I went by myself for a week to Mégève in Haute Savoie. I had never skied before and found that skiing slowly in deep new snow works on exactly the opposite principles to skating on hard ice. To turn to the left on ice, one leans to the left with the weight on the outside edge of the left skate. To turn slowly to the left on skis in fresh snow, the skis are pointed towards each other at the front to form a V. The weight is put strongly on the inside edge of the right ski while leaning to the right. As with the mathematical problems and when learning ice-skating, having assimilated these principles from a book and with a minimal amount of time on gentle slopes, I made enormous progress by what would now be called 'virtual skiing' in the head overnight. Within a couple of days (and nights with subliminal learning) I had advanced from the nursery slopes onto the mountain side and was soon promoted to an advanced class.

At the end of my eight days I had made friends with a group of instructors who were medical students from Innsbruck earning a bit of holiday money. They invited me to go to Innsbruck for the university semester and join them skiing each weekend until the end of the season. I leapt at the suggestion and managed to arrange student accommodation with a family in Innsbruck. I arrived for the five-month semester on 10 February. I was 23 years old, an ideal age for such adventure.

The weekend after my arrival in Innsbruck, I was within yards of Hitler. On the Sunday the friends I had made in Mégève asked me to join them for a day's outing. We took a train from Seefeld over the Austrian border to Garmisch-Partenkirchen. It was the final day of the 1936 Winter Olympic Games. We had no tickets for the stadium, but sat on a high wall and watched Hitler as he passed below in an open car, standing upright with his arm stretched in the Nazi salute. The road was crowded with people cheering and shouting as his procession of cars drove by. We followed the crowds to the stadium and, ticket-less, found positions under the front of the main stand with a clear view of Hitler almost directly above us taking the salutes as the competitors filed past. This seemed to go on for ever and ever.

I registered at Innsbruck University for the semester. My sole objective was to obtain a student's cheap concessionary pass on the mountain railways. I wasn't in the least interested in attending lectures and there was no requirement. I enrolled for geography – not even for mathematics – perhaps because I thought I might learn more German that way, but once I had my pass I never went near the university again. Almost every weekend we went up into the mountains for long-distance skiing, our rucksacks stuffed with food, ski-skins, wax and spare clothing. With the skins fixed beneath our skis, we walked up to some high mountain hut on the Friday evening and, early the next morning, up high glacier slopes before turning for the long run downhill at whatever speed could be safely managed. The men would go down at speed, while I followed at a safe pace. No-fall skiing was essential. Righting oneself after a tumble in deep snow while lumbered with a heavy rucksack presented real difficulties and no-one could have come back to help me. Invariably I was the only woman. Local girls never thought to come on such tours. The best run of all was from near the top of Mt. Marmalata, on the borders of Italy in the Dolomites. I came to adore the great expanses of virgin snow, the only tracks being those we had made ourselves on the way up. Fortunately, we never experienced any serious mishap.

When the snow disappeared, we turned to rock climbing. The groups became smaller and I was usually roped to the same expert climber. We made some spectacular climbs on known routes: in the Karwendel Range above Kitzbühl and in Süd Tirol (as we called it) in the Dolomites, including the Drei Zinnen with the choice of dramatic ascents. My poor hearing never caused any trouble; these young Innsbruckers seemed to respect my efforts to overcome it. They spoke clearly and German is a very precise language. Those who knew some English were glad to have the chance to practise it. For dangerous climbs and always on a rock wall, we devised a signalling code using short tugs on the rope which was every bit as good, even better, than shouting instructions or warnings around blind corners. I was never afraid of heights and delighted in the sheer drops that sometimes had to be traversed – heart-in-mouth, but triumphant when accomplished. We started out from a base very early in the morning, sometimes at 4 a.m., to get to the foot of a climb by dawn. This might mean reaching a summit by midday, with all the afternoon to come back by an easier route to our base. Once a summit is reached there is a wonderful sense of elation. Then there is the descent. That is when special care and attention are most needed. There are far more accidents on descents than on ascents. At least on the way up, when head and eyes are leading, the feet merely follow. The opposite is much more hazardous.

There is a strong parallel between mountain climbing and mathematics research. When first attempts on a summit are made, the struggle is to find any route. Once on the top, other possible routes up may be discerned and sometimes a safer or shorter route can be chosen for the descent or for subsequent ascents. In mathematics the challenge is finding a proof in the first place. Once found, almost any competent mathematician can usually find an alternative often much better and shorter proof. At least in mountaineering we know that the mountain is there and that, if we can find a way up and reach the summit, we shall triumph. In mathematics we do not always know that there is a result, or if the proposition is only a figment of the imagination, let alone whether a proof can be found.

On weekdays most of my time in Innsbruck was spent learning German – that is, the soft Austrian version of German. Evenings were spent in the local cafés drinking coffee and endlessly talking politics. Most of these Innsbruck young men were Nazi sympathisers. Work was almost impossible to find. Propaganda was very heavily laid on. Not having been in contact with any British people through the whole of my five months in Innsbruck, I was shocked when I joined Father Bob, Robert and Gerry again in August in St Gilgen by how greatly I had been influenced without being aware of it by the intense propaganda. Isolated, with poor hearing and a poor command of the language, although always arguing against the people I was with, gradually and insidiously some of their thinking had seeped into mine. It was quickly expunged as soon as I was among my own people again, but the effect was to make me realise how powerful propaganda and advertising can be. It was not until 1937 that I first began to hear about the concentration camps being set up in Germany and what was happening to the Jewish people and other victims; and to witness the effect on our friends from Vienna with whom we shared our holidays in St Gilgen.

In St Gilgen, less than half-a-mile along the road from Rätz Villa was the summer villa of the Chancellor of Austria, Herr Kurt von Schussnigg. When we were still at Rätz Villa on our August holiday we knew when he was in residence there, because of the extra heavy guard along our road. In 1938, by which time we were spending our third August in Tonder Villa a little further away, the threat of invasion by Hitler was strengthening. We pretended to ignore this: racing *Ferret* as usual, going to concerts in Salzburg, trying to imagine that things were not as bad as they seemed. Schussnigg, who had been staying at his villa as usual, suddenly left St Gilgen. This was the beginning of the Anschluss. Ellie and the Weinbergers, being Jewish, had been warned not to come to St Gilgen, but Father Bob had been determined to come and to stay for the full four weeks of the holiday. In 1938 we took heed, cut short our holiday and returned home, but in a leisurely manner. Father Bob was not one to be hurried. He had fought on the Western Front in the First World War, 'the war to end wars'. There could not be another, certainly not against the opponents we had already defeated.

On our journey home through northern France we had called in at the Greno champagne vineyards. We parked the Buick in the tourist car park and spent the regulation hour in the caves. When we emerged into the sunlight, we were politely asked if we would care to come up to the château. The enamel Union Flag on the Buick had been noticed. We were greeted by a senior director. The object of this invitation, it became apparent, was to quiz these British citizens about morale in Britain and check what Ribbentrop, a one-time champagne salesman, was telling them: namely that we were a soft bet – we would give way at the slightest threat and let Hitler walk over us – as indeed he had marched into the Rhineland in 1936 with no more than a twitter from the Western allies and the League of Nations. It is not difficult to imagine the kind of answer they got from Father Bob.

With about three of them and the three of us (Robert was already back in Manchester), we sat around a table and were plied with one jorum of champagne after another on the pretext of 'tasting'. What they really wanted most to talk about was Mrs Simpson and the prospects of an abdication. About this we knew absolutely nothing – the French probably knew more than we did and we were not hot on gossip at any time. All we could tell them was that, as it happened, we had been in the second row of the stalls in a London theatre for the musical show *Blackbirds of 1935*, white minstrels with blackened faces and very popular. Just before the interval, the then Prince of Wales, along with Mrs Simpson and an equerry, arrived and took their seats immediately in front of us. The whole audience stood up. More remarkably, the show was started again from the beginning, so that they would miss nothing. I never took my eyes off this Mrs Simpson. Perfectly groomed, she was wearing a plain black tight-fitting dress, more elegant than I had ever seen before, with just one dazzling diamond brooch. We British knew nothing but, we learnt later, the French and the American press had been full of the impending scandal. Anyway, we had never before been served champagne in such quantities. We had good heads for wine, but there are limits and Gerry and I began to feel very happy indeed. Father Bob quickly brought us to heel. We hurried home to England to be greeted by pictures of Neville Chamberlain waving his piece of paper with its agreement with Hitler and his claim of 'peace in our time'.

In the Autumn of 1938 Artur Schnabel, whom mother and father had met several times when on holiday in Zermatt, came to Manchester to play with the Hallé Orchestra. He had supper with us in Elm Road before the concert and told us what was happening to his family and friends in Nazi Germany: how neighbours disappeared during the night, never to be seen again, how thousands were being rounded up and sent to the labour camps and how nobody seemed to be able to do anything about it. We sat stunned, unable to believe what he was saying. Struggling to hear properly, I could hardly put food into my mouth for horror. Was it beyond all power to stop it? After supper I drove this famous pianist in my little Morris 8 into town . . . and then listened to him in a Brahms piano concerto, his shock of white hair bouncing over his forehead. While he played I wasn't thinking of the music, but of what he had been telling us over supper.

We hoped against hope that things would not come to the ultimate crisis. Father Bob became increasingly stubborn. He refused to give up the idea of holidaying in St Gilgen. When, in 1939, it came to planning for the usual visit to St Gilgen, Gerry, still a student, and I were not the ones to gainsay him. By then I was working full-time in cotton research, but I had an agreement that I could have four weeks leave during August. Robert, now a qualified doctor and a Captain in the Royal Army Medical Corps (TA), was anyway stuck back at home, a resident house surgeon at the Manchester Royal Infirmary. Our Viennese friends remained in Vienna and warned us not to come to Austria, but we went just the same. Hitler had moved into Czechoslovakia and the threat to peace became increasingly plain. We must have been mad to go there, Gerry and I in the Buick with the luggage, and Father Bob, delayed at home for some meeting, following us by air to Salzburg a week later. Once there the atmosphere was far too tense for any relaxation, but the more agitated Gerry and I became, the more Father Bob dug his toes in and refused to be hurried back home a second year in succession.

By the middle of August Robert, in Manchester, was going berserk. He had already been called up and knew war was imminent. He started sending urgent telegrams to us in St Gilgen: 'Grandfather seriously ill, come home', 'Grandfather fading, come home immediately', none of which we received. In the event, it was the owner of the boatyard in St Gilgen who told us to leave the next day if we didn't want to risk being interned. He filled the Buick with petrol and provided us with half-a-dozen full cans so that we could make it to Switzerland and beyond. We left that night, stopped at Innsbruck and pressed on via Zürich to France. In France the Buick broke a big end and we had to wait in Tours for repairs. Father Bob then insisted that we divert down the Loire to Angers. At 3 p.m. on the afternoon of Friday, 1 September 1939 the bells of the castle began a continuous toll – our first intimation that war had begun. The German army had marched into Poland. We returned to Tours with Gerry, expert as always, at the wheel. The road was crowded with luxury cars travelling west with mattresses and other luggage strapped to the roofs – wealthy Parisians making their way west as fast as their powerful cars would take them. We made for Le Havre, although our car-ferry booking was from Boulogne. We were obliged to leave the Buick and our luggage behind and take a passenger ferry across to Southampton. During the crossing an aeroplane came down in the sea near us and we stopped to rescue the pilot – our first taste of war. I was panicking lest Robert be sent to France before we got home and he and I had time to marry. After over eight years of betrothal, I did not want to be left, a 'pensionless surplus-woman', as two of mother's sisters had been at the end of the First World War. We went by train to London that Saturday night and on to Manchester on Sunday. At Crewe station we heard Chamberlain over the tannoy at precisely 11 a.m., 3 September: 'We are at war'. I held myself tight and said an ardent silent prayer: 'Thank you for all the blessings bestowed on me for these past twenty-seven years. For any days that may still remain to me, I promise that I shall do my best to repay these gifts.' I meant it. We thought it was the end of life as it had been. In many ways it was, but not immediately. There was a future for most of us, even if it was different.

We later learnt with relief that the two sisters Ellie Kaufman and Mimi Weinberger with her husband and the 'old lady' their mother had all, with the help of Rothschild money, got away from Vienna to Lisbon in a sealed train and then to New York, saved from the holocaust by a whisker. Tonder Villa was commandeered; *Ferret* disappeared. We were offered some compensation for Tonder Villa after the war, but we never went back.

CHAPTER 9

Work and some play

In September 1936, when I was home again from Austria, I had been away for over six months. Robert was at the Manchester Royal Infirmary and Medical School and had still a long way to go before we could consider getting married. I needed a full-time job, but the deafness was a handicap. The Government had set up a scheme for encouraging sport and I applied for a post as a regional organiser. I was turned down at interview because of the deafness. Disappointed, I had a better idea. In Didsbury there was a cotton research establishment, the Shirley Institute, financed by subscription from member companies in the cotton industry. I rang their front-door bell and asked to speak to the Director. I had my Oxford first degree in mathematics and asked if I could work at Shirley as a freelance mathematician. There was no such post, but he agreed that I could work there for six weeks and see what transpired. I was introduced to the head of the statistics department, L.H.C. Tippett, got hold of his definitive text book on statistical methods and quickly learnt the basic procedures of analysis of variance and other statistical techniques commonly used in testing materials.

One of the routine jobs at the Institute was to test the efficiencies of different methods and ingredients used in weaving. Trials were set up analogous to the field trials then being developed in agriculture to test various fertilisers. While cloth is being woven the warp threads are primed with 'size' – a mixture of starch, flour and similar ingredients that is later washed out of the finished cloth. This strengthens the warp during weaving and reduces the number of breaks in the yarn. The efficacy of the different mixtures was being measured by the number of yarn-breaks per yard of cloth woven. Four different mixtures were tested on four different but similar looms. The results were then compared by an analysis of variance that eliminates extraneous causes of variation such as minor differences between looms. The procedure involved tedious arithmetical treatment of the numerical data. On my first day at Shirley, the junior member of staff who normally did this work was away sick. I was asked to do it in her place. The Institute had recently acquired a new large electric Brunswiga calculator, but there seemed to be no book of instructions. I set to work on the calculations, but after about half-an-hour I became fed up and stopped. I sat and thought, and then bicycled home for lunch. On my return, I sat and thought some more, did a bit of pencil work and tried out a few tricks on this new machine such as pressing and holding down more than one key at a time. Overnight I 'saw' how to apply a more advanced algebra to arrive at the required analysis. Whatever the method, every number representing the raw data certainly had to be keyed in once – but why not only once instead of several times as in the existing method? After some experimenting, I achieved my objective. By the following afternoon the calculations were complete and the results nicely written up. I took my folder to Mr Tippett. The task normally took at least six days and here it was completed within six hours. There was no further mention of my appointment being temporary. I did, however, manage to make it a condition of my employment that I should have every August free (without pay) to go to St Gilgen and a full week's leave during January to go skiing.

This success was the result of my long acquaintance with higher algebra. It is surprising how many research and development projects are amenable to pure, not even applied, mathematics. Sometimes one has only to stand and watch a process for a while, think a bit, and then come up with a better method. It seems to be more a matter of imagination and experience than of academic attainment, although skill is needed in writing-up and explaining a process to others. The most brilliant invention or method is of no practical use unless it can be reproduced; preferably, if it is to be a common item of equipment, as simple in construction as possible, reliable and at an affordable price.

I enjoyed every moment at Shirley. The staff were friendly and helpful, tolerant about the deafness. I was in a 'one-off' job, not in competition with anyone, attached for convenience to the Liaison Department because there was nowhere else to put me. This department's main function was to answer calls of distress from member firms and to go out to their mills on request as trouble-shooters. This was grand for me, because the deafness, far from being a handicap, could be an advantage. Those Lancashire mills were incredibly noisy, particularly in the weaving sheds, with the heavy beams crash-banging all day as the shuttles sped back and forth between the warp threads. Visitors with normal hearing were lent ear-plugs. The weavers did not attempt to talk. They used their own tick-tack language and, indeed, lip-reading. I was in my element. Moreover, with my kind of deafness I can hear better in an environment with a lot of vibration (although not in the dreadful noise of people shrieking at one another at parties).

One day we had a call for help from a weaving mill. The employee who had mixed the 'size' each morning for the past fifty years had died and the mill foreman didn't know the correct recipe for the mixture. We asked where the measuring ladles were. 'That's the problem' came the reply, 'He always used a bowler hat. It has disappeared and we don't know how big it was.'

Spinning is a matter of twists and thickness (the 'count') and the number of strands within a thread – namely 'ply' that had come into my life so early when knitting the scarf for the soldiers. The best quality cotton yarn was not spun on glorified versions of the old picturesque spinning wheels, but on 'mules'. Huge machines, all driven by coal-fired steam boilers, moved a mule of about twenty spindles back and forth in tracks. A man, usually bare-footed because of the dripping oil, moved back and forth with the mule on which the spindles were mounted; it pulled out the raw cotton into thin strands on the outward journey and wound it onto the spindles, twisting it as the mule returned. One day, the story goes, the supervisor saw that the elderly mule operator was staring out of the window, his mule neglected. 'Whatever are you doing, Sam? You've been working here for fifty years, and never before been seen neglecting your mule.' Sam turned away from the window and remarked dolefully: 'It's th' missus. She passed away t' other day an' I thought the least I could do was t' watch th' 'earse go by.'

All army tents had by tradition been made from woven flax canvas. At the outbreak of war in 1939 flax was in short supply. The only practical alternative was cotton, but cotton canvas was not impervious to water and was a poor substitute for flax. We managed to design a new weave pattern and cotton threads of special twist and 'count' to meet this challenge. This was again an example of 'ply'. It was moreover a matter of geometry – pure mathematics – a nice problem that had a neat and successful solution. The requirement was that rain falling on a tent or coat should run directly downward and not soak through the woven fabric. It fell to me to devise a new weaving pattern so that this could be achieved with cotton.

Another application of pure geometry pleased me. When weaving with the then-new rayon yarn, if a crease began to develop it steadily increased and ruined the roll of cloth. My solution was to make a smooth bar precisely in the shape of the arc of an ellipse at its point of least curvature. The two halves of the cloth as it was being woven would then tend to pull outward toward the edges, with the curvature increasing towards the two selvages. The curvature was very slight. A crease was prevented from starting and the width of the finished cloth remained virtually unchanged. I called the invention the 'Kaymo Smoother Bar', my initials after marriage being K.M.O. There was no financial reward: we were paid a salary and it was our job to invent, the inventions being the 'intellectual property' of the Institute. There were no individual patents for employees, whether in research establishments or universities: a restricting principle of considerable contention until dealt with more realistically in relatively recent times.

The cotton industry was going downhill fast, overtaken by the production levels on modern machinery in India and the Far East, developed by the young men we had taught and trained in Manchester's colleges and the University, while we ourselves, lumbered with outdated machinery that we had insufficient capital funds to replace, followed traditional methods passed from father to son in family firms over generations. Noticeable also, and well-recognised in the Liaison Department at Shirley, were the secretiveness and suspicions between rival firms: family trade secrets had to be preserved. This made the work of the Institute especially difficult and often very frustrating.

Life at home in Manchester while I was at the Shirley Institute was far from all work. I spent much of my free time with Father Bob who needed companionship. I played hockey for Lancashire and for the North of England and the Reserve England elevens. I did most of my training with a skipping rope outside the back door, starting at 50 to 100 skips and working up to 500 or more before an important match. Because I could not hear a whistle, I always umpired myself (indeed, I later qualified as a county umpire), otherwise I could have gone hairing off down the wing unaware that a foul had been given and that the rest of the field was waiting for the ball and the free hit. This also meant that I was rarely caught off-side. I normally played at left wing. I developed a knack of running at high speed just inside the side-line and, without slowing, whacking the ball across the field to the right inner who would be well-placed to score. One wet day on a muddy ground I slipped while making this manoeuvre and tore a shoulder muscle. I was never as good at this again.

I also spent what time I could at the ice-rink, concentrating on gaining the ten grade medals in figure skating. I was mad enough to join a women's ice-hockey team. With no other British competition than a women's team based on Queen's Club in London, I was selected to play in a team representing England against France in Paris. I travelled with two ice-hockey sticks in my ordinary hockey bag. This brought disaster when crossing London, trying to negotiate the then new Bakerloo Underground moving staircase (we didn't use the word escalator until years later). The long sticks stuck out of the bag and became caught in the mechanism, smashing to pieces. I had to borrow someone else's spare stick for the match – which, I am sorry to say, we lost.

In February 1939 I was runner-up in the English-style British Pairs Ice-Skating Championship. My partner had been champion before, skating with his wife, but she was pregnant and I stood in for her. English-style is more sedate and self-disciplined than 'continental-style' where, in the free-skating competitions, specific spectacular jumps and spins are compulsory. After the war I was far too old at 34 to return to competitive skating, but I am a life member of the National Skating Association and I remained on the list of competition judges for many years.

Robert's work

By 1936 when I went off to Innsbruck on my own to ski, Robert, then also aged 24, had gained his qualifications as a doctor, but he was still studying for his Fellowship and was a resident registrar at the Manchester Royal Infirmary. He was paid £50 a year, but his laundry and food were free. He served under several of Manchester's most eminent surgeons. Two in particular he all but worshiped, and was able to use his skills in photography that he had acquired at school and when at Oxford to help in preparing material for their various public addresses and lectures. Alexander Graham-Bryce FRCS, tall, thin, and at first acquaintance rather forbidding, was the first in the world to do an open resection of the lung. Robert assisted. Deep into a patient's chest, Graham had a constant cry: 'More light, more light.' Another time, stepping back briefly from the operating table, he uttered, miserably: 'I wish I'd never started.' Several of such sayings became part of our family stock of exclamations.

Professor Sir Geoffrey Jefferson FRCS was a brilliant pioneering neurologist. Late one night a desperately ill woman was brought into the Infirmary. Geoffrey ordered his team to scrub up and without hesitation cut a window in her skull, found a tumour and saved her life. There had been no X-ray guidance. Afterwards, when asked how he knew where to look, he replied: 'When I was a student I spent long hours in the post-mortem room examining in minute detail every case where the cause of death had been a brain tumour. I remembered a woman just like this patient who had died of an inoperable tumour – so I thought it worth looking in the same area.' Sir Geoffrey was also rather absent minded. One morning, after having given a lecture in Leeds the night before, his wife asked him where he had put the car when he returned as she couldn't see it. He had left it parked in Leeds and had returned to Manchester by train, as he had always done as a student.

In 1934 Robert shot the first live colour ciné-film in the world of a surgical operation when his father operated on a foot (*hallux valgus*). The risk of a light-bulb exploding would have made filming an abdominal operation far too dangerous. He used the original French Dufay film based on the three 'negative' primary colours – yellow, cyan and magenta – a great breakthrough. The following year he made another colour ciné-film, again with his father operating on a foot (*pes cavus*). This time he used the 'new' Dufay which in addition to the three negative colours had a black grid. This gave a far superior image. I assisted (also scrubbed up) lugging the lights about and stopping people tripping over the cables. I became accustomed to the usual verbal abuse hurled at lighting assistants. Both these historic films were lost during the upheavals caused by wartime bombing.

With the threat of war in September 1938 temporarily averted, work went on much as before. I was still at the Shirley Institute and Robert a resident registrar at the Royal Infirmary. Twelve months later we were into the real war. Robert and I married in the first week, on 6 September 1939, and I stayed on at Shirley until Charles was born in 1941. Then it was taken for granted that I left. Even in wartime mothers did not work in a 9-to-5 job when they had a young baby. Thrilled though I was to have Charles, I was sorry to have to leave.

CHAPTER 10

The war years

If I had expected a warm welcome on arriving home from St Gilgen on 3 September 1939, I was much mistaken. A furious Robert was on the station platform. Why the dickens hadn't we reacted to his telegrams and come home as fast as we could a fortnight before? My parents were in an equal rage. Mother had been struggling to fix black-out curtains and had needed help with a number of other urgent chores. There was, indeed, an air-raid siren warning on that first night, but it was a false alarm. I couldn't hear it. I never heard the sirens throughout the war – I had to be dependent on others. My only thought was getting to St James's Church in Didsbury and being married. I took it for granted that Robert would be posted abroad immediately – and be slaughtered in northern France as had happened to so many soldiers. I dreaded being left unmarried after so long betrothed. We couldn't hold the wedding before the Wednesday morning and I never thought to go and buy or hire a white dress. Gas masks in cardboard boxes had already been issued and it was compulsory to carry them everywhere. I drew the line at walking up the aisle with a gas mask and left mine in the West porch. Robert was already a captain in the RAMC and members of his TA Unit formed a guard of honour. It was a glorious soft sunny September morning with an azure sky and fluffy white clouds – Didsbury could not have looked more lovely, but we were not in the mood to appreciate it properly. Robert was given 24 hours leave and we went to Buxton Hydro instead of the long-arranged honeymoon visiting his mother's relatives in Canada. He returned on the Friday to his unit, then stationed at Preston. I went back to my work at the Shirley Institute in Didsbury. In the event, no-one was 'ready' and we sat out the next six months in what became known as the 'phoney war'.

We lost a first baby, prematurely, in April the next year. I thought it was the end of the world, but it wasn't. I was soon back working at the Shirley Institute. Had this child lived I would undoubtedly have been morally obliged to accept a proffered refuge in Canada. Two ships sailed from Glasgow, loaded with mothers with babies and young children. One was sunk in mid-Atlantic by a German submarine. There were no survivors. When our son Charles arrived a year later, there was no question of evacuation; the German blitzkrieg was building up: we had to manage as best we could staying where we were – in Manchester. Seen in retrospect, this was the best thing that could have happened.

There was never any question during the war of setting up house on our own. Robert was away from the start and the conditions of war made being deaf significant: I was dependent on others. I could not hear air-raid warnings, nor the radio unless it was turned up very high and I was close to it. Nor could I hear the telephone easily as there were no amplifiers for domestic phones. If, as we hoped, there was to be a baby to care for, it would have been irresponsible for me to be alone in a house overnight. My mother loved Robert dearly and they got on splendidly. The double spare guest-room at 11 Elm Road where I had lived for twenty years, was made comfortable for us. Father Bob at Broome House was only a mile away. It could not have been a better war-time arrangement.

Although Robert had several embarkation leaves (including one to go to Norway), he remained in England for over three years until being posted to North Africa in 1942. By December 1940 I was seven months pregnant with Charles. Robert was stationed in Preston and I stayed in digs there for a few weeks. The lodgings I occupied were across the road from Preston Town football ground that was being used as a prisoner-of-war camp. I was back at home in Didsbury during the big German air-raids on Manchester on 20 and 21 December. I spent the first night under the billiard table at Broome House with Father Bob, and the second under the stairs with my parents in Elm Road. After that we cut a hole in our kitchen floor, fitted a trapdoor and wooden steps directly into the cellar. This avoided having to go out of the back door and down the outside cellar steps in future raids. Charles was born on Sunday morning, 9 March 1941 in a local nursing home. During the Saturday night there were heavy raids and I was carried down into their cellar three times while in labour. Landmines (bombs dropped by parachute) demolished three houses nearby. Back in Elm Road with the new baby Charles, he and I spent 37 consecutive nights in our cellar shelter, by then made comfortable with a camp bed for me, a cot for Charles.

We were never actually hungry, but by 1942 we became short of some basic foods. British Restaurants, under the general supervision of Lord Woolton, owner and manager of Lewis's store in Market Street, Manchester and chancellor of Manchester University, were a huge success, providing plain nourishing food. It was somewhat more difficult in our town homes. We walked to the shops every day and stood in queues with our ration cards for whatever extras were available. I remember queuing for half-an-hour in the hope of buying two tomatoes. We had a wartime phrase: 'If you see a queue, join it, there may be something on offer.' There was a special ration of a pint of fresh milk a day for a baby – and orange juice could be collected from a clinic by pregnant women and mothers who were breast-feeding. My mother, brought up on a farm, was a good plain cook, but there had always been plenty of fresh food. She never got the hang of using powdered egg or dried milk. One day Charles, when aged nearly two, was sitting in his high chair drawn up to the table where my parents and I were having supper. What remained of the week's ration of cheese for the four of us was on the table. Charles leaned forward, grabbed the cheese and pushed as much as he could into his mouth. Bye-bye cheese for that week. We had no choice but to laugh.

One great joy was the food parcels we received from time to time from Robert's aunts in Canada. Particularly welcome were the gifts of waterproof baby pants for Charles that could be worn over the clumsy 'Terry' nappies. Plastic pants were a new luxury that we had never seen in the UK.

Robert's sixth embarkation leave was 'for real'. After about three weeks knowing nothing, I received a delayed letter from him headed 'At sea'. He was writing from mid-Atlantic on a circuitous voyage with his field ambulance on his way to the Mediterranean and North Africa. The shock on receiving this letter was so great that I promptly had a miscarriage. I cried non-stop for three days and then picked myself up and took the tramcar to the University to see how I could best use my mathematics (notwithstanding being deaf) to help in the war effort.

Based on the experiences of the Great War, I assumed that Robert would not come back alive. He nearly did not. He had hepatitis three times in North Africa and also an endemic malaria. He was blown up twice when in tanks but on both occasions escaped with only minor injuries. He survived the trauma of the Battle of El Alamein in November 1942 and, nearly a year later, the landing at Salerno in Italy, only to be taken prisoner when crossing a river to try to assist some members of his unit. He escaped when British gunfire hit the German headquarters where, stripped of all insignia, he was being interrogated. He then had the perilous task of getting back across the river. He was no swimmer, but managed. It was pitch dark and there was still the worse hazard of being shot by suspicious British sentries guarding against German counter attacks. His ruse was to shout in a simulated broad Lancashire accent every swear-word he could think of – he couldn't be anything else but British and it worked. I knew nothing of this until, mercifully, when the war was over he did eventually return home more or less in one piece.

I had to leave the Shirley Institute when Charles was born; I was content to be looking after him full time. I was not unduly worried about money and the idea of a career never entered my head; the future, if there was to be one, was far too uncertain. At the worst I would be a pensioned war widow. I kept in touch with the head of the mathematics department at Manchester University, Professor Louis Mordell. He suggested that I should chat with Dr Kürt Mahler, a refugee from Hitler's Germany who had come to Manchester in 1938. Mahler's room was on the same ground-floor corridor bordering the main quadrangle where I had the tutorials with J.M. Child before taking the Oxford scholarship exams some thirteen years before – and no less dismal. A brilliant mathematician, Mahler spoke only broken English; his post had no teaching or departmental responsibilities. His main interest was in number theory and he was engaged in work in the geometry of numbers. This was most propitious; almost as though the clock had been turned back to the time I had spent with J.M. Child.

Mahler outlined to me an unresolved problem concerning 'critical lattices' and I took it home. Critical lattices relate to whole numbers in two or more dimensions and lead, by geometrical methods, to solutions concerned with 'close packing', for example, how best to stack tins in a cupboard or oranges in a box.

These are just the sort of mathematical conundra that I enjoy: nice, symmetrical, geometrical figures (not necessarily convex, but always 'bounded'), and positive whole numbers – right up my street. Without any background knowledge, I solved the problem that Mahler gave me within a couple of days and took it to him, surprised that it had seemed so easy to solve. He was even more surprised and said that, if expanded, it would merit a PhD at Manchester. Being an admirer of Oxford, he suggested I go back to my own university and work for an Oxford DPhil.

Although a reserved scientist, the deafness limited what war-work I could undertake. I could work on my own anywhere I wished or not at all, but to be a registered student (and I had to be registered if I aspired to a higher degree) an official permit was required. This would be difficult if not impossible to obtain. Undaunted, I took the train from Manchester to London the next day, went directly to the Ministry of Labour and, without any appointment but armed with a pithy one-page letter that I had drafted the night before, walked up to the Minister's office.

The Minister of Labour in the National Government was Ernest Bevin. In his office I encountered two civil servants and began to explain with great enthusiasm how exciting the geometry of numbers could be, pulling my working papers from their folder. I explained that being deaf meant that I couldn't undertake ordinary war-work, but that I could coach students on a tutorial basis. All that I needed to do my research in Oxford was the written permission of the Minister so that I could register. Reluctantly one of the civil servants went in to the Minister. He probably said: 'There's a woman in our office who is all excited about some mathematics and she wants permission to work in Oxford University – she insists'. The remarkable man probably said 'Why not?'. The civil servant came back and told me I could have the permission and they would send me a letter within a few days. 'Oh no,' I said, 'I am not leaving this building without that letter, here is a draft I have already made – can it, please, be signed now?' Amused, even laughing, and no doubt anxious to get rid of me, he had the letter typed and signed there and then.

The reason for my haste was that if I were not in Oxford within the week and with the signed permission, I would miss the remaining six weeks of that term: I needed those weeks to fulfil the required minimum number of nights-in-residence in Oxford to obtain the DPhil. There had to be six such terms of residence to qualify. As it happened, when the war in Europe ended I had just completed the time required. I would never have stayed in Oxford after Robert returned home. Had I not been as insistent as I was that day, it is probable that I would never have achieved the Oxford DPhil that has been such an important and useful part of my credentials ever since.

Within a week of my visit to London I was admitted to Somerville as a member of the Senior Common Room, entitled to eat at the High Table. On the advice of my former tutor of undergraduate days, W.L. Ferrar, I was directed to Theo Chaundy as my DPhil supervisor. He worked mostly at his home in Headington in south Oxford, but as a Student (i.e. Fellow) of Christ Church his rooms, I was pleased to note, were those once occupied by Charles Dodgson (Lewis Carroll) in Tom Quad. Chaundy was often poorly and I would stand in for him and give the tutorials. Although nearly all male undergraduates (and the majority of younger male university staff) had been called up, there was always a trickle of students on 'emergency' one-year mathematics courses, whom I helped. I could manage the one-to-one tutorial teaching with the help of lip-reading, together with the ubiquitous pen and paper of any mathematician.

Theo Chaundy's field was the calculus and differential equations, not number theory. Through me, he began to be interested in critical lattices. We exchanged pages of written mathematics each day using the Oxford colleges' messenger system – a man on a bicycle who collected and delivered letters to every college twice every weekday and once on Saturdays. The effect was rather like fax would be today: a continuing stream of interacting handwritten correspondence.

My conscience pricked me that I was spending my time wallowing in pure mathematics. I asked if I could change my DPhil registered work-scheme to do something 'more relevant to the war effort', but this was refused. 'Who knows?' came the response: 'Sometimes pure mathematics makes greater contributions than any applied mathematics'. I gave up the idea of changing my thesis plans and continued working on critical lattices.

Every true mathematician sees mathematics everywhere – in a child's swing or a pendulum, in the outline shape of a tree and that of its leaves, in the clouds, in the way a circular tube is made from straight strips of paper. As a wartime fire precaution, Somerville had erected a large emergency static water tank in the front quadrangle. It froze solid during the winter of 1944. As an experienced ice figure skater, I could not resist donning my skates and carefully tracing and retracing an extended figure-of-eight several times so that it would be clearly seen until the thaw. It lasted at least a fortnight and I used it as the base of a new critical lattice problem, the solution of which became one of the published research papers that constituted my DPhil thesis.

When I was working at my mathematics our growing baby son Charles was never an interruption. I played a continuous stream of children's gramophone records or helped him with whatever he was making, while my line of thought continued undisturbed, because we were not cerebrating on the same level. When I found a good mathematical result, I jumped around in glee with Charles, then about four. If we then went out for a walk, he would stop people we knew with a proud announcement: 'Mother's got a sum right, mother's got a sum right'. He took as much pleasure in this as I did. In all, I had five original research papers published within the two years, sufficient to gain the DPhil without any formal written thesis. Looking back, I know that I did not make the best use of my undergraduate years mathematically, but I certainly made the best use possible of this second opportunity.

The wartime food in Somerville was good, although I remember a seemingly perpetual smell of boiled cabbage emanating from the kitchens. The college became popular with male students who cadged invitations to dinner. They had to bring their own ration vouchers. One of Oxford's leading mathematicians, Fellow of Merton and deputising during the war as bursar, H.O. Newboult, went to his college chef, 'Our undergraduates are hungry', he said, 'They always want to go to Somerville for a meal if they can. Why can you not produce something filling like "toad-in-the-hole"?' The Merton chef, in his tall white hat, who was used to cooking dozens of chickens on the traditional college kitchen spits, drew himself up to his full height and pronounced, 'Sir, gentlemen don't take toad-in-the hole'.

My two years at Somerville during the war coincided with the arrival there of Margaret Thatcher (then Margaret Roberts), thirteen years younger than I am. I came into regular contact with Dorothy Hodgkin, already famed for her achievements in crystallography, who was Margaret's tutor and often dined in College, but, except for the Senior Common Room friendships, I was totally absorbed in my mathematics and I had no special interest in politics. There was little social life in Oxford during those war years and few contacts between members of the Senior Common Room and the undergraduates other than through academic work. My strong links with Margaret only developed twenty years later when she was Shadow Secretary of State for Education in opposition to the second Wilson government.

In Oxford I lodged at the Parsonage, No.1 Banbury Road (then divided into two privately owned houses), a few minutes walk from Somerville. One traumatic memory is of the evening of the Normandy Landing, 6 June 1944. The route from the army barracks at Kidlington to the air-field at Didcot was along the Banbury Road and straight through the city. British soldiers in full battle attire were driving motorbicycles with a colleague in a side car, the vehicles stuck in a slow-moving tail-back. They were to be crammed into gliders towed in threes by huge American aircraft and unhooked on arrival over France, their motorbicycles being dropped by parachute from accompanying cargo planes. The long column of motorbicycles crawled past our gate. For several hours, my landlady Mrs Nelson and I brewed strong tea (not rationed) and carried mugs to them as they slowly drove past. Before the trail had ended, we saw the first United States planes passing overhead towing the gliders with our troops in them. How many of those now drinking our tea would still be alive in twenty-four hours time? Some, we learnt later, were unhooked prematurely, meeting immediate disaster at the hands of the German troops waiting on the ground

Oxford became swamped with American troops prior to the Nor-mandy Landing – welcome reinforcements. Young girls, with our own young men all away, fell like skittles for these tall, handsome, well-fed young men with their 'priceless' gifts of silk stockings (nylon had not yet been developed) and chocolate (rationed and almost unobtainable). The situation in 1944 and 1945 on the home front was much more critical than those, like Robert, fighting their way up Italy, ever fully realised. Food was limited and restricted. We were weary of war. The enemy V1 unmanned flying bombs and then, worse, the V2 rockets falling mainly in and around London, were sapping the morale of civilians. We glued ourselves to the wireless to listen to Winston Churchill when he spoke to the nation, boosting our spirit with his stirring oratory.

Shortly after VE day in 1945 the telephone rang, and a by-then unfamiliar voice said, 'I am at Paddington Station and I shall be arriving in Oxford at half past four.' It was Robert. I jumped in ecstasy. I thought he was in Palestine, having been sent there directly from Northern Italy without coming home on leave. I was on the platform to meet this stranger with a bright aluminium front tooth, made to protect the stump left when he had been blown up in a tank. I took him into College for dinner. My chief memory is of his impact at the High Table. Every other word he uttered was a virulent army swear word. It had become such a universal habit among our troops that he was totally unaware of it. This did not go down well.

The reason for this sudden appearance was simple. Robert was by now a full Colonel. The army had decreed that any officer above the rank of Lieutenant-Colonel who had had no home leave for more than two years should be allowed to hitch a lift on the first available RAF plane for a fortnight's special leave. We returned home to Manchester the next day and Robert had about ten days to try to get to know Charles, whom he had not seen for over three years. After the fourteen days were up, we went back to London together for him to await a seat on a returning RAF plane. We stayed at a boarding house behind Harrods, while Robert reported each morning to see if there was an RAF flight to Palestine, where he was to become stuck for another six months. The formidable landlady refused to allow us to occupy a double room, despite my wedding ring and ration card, until we showed her proof of marriage. The outcome of this happy and unexpected fortnight was that nine months later Florence was born, just after Robert had at last come home for good.

A minor misfortune was that he infected me (and through me, Charles) with scabies. This was a scourge of the armed forces towards the end of the war. Robert had picked it up from unwashed army blankets on a stop-over in Rome. The infestation does not become apparent for about six weeks until eggs buried under the skin hatch and little yellow spiders begin to burrow. Because we kept ourselves clean, the symptoms were unfamiliar and we were scratching for no obvious reason. Only when I wrote saying that I had scabies did Robert realised it was this that was causing him such discomfort. Once diagnosed, the treatment, although unpleasant, was simple and effective.

In the last phase of the war in Italy, Robert was offered the appointment of Brigadier to take up command in the RAMC in the Middle East. This meant joining the permanent regular army with no release when hostilities ceased. I knew nothing about this and he did not consult me, but made up his own mind that he wanted to be free to return to civilian life and to be in this country with me and Charles and any other children we might have. Robert was very happy in the army and it was a great temptation. Had he accepted, I would unhesitatingly have supported his decision and shared my life with him as an army wife in service abroad.

Robert was one of the last serving non-regular medical officers to be demobilised and the best posts in Manchester had already been filled. He decided to qualify as quickly as possible as a radiologist so that he could earn a proper civilian living at last. There were more exams to take and, intriguingly, his greatest deficiency was in some of the mathematics. Here, for the first time, my knowledge came in useful for him and I was able to help. He was offered a post in London. We had to make a decision: to pack up and go to London, accepting an attractive post there, or stay put in Manchester with something less ambitious. We were of absolutely like mind. We would stay where our roots were – in Manchester – but with one caveat: 'whenever either of us wishes or needs to travel to London, we will never let any expense or other obstacle prevent us'. Travel expense would be nothing, anyway, compared with the costs saved by not living in London. It was absolutely the right decision. We were equally in full agreement that we would never be persuaded to leave Didsbury. Relatives and friends were moving out to lusher areas in

Cheshire, or to the attractions of the Peak District we both loved, but we preferred to remain within ten or fifteen minutes' car drive from the city centre, from Hallé concerts, the Manchester Royal Infirmary where Robert became established, the University and its library and other places that mattered most in our lives. Over the years and particularly now, when I am perforce alone, it has proved to be the ideal place to live.

There were some raised eyebrows when Florence was born on 21 February 1946 as not everyone had known of Robert's short surprise leave nine months before. My parents felt that we should have 11 Elm Road to ourselves once Robert had returned. They bought a smaller house a hundred yards away around the corner in Pine Road. When Father Bob died in May 1948, this meant the end of Broome House for us. The main task of selling and moving out fell to me. We soon decided that 11 Elm Road was too big. The solution was for us to move to Pine Road and to live next door to my parents. So we built a house in their garden, sold 11 Elm Road and moved in to Pine Road ourselves on 2 June 1953 – Coronation Day! We had a blissfully happy two years under this arrangement, but then mother was diagnosed with cancer and she died in October 1954, aged 74. Because the houses were next to one another with a common garden, we were able to look after my father there until he fell ill and died thirteen years later.

CHAPTER 11

Hearing at last

In 1949 one of the greatest blessings I could imagine was granted me. Technology had advanced – viable hearing aids had been developed and I acquired one. We had come through the war. We had two children. I had a higher degree in mathematics and a range of new opportunities – and now, miracle of miracles, I could begin to hear almost properly.

The development of hearing aids was due to the invention of the transistor by William Shockley in 1945. Miniaturisation of electronic equipment in general was the priority. Hearing aids and other gadgets were largely spin-offs from the work on the hydrogen bomb and from efforts of the USA and the USSR to be first to put a man on the moon. Their invention opened up the world for me; I can never be more grateful. I was approaching my 40th birthday. I had 'got by' relatively successfully with lip-reading and other people's general kindness, but with hearing aids there could perhaps be a different prospect.

My first hearing aid was a crude contraption. A cable ran from the ear-piece to a bulky microphone worn strapped to my midriff beneath my clothes, causing appalling rubbing noises with every movement. From the microphone more wires led to heavy batteries for which I made a bag strapped to my thigh. The batteries lasted at most for a day, but it was wonderful. When I walked down our hard-wood stairs I heard my footsteps for the first time and nearly fell headlong. I heard birds sing. To hear cars in the road came as a shock. At last, I might begin to live a normal life.

Hearing aids gradually improved, in quality of tone and in the volume they could give. They also became smaller. The Achilles heel of hearing aids for me has always been the ear-moulds and the whistle created if the volume is set too high. Ears have highly sensitive cartilage. If the mould is made to fit tightly, wearing it soon builds up to agonising pain. If it does not, then there is a tendency to have a socially unacceptable feed-back whistle. This problem has still, in the year 2004, not been satisfactorily solved and, worse, the skin becomes tender when age increases. There is hope that this may yet be resolved, but it is unlikely to come soon enough for me. An aid cannot be worn at night; the pressure of laying the head on a pillow is too great. For the partially deaf, this may not matter; for the seriously deaf like myself, this presents a major problem despite all modern technological advances.

I had no immediate thoughts about the difference that this sudden miracle entry to a land of normal, or at least near-normal, hearing would bring. I was too surprised and there was so much to absorb and learn, but opportunities presented themselves as if by magic. The habits I had acquired in order to manage stood me in good stead in the life that opened up as the months and years went by. It was now up to me to meet new challenges.

Even with hearing aids there can be social problems, apart from the perennial panic of being caught without spare batteries. I still needed the advantages of lip-reading to get full comprehension of ordinary conversation. Group discussions can be very difficult. If the environment is quiet and people around talk in a normal way between each other, the level of sound is usually beneath my threshold and I cannot join in. This results in a tendency to try (often unconsciously) to command the conversation myself so that others turn their faces toward me. Also it helps if I know what a conversation is about and have some knowledge of the substance. As I spend a lot of time alone or create an ambience of silence around me, inevitably I have done a good deal of thinking and have much that I would like to communicate and share with others whenever the opportunity arises. This, too, can be anti-social, as it means that when in company I talk too much myself. Before I go out to some engagement, I say to myself twenty times, 'Listen, don't talk', but it rarely works. The target should be to let others talk for at least twice as long as one talks oneself. When I have returned home, I realise with shame that it has been the other way around, despite my good intentions. I have done well if I have talked for less than two-thirds of the time. The alternative of mentally switching off and not trying to join in can be socially worse.

I have never been able to enjoy radio or television in the company of others because I need too much volume. The exception to this was with my husband Robert who became rather hard of hearing but would never admit it and, even when at last persuaded to acquire an aid, usually declined to turn it on. There are ways of overcoming this with closed circuits or other techniques, but only at the expense of cutting myself off from normal hearing, which may not be an advantage and can set me at risk if I am alone. In modern lecture halls I try to sit within the range of a public address loudspeaker; otherwise I depend, as I have always done, on the kindness of friends who repeat to me either then or later what is essential for me to know. At concerts I inevitably miss a lot, but there is always enough for me to enjoy every moment – the important thing is to be there, seeing events for oneself, and never giving up.

Apart from the actual lip-reading, Professor Ewing had taught me all manner of strategies. Although I was then only a child, they have been a keystone of my way of life ever since. For example: always to try to arrive early for any assembly of people and to choose a seat with its back to the light, so that those one needs to be able to hear will have the light on their faces. In order to avoid having to write from dictation, always to have a pencil and paper handy and ask others to write down their name, address, or a required telephone number. It is almost impossible for someone who is deaf, even with today's modern aids and telephone amplifiers, to pick up numbers and letters of the alphabet said separately – we need to have them in some context and to be able to see a speaker's face. It is helpful when people talk clearly, perhaps louder than normal, but any exaggerated 'mouthing' or very slow speech is detrimental – the speech has to be natural to give the natural lip movements. Above all, do your homework. If one knows in advance what people are likely to say or be talking about, then it is all that much easier to lip-read what they are saying. These are good disciplines in any circumstances; it means only that if the deaf are to keep pace they have to work that much harder than others and try not to become over-tired.

It is my custom to turn my hearing aids off when travelling in a train or on an aircraft. This gives me peace and quiet however noisy the environment. For courtesy's sake and safety I tell any passenger in a neighbouring seat (and attendant staff) that I shall be totally deaf unless warned and that a tap on the arm will alert me to switch on and have hearing again. On one journey to London in a crowded carriage I did just this. When we arrived at Euston station, suddenly I was verbally attacked with violent language: 'You are the rudest person we have ever met. You should be ashamed of yourself.' Apparently I had been asked to make room for some relative and, not hearing, had ignored the request without reacting. The lady was so loud and strident, shouting at me in this way, that other passengers as well as myself were shocked. I waited until the carriage had emptied and wended my way alone along the platform to the exit. I did not let it worry me too much: this was the price I paid for being able to hide the deafness most of the time.

CHAPTER 12

New horizons

In 1952 I bumped into Isabel Graham-Bryce. Ten years my senior, she was the wife of the thoracic surgeon for whom Robert had worked as an assistant before the war. She asked what I was doing 'for my fellow men and women'. I explained that Robert was now at last back at home and working at the Infirmary, that we had two children who had to be taken to and fetched from school each day, that I filled in as a part-time lecturer in mathematics at Manchester University, a position that rapidly expanded when they were short-staffed, and that I was keeping up with my own mathematics research. 'Oh no', was her reaction, 'That is not what I mean. Not for a St Leonards girl. What are you doing for the community?' Isabel, who had also been at St Leonards, was chairman of the local Manchester branch of the National Council of Women (NCW). Before I could say Jack Robinson she had enrolled me as a member.

I was asked to address a monthly meeting and was at a loss to know what to talk about. There had been articles in the local press about the bad conditions in many of our older schools within the city. I was given permission to make some visits and prepared an unofficial report. At this NCW lunchtime meeting, in the basement of an office in central Manchester, perhaps ten or at most a dozen members were present. No journalist was there. I had sent a copy of my report to the leading newspapers in advance and I felt rather deflated after so much effort. To my surprise, that evening the *Manchester Evening News* and the leading national newspapers next morning had banner headlines *Shocking state of school buildings in Manchester.* This was my first experience of a useful procedure: give the press a script in good time before an event so that reporters can prepare their account at their convenience. They have then only to check that the speech has actually been made, submit their copy and go home without being obliged to attend the meeting. But the headline horrified me. Here was my beloved Manchester being vilified as a result of my press release when I knew that, even though things were bad in Manchester which prided itself as a caring city, they were certainly equally bad or even worse in most of our big cities. The press reports prompted an invitation to address the national conference of the NCW in Edinburgh. In order to save Manchester's good name at this conference, I set about finding the facts over the whole of England and Wales. This was easier than might have been thought.

Before 1950 there had been four great Education Acts: the 1870 Act that made elementary education compulsory for all children from 6 to 12 years old: the 1902 'Balfour' Act that made legal what Manchester had been doing illegally for several years, namely providing post-elementary education on the local authority rate for the more able children who wanted it; the 1918 Act which raised the school leaving age to 14, extending opportunities for post-elementary education; and the 1944 'Butler' Act with the promise of 'secondary education for all' from the age of 11 and provision for raising the school leaving age to 16 as soon as possible. The last three Acts were the result of wars that had exposed the inadequacy of the public education system in England and Wales, compared with that in other leading European countries (and in Scotland). Each Act in turn resulted in rapid expansion, with school buildings largely following uniform architectural patterns – one type in rural areas, and another, of larger and more austere buildings, in urban areas. The pressing need of each generation was to build schools for new populations, rarely modernising existing buildings. It was customary to have a ceremony for laying a foundation stone on which the date was inscribed. Almost without exception, pre-1944 school buildings, apart from repairs and minor extensions, were standing in 1953 exactly as when they were first opened, some of them over eighty years before – with outdoor lavatories and, in rural areas, still the original earth closets. Two world wars and an economic slump in the intervening years had made this almost inevitable, but this was now 1953.

Most fortuitously for my purpose, on a specified day early in each New Year (traditionally the third Tuesday in January) every school must by law make a return of all pupils on its register. These returns are used incidentally as between-census checks on population size and movements from one district to another. I had a trained mathematician's keen interest in the census, and in methods of checking grand totals by controlled random sampling. When numbers mean money, whether in grants or salaries, it is only human nature to round upward (and official bodies can sin as culpably as individuals), whereas in a census, even in the days when this was every two years and far simpler and less inquisitive than now, the tendency is to default, which leads to 'undercounting'. In a small project such as I was pursuing, the errors would not be significant, and the checks I used reduced them still further.

I wrote to all 130 chief education officers in England and Wales (80 county boroughs and 50 'shire' counties) inviting them to co-operate by asking their head teachers to add to their returns the date on their school's foundation stone. It was then only necessary for one of the local education office staff to add the totals of children in the schools built in each of the five periods defined by the Education Acts: namely pre-1870, between 1870 and 1902, between 1902 and 1918, between 1918 and 1944, and after 1944. To my delight more than a hundred chief education officers did precisely this without any further prompting and sent me the totals, divided also between voluntary-aided church schools and 'county schools'. They must have been pleased to see an effort being made to assemble information which might persuade Government to allocate resources for improving their old school buildings.

Follow-up letters to those who had not provided figures, telling them of the spontaneous compliance by such a high proportion of their colleagues, bore further fruit. By September 1955 I had up-to-date statistics for over 90 per cent of all schools in England and Wales. The missing 10 per cent could then be reliably estimated by interpolation. The survey covered pupils attending local authority (state and church) schools only – ignoring the 4 per cent or so of pupils attending private, direct grant and 'public' schools. The totals came as a shock. In January 1955, 20 per cent of children under 11 were attending schools built before 1870, that is over eighty years earlier; and over 32 per cent were in schools built between 1870 and 1902. The statistics relating to pupils over the age of 11 were not much better.

I took my analysis to the editor of the influential journal *Education* – the official organ of the then powerful Association of Education Committees, led by its indomitable chief executive, William Alexander. I remember quaking in my shoes at the prospect of meeting such an important editor, and being astonished to be welcomed by a young man, Stuart McClure, who, as it turned out, was happy to be presented with such a paper for publication – without any request for payment. The impact of this article *Old School Buildings* was great. The Government (Conservative at the time) relaxed restrictions on the capital funds that could be spent to make good or replace the worst school buildings. For ten years until then, all school capital building programmes had been directed to the battle to provide 'roofs-over-heads' for the inflated birth-rates of the immediate post-war years (of which our daughter Florence was a part), for raising the school-leaving age and for children living on new housing estates. Now, in 1955, it was at last the turn of those who had been there longer and had been somewhat left out.

This, almost by accident, made my name well known to those engaged in the administration of the education service. It strengthened my belief that, if one hopes to influence governments on social issues, it can only be done on the basis of accurately established numerical facts, not on mere opinions and protests. This had been demonstrated by Florence Nightingale after the Crimea War in 1856 and by Beatrice and Sidney Webb at the beginning of the twentieth century. I became thought of as a statistician rather than as a mathematician. It was this survey and the publicity it attracted that led to my being described nationally as an 'educationist' involved in a broad range of educational matters.

Mother's youngest sister, Vera, had married a city alderman of St Albans in Hertfordshire. A widower with four children, Jim Baum was chairman of the governors of St Albans High School for Girls and invited me to be chief guest at their speech day in the summer of 1953. I took enormous trouble over this, my first big public speech – writing, editing, learning it by heart. As the years went by, the innumerable speech-day addresses that followed had to be undertaken in a very different way, but this was the first. In the audience was the Chief Education Officer of Hertfordshire, John Newsom. He wrote to his friend,

Norman Fisher, the Chief Education Officer for Manchester, saying that if Manchester was ever looking for a co-opted member for their education committee, here was someone who might be suitable.

That I had received my schooling through the private system was largely because mother, having never been to school, was determined that Betty and I should have the best education available. I had been so happy in my two schools and so well taught, it was natural that I should want to see that the 94 per cent of children who attended local authority and church schools within the state system should have as many as possible of the opportunities that I had enjoyed. I did not know that my visit to St Albans would lead to activities based on this desire that were to dominate the rest of my life.

In May 1954 a Conservative co-opted member of the Manchester education committee died. The leader of the Conservative group in the city council, albeit in the opposition party, had the right of nominating a successor. The Butler Education Act of 1944 laid down that only two-thirds of the members of a local authority education committee could be elected members of the authority's council; the remaining one-third were to be co-opted members with special knowledge or expertise in education. I was not a member of any political party, although I admired our Member of Parliament Evelyn Hill, a Conservative, and I had helped in her election campaigns. I was asked if I was prepared to be nominated to fill this vacancy on the education committee. I was astonished and delighted and accepted without hesitation. To serve on the Manchester education committee seemed an ideal way of giving the public service that I had been brought up to believe should be a main objective for those not obliged to earn their own living. I had no other positive plans, the deafness until so recently having ruled out most possibilities. Nor, married and with young children, did it seem possible to apply for any permanent post as a mathematician in a university or research establishment. Here, as I thought, was a part-time volunteer interest very much to my liking.

Becoming involved in public life had never entered my head as a possibility. Admittedly, in 1951 I had accepted an invitation to become a member of the governing body of my own school, St Leonards, and subsequently to being the school's representative on the Association of

Governing Bodies of Girls' Public Schools, but I did not see this as public service, merely as service to my school. Having come through the private system, I had no special knowledge of state education or of local government, but the Oxford doctorate in mathematics always brought its own kudos and recognition. The new challenge attracted me: given this chance, I grabbed it. I set about reading current journals, and learning fast. Education officers said that they had to read the *Times Educational Supplement* immediately it arrived, otherwise I would be ahead of them at the 10 a.m. morning meeting.

In becoming a member of the education committee, I was entering a new world where few people knew I was deaf. For comprehension of speech I still needed to lip-read and I used all the techniques on which until then I had been utterly dependent. I needed to be able to see a speaker's face clearly, which meant having a good position at any committee table. The established tradition was that a new member had to earn a good position by seniority. For my first meeting, I arrived early (always an important strategy for any gathering), surveyed the lay-out, taking special note of where the chairman would be sitting – and then chose a seat as near as I dared to the chairman and with my back to the windows. This ensured that I would have the best view of the faces of those who were speaking to the chair. Gradually other members arrived and glared with surprise at this bumptious new member seated determinedly in a key position without any sign of moving down the table to somewhere more humble. I can still see the indignation of the lady member (later a great supporter and friend) who regarded this as *her* position as of right. We squashed up and I stayed put. As time went by, people became used to me sitting there, but I made certain that I earned the privilege by reading committee papers assiduously before every meeting. It is much easier to hear if one knows what is likely to be said. I once commented to a respected member, Alderman Dame Mary Kingsmill-Jones, on how few people actually read their committee papers. 'Be grateful' she replied, 'If everyone read their committee papers, we'd never be home for tea'.

Between 1945 and 1948 there were about 2,200,000 boys and girls aged 15 to 18 in England and Wales. In 1965 this total had risen by over half to nearly 3,500,000. In 1958 only about a quarter of both boys and girls aged 17 were in full-time education, and the opportunities for girls in part-time education after 17 were minimal. Whereas there were almost as many boys in part-time apprenticeships at 17 and 18 as had been in full-time education at 15, only 5 to 6 per cent of girls aged 17 had part-time day-release or any access to further education. We had belatedly raised the school leaving age to 15 and were committed by the 1944 Education Act to raising it to 16 'as soon as possible'. The pressures on the education system were enormous and the insistence of the majority of parents that the hazards of selection at 11 for grammar schools be removed was strengthening; it seemed sometimes almost like a lottery based on where one lived. In cities such as Manchester, which had suffered heavy war-time bombing, the problems were acute. In our industrial heyday, leading the country in the creation of national wealth, we had built large, substantial schools to provide elementary education and then secondary education for all. Despite massive slum clearance and a considerable exodus of the more affluent citizens to greener fields, these buildings, now well past their prime and in the wrong places, remained and had to be used. It has taken fifty more years until these and some of their immediate replacements are being demolished. The sad part of this is that in this process so many of the extensive playing fields surrounding these schools that were once our pride have been lost to blocks of flats and shopping centres.

Being a co-opted member of the education committee was a good introduction to local government, but, as the months passed, it brought considerable frustration. City council members and others grumbled: 'You and your education, you are forever asking for more money.' My retorts would fall on stony ground: 'There are more children. Parents are demanding a better deal.' There was support in the first paragraph of the Crowther Report of 1963:

> This is a report about the education of boys and girls aged from 15 to 18. Most of them are not being educated . . . The passage of this tidal wave [the post-war high birth-rate] through the narrows of the 11-plus has increased the public clamour against a competitive element in grammar school selection which seemed to parents to

be contrary to the promise of secondary education according to age, aptitude and ability.

Government, whether at national or local level, always involves the distribution of public funds. First, raising the money through taxes and local rates and then spending it according to perceived needs and priorities. It is always difficult to raise money without controversy, but distributing it fairly to meet disparate needs is far more difficult. When it comes to spending large sums of public money, the one check in the end is the approval of the general electorate – after all it is their money. The best way to earn the right to determine how to spend other people's money is to submit to public election. If I was to play a full part in developing educational opportunities for all, it was no use being only a co-opted member of the education committee, I needed to be an elected member. There came a chance in May 1955. Robert took a telephone call while I was out. 'If Kathleen will agree to come to Whalley Range to a meeting this evening, we will adopt her as our candidate for the city council.' At that time this was a safe Conservative seat. Robert reported the message, adding: 'If you say Yes, I shall walk out on you'. He saw me in the image of his adored late mother, looking after the house and him and the children, organising bridge parties for charities and arranging the flowers – not in public life, although he was content enough that I should be so happily busy at home, always engrossed in my mathematics and part-time lecturing at the university. He regarded the mathematics as a hobby, which was true as I was not in a full-time job. To be a co-opted member of the education committee was bad enough – a full city council, 'No'. I accepted his reaction without demur. This surely was the marriage contract and we had waited a long time for that. I did not reply to the telephone call.

A full year went by. Apart from his work at the Manchester Royal Infirmary, Robert's passion for the Territorial Army took him out of the house a great deal, and this time I came to regard as 'my time', to spend as I liked on 'my hobby', the mathematics. When he went out to a TA training evening, I left the supper things in the sink to be washed up later (no dishwashers for years yet), dashed to my desk and worked like crazy at my current mathematical problem, producing a steady flow of published papers, mainly still on critical lattices.

Then, in 1956, when I was about to complete my second year as a co-opted member of the education committee, a vacancy occurred in the Conservative-held inner city ward of Rusholme. The incumbent, Councillor Bobby Rodgers, was to become an alderman. Robert and I were attending a civic reception in the town hall when Bobby came up to us and suggested that I should allow my name to go forward as a prospective candidate. Robert by then had become inured to my constant occupation with the work of the education committee. Perhaps he was ashamed to show his opposition. I looked at him. Within the hearing of everyone, he came out loudly with 'Darling, why not?' Many years later I asked him why he had opposed the idea so ferociously for so long. He replied rather meekly, 'You have to give a chap a chance to adjust. We cannot stomach such fundamental changes all in one go.' Perhaps it was the same for most wives of my generation and background. We had grown up with a set of ideals and objectives. We had been caught up in a world war and, eventually, had won it. We had expected to return to a world as it had been before. This was an illusion: everything had changed, particularly in social mores, in attitudes to women and in the way we ran our daily lives.

Being elected a member of the city council could hardly take up any more time than I was already giving to the education committee – or so we thought. I was responsible for looking after my by then widowed father and therefore tied (willingly) to Manchester. No amount of cajoling would have persuaded me to stand for Parliament. Charles was already away at boarding school in Oundle, following in his father's footsteps. Florence, ten years old, was a day pupil at the Manchester High School's preparatory school – just across the road at the end of Elm Road where we lived. (She went on to Manchester High for two years before following in my footsteps to St Leonards School, St Andrews.)

To stand for election to the city council seemed a reasonable decision. So I submitted my application to the selection committee for Rusholme ward. There were three applicants. I wore a neat little hat – hats were compulsory on formal occasions – which disguised the hearing-aid cords. If it were known that I was deaf there would be no hope of being selected. I remember being shocked when I was asked my religion. I had always felt that to be my private business. Later I realised that the selection committee wanted to know whether I was Roman Catholic. There was a large Catholic community in Rusholme, mainly descendants of immigrants from Ireland during the Potato Famine and of the navvies who found employment digging the Manchester Ship Canal in the 1890s. I stammered 'non-conformist' and left it at that.

I was delighted to be selected. In the local elections in May 1956 I had a 1,666 majority. (I liked this; it is the date of the Fire of London and a favourite number of mine as it can be written pictorially to represent rising smoke.) This was a good majority for a local government ward. I never achieved as good a result again in the next 25 years, given the diminishing majorities common to all Conservative candidates in inner city areas. I lost the seat in 1981 when there was a massive party political swing to Labour in local elections over the whole country. So it came about that in 1956 I was a full-blown member of the city council. I retained my place on the education committee, now as an elected member, with more influence than as a co-opted member. Perhaps I can best give an idea of what being a member of Manchester city council meant to me during those years by quoting the words of a political opponent – the late Edmund Dell in his biography published in 1999 just before his death, aged 78:

> During the fifties I was for seven years a member of Manchester City Council. It is a time to which I look back with pleasure. Manchester was an important local authority and it succeeded at that time in conducting its affairs without the intervention of much party dogma. The Labour group on the City Council considered that the use of the whips, except on rare occasions, would be an insult to its dignity because councillors were entitled to make up their own minds on the basis of the arguments presented. The Conservatives took the same view. This freedom, extraordinary by modern standards, was probably the result of a residual influence from Manchester's great days as a centre of liberalism. Serving on the Manchester City Council was, therefore, an experience of a kind that Members of Parliament, marching to and fro under the instruction of whips, seldom enjoy.

CHAPTER 13

Hodge Close

In the early spring of 1954, just before I received the invitation to join the Manchester education committee, Robert and I, remembering our pre-war holidays in St Gilgen, began to look for somewhere in the Lake District, which we both loved, to spend weekends and holidays. Florence was by then 8 years old and Charles at boarding school. After searching during weekends throughout the summer, we came across an unoccupied 300-year-old road-worker's cottage, Hodge Close. It lies north of Coniston, up a one-and-a-half mile single-track road leading, principally, to a large worked-out slate quarry. Within a few days we bought it, freehold, for an almost give-away price. It has been an escape haven and retreat ever since.

The cottage had no amenities, but the three-foot solid stone walls were built to resist rough weather. Five derelict lofty Lakeland hay barns were a liability and two of them had to come down immediately. When a heavy slate from a third barn fell within inches of my head, we decided something more had to be done. This barn was converted into a double garage. Another, when we had re-built the roof, Robert turned into a well-equipped workshop. At Florence's insistence, we made the smallest into a space where I could be banished to do my typing without the clatter in the one living room (no nice silent laptop in the 1950s). With a minimum of outside help, we gradually made things comfortable, channelling water down from the fells and piping it under the road, replacing the earth closet, installing a bath, removing the low ceilings upstairs and, much later, re-roofing.

After the first ten years with only Calor gas for light and cooking, we were contacted by the Electricity Board seeking permission to erect on our property a pylon to carry grid electricity from Little Langdale to Coniston in return for a 'way leave' of what was originally about 50p a year. We were able to link to this mains supply line. Although the ugly pylon spoils snapshot pictures of the cottage, the gain in comfort and day-to-day convenience was tremendous. With electricity we could spend weekends at Hodge Close, and also Christmas and the New Year, although most years we had to hurry home during the first week in January before being iced in. The distance from our home in Manchester is precisely 100 miles from door to door. As the motorways and by-passes developed, the car journey time shortened from a tedious four hours on holiday weekends to an average two hours. Having Hodge Close meant that, as we could take my father with us, we could always have breaks away from Manchester that otherwise would have been impossible. From the start Hodge Close became my hide-away for doing mathematics. Through all the ups and downs of life it has remained that way for fifty years.

Hodge Close is quarry land, but the quarry at our doorstep was finally abandoned in the late 1950s. Every weekend the sheer unstable walls of the huge cavity bring rock climbers, while down at the bottom a deep reservoir of stagnant water attracts dozens of divers. Despite all warnings, barriers and the efforts of clubs to impose discipline, there are accidents and tragedies. Even now, with telephones, it takes at least half-an-hour before expert rescue help can arrive. It blights any holiday to have a death, especially of a fit young man, and we have had too many.

About a mile distant over the brow is a farm, Oxenfell, one of the many small-holdings in lakeland bought by Mrs Heelis, who was born Beatrix Potter – creator of Peter Rabbit. She married an astute Manchester solicitor and, as an investment, bought up many local farms. Mrs Heelis was a fierce landlord and imposed a condition that her tenants could remain in occupation only while they could still actively maintain their farms.

The occupants of Oxenfell were Jack and Marion Brown. Jack had been a tackler in a cotton mill in Colne, a small and at one time flourishing Lancashire mill town. Marion had been a weaver in the same mill. They had courageously taken the plunge to get away from the tyrannies of a Lancashire mill and escape into farming. They had no children, no income except from the farm, and no future when, at 60, they would be forced by Mrs Heelis to leave.

I used to walk over to Oxenfell with Florence every day to fetch our milk. One afternoon I asked Jack and Marion if they would like to help us re-build the derelict forge, the ruins of which lay behind the largest of the barns at Hodge Close, converting it into a bungalow, and then be our caretakers, finding other casual jobs to supplement their income. The remains of the outer walls of the old forge still stood, but the floor areas were a rubble of stones and fallen roof slates. The only structure still intact was the sturdy anvil column, set deeply into the ground at the centre of what had been, perhaps a hundred years before, a considerable workshop for the quarries. Their answer was an enthusiastic 'Yes' and we obtained planning permission with ease. It took just under three years to complete the building – Jack, Marion, Robert, myself and Florence, but mostly Jack, with no other help – in Jack's spare time and our holidays.

Marion was extremely gifted. She could make flowers grow from nothing. She created a spectacular rockery outside the finished single-storey bungalow and grew vegetables for us all. Jack, too, was a 'natural', who could turn his hand to anything and was an indefatigable worker. He had an irrepressible sense of humour and a great store of Lancashire 'tackler' stories. He used to pop over to us for a beer and keep us in fits of laughter.

In 1961 there was a nuclear waste accident at Sellafield, the nuclear processing complex on the west coast of what was Cumberland. The sale of milk from farms over a large area was banned, but the cows needed to be milked and the milk had to be thrown away, the Government paying compensation. Jack, who drank milk in large quantities, ignored the warnings. On Christmas Day 1964 I went across to the bungalow and was shocked to see him, white faced and unable to get up from his chair to greet me. His doctor had given him pills and told him to come back the next Tuesday. I hurried back to my doctor-husband and demanded that he take some urgent action. An ambulance was called and Jack was taken down to Kendal. It was myelomatosis – a virulent cancer of the marrow, like leukaemia. Blood transfusions followed and he came home three times, until everything collapsed and he died on Easter Sunday. This was a most fearful blow. Marion struggled on alone for a couple of years, but it was too isolated and she eventually went to live down in Kendal. She died there in 2001.

People say that rural areas are commandeered by town dwellers seeking second homes, pushing up house prices and making little contribution to the local community. Not us. At first, after Marion left, we could not persuade anyone to take up residence in the bungalow, except as a holiday home. After one serious failure, we were lucky to find a local family, the Adams, who wanted their younger children to go to the school in Coniston, not Ambleside. So it was education that came to our rescue. A school bus (actually a taxi) had to come up every day to transport the children to and from school. This meant that the narrow road had to be kept in reasonable condition, which did not necessarily mean just keeping it clear of snow in mid-winter. One of the now grown-up Adams children, John, together with Elisabeth his wife and their two children, took over some fifteen years later. Without John in residence in the bungalow, I could not now still have Hodge Close as a viable retreat.

Being at Hodge Close whenever possible did not mean isolation for me, even after Robert died. I could enjoy recorded music to my heart's content, set at a volume right for me with no-one to disturb. Every August there was also the Lake District Summer Music fortnight. My involvement in the years to come with music in Manchester spread to the Lake District. Renna Kellaway, wife of John Manduell the first Principal of the Royal Northern College of Music, had for several years been a director of, and participant in, the summer music school at Dartington in Devon. John and Renna thought to establish a similar summer school in the Lake District, with Renna the artistic director. Accommodation was found at Charlotte Mason teacher training college in Ambleside and sponsorship was obtained for five years from British Gas and for a second five years from British Telecom. This meant that almost every evening for a fortnight each August since 1984, I have had the pleasure of attending concerts given by the professional performers engaged to tutor the summer music school students. The standards remain high, seats for the concerts are heavily over-subscribed and the Lake District has a fine music asset during the first weeks in August for the enjoyment of both residents and visitors.

From the start, I made Hodge Close an escape haven from committee demands and other forms of public duty. Almost all my mathematics was done there, and the public speeches and books I wrote were drafted there. Every path, every steep hillside and grassy slope, every familiar rutted road has its memories of moments of insight when the solution, or at least a way forward for some problem that had been holding things up, suddenly became clear. After Robert died I was mostly alone at Hodge Close, and when taking my two little dogs (Max and Min – what other names could have suited a mathematician better?) for a walk, I would have one of my flashes of enlightenment, seeing what was needed to solve a problem just as I stepped on a stone in the middle of our nearest stream. 'Sorry, little dogs – no walkies' I would say, turning back and hurrying to put on paper the fleeting idea before it slipped away. As I ran I held my fingers crossed, hoping I would meet no-one expecting me to stop and pass the time of day and interrupting the flow of the logic.

When the weather is good, Hodge Close is to my mind one of the most beautiful spots on earth, with the majestic slopes of Wetherlam seen from our windows, and, from the level tops of the old quarry wastes that surround us, wonderful views over the bracken-covered fells and valleys, to Helvellyn in the north and the Langdale Pikes to their west.

The water coming from the fells is superb, just as we used to have in Manchester when I was a child, direct from the Lake District with no intervening treatment. In a hot summer it dries up and has to be carried from Coniston; in a harsh winter the supply pipe freezes under the road coming into the cottage. We learnt long ago how to manage with very little piped water when supplies run dry. It is not unusual in a drought for teenage campers to bang on our door asking us to fill their drinking-water bottles. They can be astonished that any dwelling, even if two miles up a hillside, does not automatically have mains water supply. Hodge Close lies on a listed 'walk'. We say that if we sit on our deckchairs long enough, everyone we know will sooner or later come by.

CHAPTER 14

The comprehensive dilemma

Becoming a member of the city council broadened my commitments. I retained my membership of the education committee – now with much more influence than as a co-opted member. I also became a member of the city council's finance committee, the first and the only woman member for many years. I was drafted to the establishment committee that dealt with the salaries and wages of all the council's employees. This was an unpopular committee to be on (there were no lunches and no visits), but it had advantages for me as a newcomer: it gave an overview of all departments of the city council and it brought me into direct contact with the workings of trade unions, which was useful ten years later when I had to lead for all urban authorities on the Burnham Committee, the negotiating body for teachers' salaries.

For reasons that I do not know, Manchester education committee had not set up separate governing bodies for its secondary and primary schools in full accordance with the 1944 Education Act. Independent and voluntary aided schools all had their governing bodies to which representatives of the education committee were appointed, but for our own local authority schools the secondary education sub-committee and the primary education sub-committee were officially constituted governors of the secondary and the primary schools respectively. The legal requirement that one-third of members must be co-opted meant that there were usually sufficient members with special interest in education able to give most weekdays to the work. We came in to the education offices on most weekdays as well as being invited to visit the schools. Members of the sub-committees came to know the schools and their senior staff well. As all headships were made by the sub-committees' staffing committees, members became very experienced indeed in interviewing and selecting new appointees. At some times of the academic year I spent as many as three mornings a week interviewing at the education offices. In this we were magnificently supported by our local education inspectors who vetted all applications before selecting a short-list of at most five candidates for interview. I 'learnt' my education that way. After a brief welcome by the chairman, the chief inspector asked the initial questions, and then each member was expected to ask supplements, the chairman never indicating any personal opinions until last. A newcomer to the committee had no opportunity to hide behind (or 'just follow') others; it was a personal test, more experienced colleagues judging the newcomer by his or her questions and reactions. In all the years and different situations since then I have never witnessed a fairer or more unbiased interviewing procedure than that adopted by our education sub-committees in Manchester. It was an invaluable training for newly elected members. There was never, but never, any collusion, and it was an unwritten law that we never discussed any candidate privately in advance of an interview.

The main job of members of the education committee was to prepare and gain approval for the annual budget for the whole education service and to provide and maintain the buildings. Schools did not have separate budgets of their own, although heads might have a *per capita* allocation of money to spend for special purposes. Staff/pupil ratios were fixed as a policy agreement. Decisions concerning the curricula were the responsibility of the professionals whom we had appointed; members did not interfere. Despite my keen interest in mathematics education, I never went into a mathematics classroom in one of our own schools, but accepted frequent invitations to visit schools (and classrooms) in other local authorities. It was our responsibility to decide only overall policy: what kind of schools should be provided and where, and the criteria by which children were allocated to different schools when there was competition.

The emphasis in the 1950s was on building new schools to keep pace with the 'bulge' in the number of children born in the immediate post-war years. Manchester was one of the few local authorities in England and Wales (and, I believe, in Europe) which succeeded in never having to introduce shifts, that is one group of children attending in the mornings and another in the afternoons, or sharing buildings between neighbouring schools. We built to the patterns of the 1944 Education Act: primary schools often divided into infant schools (up to 7 years of age) and junior schools (from age 7 to 11), with the change from primary to secondary schools at the age of 11. Secondary education was to be provided (in the heavily populated urban areas anyway) by a tripartite system of grammar, technical and modern schools. On a new housing estate of 100,000 people in south Manchester we built, almost from scratch, entirely on this pattern. In the older areas of the city we did our best, as we had done since the first Education Act of 1870, to adapt buildings to fit the current requirements.

Although all building had to be kept down to a price, the education committee did have its ideas about art – and we stipulated that at least one original work of art should be commissioned for every new secondary school building. In one new grammar school the work was a sculpture representing a man and woman lifting high a young child. A humorist in the city council, in a political debate about wasting rate-payers' money, described it as a 'plucked turkey standing on its parson's nose'. We never ventured into sculpture again.

The difficulty with the tripartite pattern of secondary education was that it necessitated a decision at age 11 about which school a child should go to. The 1944 Act had promised 'secondary education for all according to age, aptitude and ability'. In general people interpreted 'secondary education' as 'grammar school education' whereas it was planned from the start that only about 25 per cent of children would be deemed suited to a grammar school. To make matters worse, in the large cities such as London, Manchester, Liverpool, Birmingham, Newcastle and Leeds which had pioneered secondary education throughout the previous half-century, those youngsters who had not gained entry to grammar schools were in 'elementary' all-age schools, mostly in very old buildings. These had to serve as 'modern schools' with many of the same teachers teaching in the same old ways and with few if any updated amenities. The public demand for change grew so great that no government could withstand it.

In 1960 I received an invitation from the Minister of Education to serve on the Central Advisory Council for Education (England) with the remit to consider the education of pupils aged 11 to 15 of 'average and less than average ability'. The original chairman, Lord Amory, became within a few months the High Commissioner for Canada. John Newsom, the chief education officer for Hertfordshire, took his place and the Council became known as the 'Newsom Committee'. John had written a book about the education of girls, as I did a few years later, and we became great friends. I thought it must have been his recommendation that brought me an invitation to be a member of this prestigious, statutory and advisory council. Our report, entitled *Half our future*, was published in October 1963, after three years of visits to schools not only in England but, for comparison, in Scotland and France as well.

Eight or nine members of the committee, including at least one of Her Majesty's Inspectors, travelled to a local authority area and spent one or two days visiting schools for pupils of secondary school age who had not been selected at 11 for a local grammar or technical school. (Technical schools were later discontinued, but had been a useful feature of pre-war secondary-school provision.) Most of us lay members, the products of grammar schools and without direct experience previously of what less able children of secondary-school age could achieve, were almost invariably shocked by what we saw. We had considerable difficulty in coming to terms with the content of the curricula, and the lack of competence and general knowledge of many classroom teachers. Although there were notable exceptions, we found teachers writing sentences on the blackboard in meticulous copper-plate handwriting, and a whole class of forty or more pupils sitting in rows copying (yes, copying) the sentences – handwriting having precedence over content or meaning. They were all, however, taught some English grammar and the difference between a noun and a verb. Spelling mistakes were ruthlessly corrected and pupils were made to write corrected spellings six times. As for the mathematics, it was in the main 'arithmetic only' at its worst: long columns of addition in pounds, shillings and pence.

In contrast, if we were in a new building with a biology laboratory (with almost all girls, even in mixed schools), a physics and chemistry laboratory (with almost all boys), a workshop (for boys only) and a cookery room (for girls only), then it was different. This was deemed to be 'modern school' education.

There were many inspired head-teachers, particularly headmistresses in large girls' schools who were doing excellent social work in poorer areas and bringing self-respect and promise for the future into the girls' restricted lives. The overall impression, however, was of abysmally low standards. In general, if a youngster was not among the top 20 to 25 per cent or so who passed the 11-plus and gained entry to a grammar school, that was it. In theory, there could be transfer upward to a grammar school at 13. In practice in urban areas this almost never happened – at the modern schools there was no opportunity to catch up. The only hope then was to gain an apprenticeship to a trade at 15. Girls whose mothers before them had been condemned at the age of 12 to the tyranny of the mills or menial domestic service, if they did well in a post-war modern school, looked for jobs in offices, shops or restaurants, but not much else if they had failed to make a grammar school at 11. To call these schools in the older buildings 'modern schools', or suggest that they were offering a modern secondary education, made a mockery of the system as a whole.

It was the mathematics, or lack of it, that interested and frightened me. Pupils in most of the schools we visited were allowed to drop maths after the age of 12 if they disliked it or felt they were no good at it. This had a knock-on effect that was to damage a whole generation of children during the next decade. Full-time teaching staff in secondary schools were required to have either a degree (in any subject) or a recognised teacher training qualification that included a pass in mathematics at 'Ordinary level' in School Certificate or an equivalent. For teachers in primary schools this was not a requirement. The usual pattern in state-provided primary schools was for 'class teaching', not 'subject-teaching', so that a child had one classroom teacher for a whole school year. This may have special advantages for young children up to 7 years needing the stability of having just one teacher, but hardly seems necessary on those grounds as they grow beyond the infant stage. Although head-teachers could organise classes differently, class teaching through the primary school was the norm. Teachers in large urban primary schools preferred this, having more chance of getting to know the children in their class, but for mathematics this could be disastrous.

Immediately after the end of the Second World War, the school-leaving age was raised from 14 to 15 and then, in 1967, to 16. In the middle 1960s teacher training was increased from two years to three years for those without a degree. This coincided with a determined effort to reduce the size of classes: in total this was too much over too few years and too late. The restriction on married women teachers had been abolished and the retirement age delayed, but there developed a chronic shortage of teachers which lasts to this day. Raising the school-leaving age exacerbated the problems of indiscipline among unruly teenagers of increasing physical size and strength. Over-stressed teachers took early retirement. Great efforts were made to persuade qualified women teachers who had left teaching for marriage and child-bearing to return to teaching with retraining courses and salary incentives, but success was limited. Teaching in large secondary schools with high truancy, where help was most needed, had little attraction.

All this required a great increase in entries to teacher training colleges and considerable expansion of the colleges themselves. For training as a primary school teacher, entrance was accepted without any examination pass in mathematics (or even in English). Indeed, school-leavers opted for teaching and training for primary schools because they had given up maths at 12 and teaching at a higher level was barred. Teaching was a good job-choice for girls and had better prospects than shops or offices or nursing. Their lack of even a basic competence in mathematics would not have mattered so much in a secondary school where there would be subject teaching and they would not be required to teach mathematics. In a primary school a whole class of children could be stuck for a complete year with a teacher who admitted hating mathematics – and it showed. Mathematics is a progressive subject. If, for example, multiplication tables are not known then it is useless to try to teach long-division or how to understand and calculate a percentage. When the teacher in the following year cannot proceed to the next stage because of poor foundations and presses too hard to try to make up, a child can develop an even more positive dislike or fear of mathematics.

Unlike music, where almost every child can get some idea of a melody, numbers do not have the same general appeal. Moreover, when an underlying talent for mathematics exists, it needs to be activated to bring it to the surface. This may come about spontaneously, but in general it needs to be triggered by something or someone: perhaps noticing the ripples on a pond, a spider's web, a snow flake or a snail's shell. If a teacher knows nothing of the wonders of mathematics or science, a whole class or age group of children can be deprived.

In an international study of attainments in mathematics at ages 7, 11 and 14, undertaken between 1965 and 1969 by Stanford University in California, England came among the lowest of all advanced countries, with America actually lower. This was no surprise. I fought this issue about a basic 'Ordinary level' qualification in mathematics as a requirement for primary school teachers without success until, at last, in 1972, I was supported by the then principal of Huddersfield Polytechnic, Eric Robinson, a staunch and committed member of the Labour Party. He had been appointed a member of the Council for National Academic Awards, of which I was a member for ten years from 1964 to 1973. When the CNAA was about to introduce a new degree in education (which served as a qualification for teaching), Eric and I succeeded in ensuring that a pass in GCSE at Ordinary Level in mathematics should be an entrance requirement. It was another two years before this was made a requirement for all entrants to teacher training.

This serious deficiency in mathematics teaching was exacerbated by another factor. Teachers, once qualified and through a probationary year, had almost absolute tenure. Short of criminal behaviour, they received, irrespective of performance, automatic increases in salary every year for their first fourteen years until the maximum of their grade was reached. The teacher unions were unanimous in their insistence that the right to tenure should not be eroded. Tenure, which had also obtained in further and higher education, began to crumble in universities. In 1971, Sir Keith Joseph, after a spell as Secretary of State for Education, resigned from the Shadow Cabinet to take time away from active politics to re-think Conservative education policies. He challenged the right of tenure for teachers in schools and gradually it was withdrawn. Inadequate teachers in primary schools who 'hated mathematics' had until then remained in post unscathed until retirement, albeit without promotion.

Truancy was a big problem, then as now. Parents of persistent truants were required to present themselves before a School Attendance Officer, or School Welfare Officer as they came to be called, to explain why their child was never in school (it was more usually a boy than a girl). Time after time the parents would not show up. After three non-appearances they were referred to the magistrates' courts and fined. This made no difference to the child's attendance. When I was still a new member of the education committee, it fell to me to accompany the welfare officer on this thankless task. It was a good introduction to real life and I learnt a lot from the welfare officers, who knew it all. After I had experienced about two years of this, it had become such a time-wasting farce that the presence of a member of the committee was allowed to lapse. Schools varied in what they could do for themselves. In Nichols Ardwick, an old and impressive one-time charity school, a dedicated deputy headmaster who knew all the boys and where they lived, went to their homes if they had not turned up for morning assembly and literally got them out of bed and frog-marched them to school – both parents having left home hours earlier to go to work. This is not a story of the nineteenth century, but of when I was first a member of the education committee in the 1950s.

If grammar schools were to remain, then 'selection at eleven' seemed inevitable. This became totally unacceptable. For the one-in-four who 'passed' the 11-plus it was fine, but for those who failed to do so, even when it was through no fault of their own or of their parents, it could spell the end of all hope. The theoretical transfer upward into a grammar school later, at 12 or 13, rarely happened. In effect this meant that any chance of going on to university or entering a profession was almost written off at the ridiculously early age of 11. Moreover this applied to more than 75 per cent of children. Not only were parents indignant, but so were grandparents, relatives and friends who made up a high proportion of the electorate when it came to a General Election. When dissatisfied, those parents who could, chose to move house, or go to any lengths to send their children to a direct grant school (if the children were clever enough or could be well-enough coached to gain entry) or into the private sector. Except in some die-hard better-off, usually Conservative-dominated, local authorities the change to comprehensive secondary education with no selection by ability was inevitable.

In Manchester, Labour-controlled and becoming increasingly party-politically led, it took until 1966 to devise a plan for the re-organisation of secondary education into a comprehensive system. It took another year to implement it. The first plan (probably the best – it involved middle schools) was thrown out by a majority vote; the second was plainly worse and was scrapped by the Labour Party itself. The third plan, a compromise, was accepted almost in desperation. We were the victims of our own previous virtues, with nine local authority grammar schools of our own and nine direct-grant grammar schools (four Roman Catholic and five non-denominational). The direct grant schools charged fees, mostly on a means test basis, although there were bursaries. Neighbouring authorities that were short of grammar school places regularly took up some places in these Manchester direct grant schools, as did Manchester itself on a competitive basis for pupils who did well in the eleven-plus exam and had attended a state primary school for at least two years. The direct grant was later withdrawn by the Labour government and so that privilege ceased. Manchester's compromise plan, at least in the short term while the post-war birth-rate bulge passed through secondary schools, was to link each of its established grammar schools to a nearby modern school (occasionally even two), sharing staff under one head. Pupils already in the combined schools would work their way through, following their previous courses, but as new intakes came in they were treated as single groups, usually accommodated in the secondary modern building (which became the lower school of the new comprehensive). The ex-grammar school, with its better facilities, usually became the upper school. It was never satisfactory. Specialist staff had to travel from one building to another, sometimes over a mile apart, and did not feel an integral part of either. In particular, science teachers no longer had their own laboratory and there were not enough teachers with qualifications in mathematics to look after pupils in two buildings.

Good teachers, particularly if led by a good head and given freedom, can usually make a success of any school, but standards varied enormously. Discerning parents quickly became aware if there was little chance of success for their children in their neighbourhood school. If they doubted whether their offspring would succeed in gaining a place at one of the direct grant grammar schools (or they could not afford the fees), they moved out of Manchester to the surrounding areas within commuting distance of the city, altering the social structure of the city for a generation. The effect showed very quickly. Relatives, friends and colleagues moved out too. My sister did this, and Robert and I could have been tempted to follow. Against the tide, we stayed determinedly where we were, preferring to live 'above the shop', but then we had sent our two children when they reached the age of 13 to the same boarding schools as we had attended ourselves a generation before – in the private system. The erstwhile direct grant schools in Manchester remained, but on a fully fee-paying basis. The prospect for the Manchester comprehensive state system was bleak. Things change. Fifty years on, a new generation is returning to the city, but not necessarily people with children. House prices near new and popular schools have risen beyond all common sense, the mortgagers being the beneficiaries.

The secondary schools sub-committee on which I served worked for months during 1966–67, appointing heads for the re-organised schools, reshuffling other staff, allocating pupils coming up from the primary schools (mainly on the basis of precisely where they lived) and having the new plan up and ready for the start of September 1967. In the General Election of October 1966 Harold Wilson was returned as Prime Minister for a second term with a big majority. In the local election the following May, Labour supporters, disillusioned when General Election promises were not fulfilled (as they rarely are), stayed at home, abstaining. There was a huge swing to the Conservatives throughout the whole of England and Wales. In Manchester another factor contributed to this swing: at six o'clock in the evening on polling day, there was a tremendous thunderstorm – a cloud burst – followed by torrential rain until the end of polling at 9 p.m. Traditionally, Conservative businessmen vote early on their way to work and their wives during the afternoon or on their way home from work. In contrast Labour supporters vote after they have returned home from work and have had their tea, husband and wife then going out to vote together. The storm kept everyone at home that evening. In the city's thirty-three wards the Conservatives had a net gain of fourteen seats from Labour and secured majority control of the city council for the first time for many years. I should have been cheering. In fact, I sat outside the committee room in the town hall where my Rusholme ward count was taking place (it was not my turn for re-election) and could hardly suppress my worries as the news grew of the phenomenal swing to the Conservatives. I knew what this could (and did) mean for me. I had my activities nicely organised and was enjoying an interesting existence with time to look after the family as well as keeping up with the mathematics research. Now everything would be changed. I would be expected to take on massive extra responsibilities and new time-consuming commitments – probably in London (as indeed it turned out) as well as at home in Manchester. There would be little or no time for the mathematics. I could lose a lot for something that was likely only to be short-term. There would almost inevitably be a party political swing back to the left at local levels if Labour lost to the Conservatives in a future General Election. In the event, the Conservatives remained in control of the city council for four years.

I was dead tired, as after any election campaign, but on waking up next morning I made my decision: I would not resign from anything merely to make time, but take on whatever came my way and find the time somehow. Before June was out, I found myself chairman of Manchester education committee, chairman of the education committee of the Association of Municipal Corporations meeting in London with a heavy schedule, and on other national advisory committees concerned with further and technical education. Since 1964 I had been a member of the Council for National Academic Awards, set up to validate degree courses in the newly designated Colleges of Advanced Technology (CATs) that later became full universities. I also had my own special interests in the further education colleges in Manchester, in particular the creation of a new academy of music that became the Royal Northern College of Music. I cheated the clock by making all journeys to London by sleeper, so much so that I once said my address could be taken as Euston Station. This is where the deafness paid dividends. In a sleeper I took out the aids (I always wore two) and, having complete silence, was able to sleep soundly from 11.30 p.m. until 7 a.m., having a longer undisturbed night than in my own bed at home, with the advantage of arriving early at morning meetings in London, with the newspapers read and being able to stay on for any official dinner. I often travelled to London twice in a week for several consecutive weeks without anyone in Manchester knowing that I had been away – and I was never tired.

Elevated to the chairmanship of Manchester education committee in May 1967 with all its accompanying extra commitments occurring at the very moment of the change to comprehensive schools, I was the recipient of considerable flak for not immediately stopping and reversing the plans to go comprehensive in September. This in my view would have been totally irresponsible. New appointments had been made, and pupils allocated their places. Besides which, I had for some time felt that selection at 11 to grammar schools could not continue on the old criteria indefinitely. The task seemed to me to be to limit any damage and to make the new scheme work. There was however a major weakness, the full impact of which did not perhaps strike us at the time. As a nation we were trying to do too much at once. We wanted to get on with real improvement. Manchester was in the middle of a huge slum-clearance scheme and large-scale movements of people. The population was falling fast – from 700,000 in 1948 to a meagre 400,000 ten years later, the older generations following their offspring into the new overspill housing estates beyond our boundaries. There was also the significant migration of middle-class people. We were accepting large influxes of immigrants into our own new system-built high-rise flats of Hulme and Moss Side which were replacing the slums, creating, had we known, a new underclass of unemployed young people.

Even more catastrophically from an educational point of view, the drive to reduce the size of classes nationally coincided with the extension of teacher training from two to three years. This meant that provision in the teacher training colleges needed to be almost doubled. Manchester was proud to take an active part in this expansion. Within six months we had set up a completely new teacher training college in the building vacated by an inner-city boys' grammar school. The result of all this was that senior staff in our nine local authority grammar schools, facing drastic reorganisation, applied for and were appointed to posts in the expanding new colleges. The planned merging of our grammar schools with modern schools to form comprehensives was a daunting and depressing thought for committed sixth-form career teachers. Pay and conditions in the colleges were far more favourable than in schools. Although women grammar school teachers mainly stayed put, loyal to their schools, the men moved away. Almost overnight, the boys' secondary schools in Manchester were stripped of their leading science and mathematics teachers – the very teachers whom the new comprehensive schools needed most. They took up lectureships and became principals in the teacher training colleges and the expanding further education colleges.

As the years passed and the child population of Manchester continued to fall, it was gradually possible to finish with schools on split sites, but it has taken forty years. In the shire counties it was often easier to create comprehensive schools without too much disruption – their existing grammar schools became sixth-form colleges and their (mostly new) modern schools became the feeder 'lower schools'. In the cities, having to make-do with our older school buildings, the brighter pupils rarely had the full benefit of teachers of grammar-school standard. It was always hoped that pupils' achievements would 'level-upward' and in the main they probably did, but this took time. One extraordinary and unex-pected phenomenon has occurred as a compensation. As, gradually, girls have had genuinely equal opportunity with boys, the superiority that they used to have over boys at 11 in mathematics tests has spread up through the age ranges. We used to moan over the comparatively few girls taking advanced mathematics. Now they are outnumbering boys. Unfortunately for these ill-prepared schools, the job-opportunities for those with qualifications in maths are also expanding beyond earlier imagination. Whereas in my day the girls taking a degree course in mathematics had school teaching as almost the only career outlet other than to become a professional researcher, there is now a whole range of other choices.

While I was chairman of the Manchester education committee, heads of secondary schools were required to report to the secondary education sub-committee each year. After re-organisation the reports became increasingly gloomy. Almost every head reported that their disappointing results in external examinations were because of their poor, below-average intelligence intake. To me this seemed ridiculous. The same children were entering secondary education as would have been anyway, so where were all the brighter children who had previously passed the 11-plus and gone to the grammar schools? Perhaps the schools were too isolated and did not know what their colleagues were reporting. I called a special meeting of all twenty-six heads of the newly created comprehensive schools, so that they could hear each other. Each head in turn gave his or her report – all with this tale of poor intake. By the middle of the afternoon, the penny had dropped. Were we saying that all the brighter grammar school children had disappeared from Manchester? Admittedly many had moved away to surrounding areas – but surely not all and in such a short time. After that traumatic afternoon, we heard no more grumbles about sub-standard recruitment.

The work of the education committee took an immense amount of time and anyone in full-time employment could rarely take this on. We were paid no expenses and there were no attendance allowances, free telephone or postage. This, in general, limited membership of the city council and of the busier committees largely to women who were not in full-time employment and had no young children at home to look after, to men who were retired or managers of their own businesses or firms, and to trade union officials who were encouraged to give time to become elected members of local authorities and given paid time-off for meetings. All council and committee meetings took place during the daytime; evenings were for work in the wards and party political commitments. Members of a committee, other than co-opted members of the education committee, were essentially laymen. If they had a professional interest in the subject matter of a committee, this was incidental. Their role was to represent with intelligence and sympathy the ordinary man in the street. We appointed a professional chief executive, heads of schools and colleges and other qualified staff, and it was for them to run the service. The committee chairman needed to be capable of taking the chair efficiently, getting through the business quickly and seeing that clear decisions were reached, when making the senior appointments. It was best when there was a strong partnership based on integrity and mutual respect between a chairman and the chief officer.

From my own background and through my membership of national advisory committees, I began to acquire a certain expertise, but in Manchester itself I made a point of never interfering in what was happening within the schools and colleges – it was my function to persuade those in political control and the general public to provide the money for them to do their job, and then to leave them to run their own show.

Looking back now, forty to fifty years on, we probably did as good a job as we could for the schools in Manchester in those post-war years. The traditions and pride were there, but no society can live on tradition alone. There is no such thing as a stable state – not only statisticians and economists know that. Ideas and action begin to take place, then accelerate in what the mathematician describes as a 'normal curve' until gradually the acceleration slackens and the curve begins to level off. This curve of achievement rarely remains steady. Having reached its summit, it starts to fall in a mirror image of the earlier ascent until a new advance or fashion takes over. I had a stock lecture entitled 'the fashion factor' that illustrated this social phenomenon. The knack of the successful business manager or entrepreneur lies in recognising the start of the levelling off. Large cities and even nations can become trapped by their own successes and develop their own inertia, unable to change track as new fashions and needs emerge. No-one a hundred years ago would have predicted that the great leading industrial cottonopolis that was Manchester would find itself in such decline within fifty years. The years following 1956 when I became a member of the city council were largely make do and mend, doing the best we could in a way that seemed appropriate at the time. The mistakes we made were not for want of trying, more from trying too hard, with too few resources, to meet the needs of an understandably impatient and demanding populace.

Attitudes at home

Being in public life rarely runs smoothly. It is often said that when a women takes an active role of her own it is a great help if she is married,

1 The Stops family in 1906 at Tiffield
Back row l to r: Sidney, Mary (mother), George, Westley, Jessie, John
Middle row: William, Vera, Thomas (grandfather), 'Bessie' (grandmother), Winnie
Seated: Alfred, Lady (the dog), Neville

2 William Timpson (grandfather) in the 1920s

3 'Granny Stops', Elizabeth (Bessie) Ann, born in 1854

4 With sister Betty on the beach at St. Anne's-on-Sea in 1920, with a holiday friend

5 Dressing up with Betty c.1918

6 Robert, with his arm around
Kathleen, in 1918. Betty is behind them

7 Florence Eleanor Ollerenshaw,
Robert's mother, taken in Didsbury in the
late 1920s

8 At the summit of Hafelaka, above Innsbruck, in 1936

9 Tonder Villa in St Gilgen, Salzgammergut, 1930s

10 Hodge Close, Coniston, Cumbria, 1954 to date

11 Charles and Florence in 1951

12 Charles and Florence in 1971

13 Dame Kathleen on the occasion of her investiture, with Charles and Florence, near to Buckingham Place, January 1971

14 With Robert, 22 May 1975, at the start of the year of office. Reproduced by permission of the *Manchester Evening News*

15 Opening the nursery at the Manchester Royal Infirmary in July 1975. Reproduced by permission of the *Manchester Evening News*

16 At the opening of the roof garden at the RNCM dedicated in memory of Florence in July 1975. With Dame Kathleen are the Lady Mayoress (her daughter-in-law, Margaret Ollerenshaw) and the Principal. Reproduced by permission of the *Manchester Evening News*

17 Being greeted at Manchester Airport on return from the inaugural flight of Concorde from Beirut (September 1975). Reproduced by permission of the *Manchester Evening News*

18 The menu of the luncheon served on board

CONCORDE

Flight from Beirut

Menu

Brook trout in champagne aspic
Truite de ruisseau en gelée

Grilled fillet steak with savoury butter
Tournedos Café de Paris

Fresh vegetables in season
Légumes en saison
Small roast potatoes
Pommes olivette

Salad bowl . Thousand Island dressing
Salade panachée . Mayonnaise epicée

Assorted cheese
Choix de fromages

Fruit tartlet
Tartelette de fruits

Coffee
Café

———————

Champagne Brut
Grande Marque

Bordeaux
Château Mouton Baron Philippe 1970

A selection of spirits and beers on request

19 With the artist Michael Noakes and his portrait of The Queen in September 1975, commissioned for Manchester City Council by Dame Kathleen in Her Majesty's Silver Jubilee year

20 At Manchester Steel with Anne Kristin Sündt, 14 January 1976. Reproduced by permission of the *Manchester Evening News*

21 With Margaret Thatcher then Shadow Secretary of State for Education and Science, at the town hall, February 1976. Reproduced by permission of the *Manchester Evening News*

22 Celebrating Manchester City's winning of the League Cup in 1976 with Peter Swales (Chairman) and Tony Book (Manager). Reproduced by permission of the *Manchester Evening News*

23 With Sir Matt Busby, 25 July 1975. Reproduced by permission of the *Manchester Evening News*

24 With the gift she presented to the Manchester and Salford Universities OTC on her retirement as Honorary Colonel in 1981. Reproduced by permission of the *Manchester Evening News*

25 Being given the Freedom of the City of Manchester in 1984, overlooked by Sir Bernard Lovell, FRS (already a Freeman of the City). Reproduced by permission of the *Manchester Evening News*

with a husband and family to share the bad times. Robert's attitude, at least in the first years when I was on the city council, was a tolerant acceptance, glad that I was happily occupied and making few demands on him. When I became chairman of the education committee and sometimes, inevitably, became the object of media flak, he did not like this one bit, and certainly gave no sympathy. 'If you will get involved in politics, then that is your fault.' His attitude changed substantially for the better when a senior army officer, visiting his Field Ambulance, asked him if his wife was Kathleen Ollerenshaw, the Manchester educationist. From that time onward he took more notice of what I was doing and was more sympathetic when things went against me. He enjoyed accompanying me to civic events where there were important and interesting guests.

My commitments took me out of the house a great deal, but Charles and Florence were growing up and studying or working mostly away from home. I tried never to bring controversial issues home and, almost as a matter of principle, I never entertained colleagues at home or had any consultations in our own house. By mutual agreement, we council colleagues never at any time used the telephone for any discussion and, mercifully, mobiles had not been invented – so our private lives were rarely interrupted. This did mean, however, that when we met socially at receptions and on other occasions we would talk to each other like crazy, exchanging views and planning our next committee moves. This could be very bad manners. Our hosts would be annoyed if their hospitality was being somewhat abused – and they were unlikely to appreciate that we might not see one another between one committee meeting and the next. There was a monthly evening meeting of our political party 'caucus' before each meeting of the city council, but rarely more often. Councillors also had to look after their wards and attend ward meetings. In all, this could take up at least four evenings in every normal week. Robert got used to it. He was very occupied himself and I always found the time to make sure that I accompanied him when he needed me. And there were the occasional weekends and every main holiday at Hodge Close together. It added up to a very satisfying way of life.

Speech days

One potential problem in the early days of my membership of the education committee in the 1950s and 1960s was the prevalence of school speech days. There were so many: my diary for November 1964 records that I was guest speaker in the Free Trade Hall as often as three times in a single week. There were not only the Manchester secondary schools, but those in surrounding areas who liked coming to this central venue. I seemed always to be driving out of our gate, dressed in my best outfit – wearing a compulsory elegant hat, at exactly the time that a tired Robert was returning from a hard day in his Department at the Royal Infirmary. 'Where the hell do you think you're going – not another speech day?' But no-one in public life, dependent on a popular vote at elections, would dare to refuse an invitation to address a captive audience of up to 2,000 people. It became for me almost a routine. At the beginning I spent hours preparing and learning a speech by heart. As time went on, it began to come naturally. However, I found that an audience can feel insulted if a guest speaker appears not to have taken special trouble, and I usually remembered to take with me a card that had at least a few words scribbled on it to give an appearance of preparation. One advantage of this was that I omitted all conventional 'buzz' sentences because I forgot to say them. I had a small watch that was my absolute boss. During the chairman's introduction I set it on the nearest hour. As I sat down I invariably noted the time before tucking it away in a pocket for the next occasion. My rule was 'one must speak for ten minutes, otherwise the audience feels cheated, but every minute over fifteen is downhill. I learnt never to go beyond this fifteen minutes – just sitting down with my best jokes untold.

This all came to a natural end. The city council, strapped as always for cash, started to charge schools the economic cost of using the Free Trade Hall. This brought these annual speech days to an instant stop. The schools, re-organised as comprehensives, chose instead to have smaller award-giving ceremonies in their own school halls.

CHAPTER 15

Everything in the name:
the expansion of further and higher education

In the 1950s most members of the Manchester education committee were more interested in getting roofs over heads in the primary schools than in further education, but from the time when I first became a member my main interest was in post-school education. Before the Second World War, although there were some adult education classes organised by local authorities in the daytime and in the evenings, the Workers' Educational Association was the leader in the field. Further education had been synonymous with night school, places that were taken up almost exclusively by boys in apprenticeships which usually spanned seven years. This was referred to as 'coming up the hard way'.

The need for a huge expansion in the number of places in universities was plain. In 1960, the Government set up a committee under the chairmanship of Lord Robbins to make recommendations. Filling in time before the committee was fully in action, he asked several people to meet members and give informal opinions on certain issues. I was flattered to be invited. Lord Robbins asked me whether I thought that applicants to teacher training colleges should be offered the prospect of a degree in education instead of the then current diploma. I naively replied that it was the content and the recognised status of the award offered that mattered, not its name. Lord Robbins came back at me like a ton of bricks: 'How wrong you are: there is everything in the name.' This proved true not only for school teachers but, as we experienced later, for top-ranking colleges themselves which insisted on becoming universities rather than being named polytechnics.

Manchester's great pride was 'The Tech', descended from the Mechanics Institute founded in 1894. Here, many thousands of young men over the years had attended night school, pouring down the huge central

staircase on weekday evenings to get to local pubs before closing time at
10 p.m., and then walking or cycling home, sometimes long distances,
before setting off to work early next morning. In 1955, for lack of any
other nominee, I was made a representative governor. This was short
lived, because in 1956 the city relinquished control of the Tech. After a
series of transmogrifications it became, in 1968, the University of Manchester Institute of Science and Technology, commonly known as
UMIST, funded through the national University Grants Committee. Years
later, in 1979, I was invited to become one of UMIST's two vice-presi-
dents. This brought me into active contact for over ten years with its
development as a leading institution of technological and engineering
research. Now, at the time of writing, plans are well advanced for the
merger of UMIST and Manchester University to form one of the largest
prestigious research universities in the world outside the United States of
America, Australia and Japan. (I am not likely to forget the date fixed for
the official creation of the new University of Manchester: 1 October
2004, my 92nd birthday.) In its own way this will bring the process of
development full circle, where Manchester's two great institutions of
higher learning and research, started through the efforts of inspired
individuals in the late nineteenth century, nurtured by citizens and
neighbours and the local authority with its tax-raising powers, moved to
independence and national funding and now combining to achieve
greater independence and undisputed world eminence, attracting both
private and public funds.

As 'The Tech' rose to university status it left a gap that had to be filled
to provide for the increasing number of both men and women students
seeking technical, engineering and commercial qualifications and skills.
It was the local authority's task to fill this gap. In 1957 an action plan, a
scheme for post-school education in Manchester, provided for thirteen
new further education colleges, including four technical colleges. I was
elected deputy chairman of the further education sub-committee of
which Maurice Pariser, one of the leaders in the city council, was chairman. I threw myself into the work.

The amount of new building that could be undertaken in each particular section of education was strictly controlled by the Government's
education building programmes announced each year. Within these

restrictions there were decisions to be made about sites and building designs, and, in due course, the appointment of principals and the arrangement of opening ceremonies.

As a first immediate step, we built the new John Dalton College, which took over from the Tech all non-degree engineering courses. We also built a replacement for the College of Commerce, the governing body of which I became chairman in 1965. In 1967 these two leading Manchester colleges, together with the long-established College of Art and Design, became the three major constituent parts of a newly created polytechnic. Party political change in control of the city council had in 1967 pitched me into the chairmanship of the education committee, and I became first chairman of the new polytechnic governing body for four years. Then party political changes again intervened and I became an ordinary member of the governing body until I lost my seat as a city councillor in the local government election of 1981.

In addition to representing Manchester on the governing body of the Tech, in 1955 I was also nominated to the governing body of what was then Salford Royal Technical College, which had been opened in 1896 by Queen Victoria on her visit to Salford to open the Manchester Ship Canal. This technical college was also destined to rise to full university status.

It was not all smooth sailing for me. In the early 1960s, partly perhaps because I became known to educationists through my membership of the Newsom Committee, I was asked by *The Sunday Times* to contribute an article about mathematics in schools. This led to several other centre-page feature articles – one, in 1963, commenting on the Robbins Report on Higher Education; another on the issue of comprehensive schools. I described myself as a member of Manchester City Council which I was. One day I was approached by the distinguished Labour co-opted member of the education committee, Dame Mabel Tylecote, an historian for whom I had a great respect. She had been asked by the Labour leader of the city council to warn me that if when writing press articles I continued to describe myself thus or as a member of the Manchester education committee, then, because I was not a member of the controlling political party, I would be removed from all governing bodies of schools and colleges where I was a city representative. I refused point blank to comply and the threat was carried out.

The local Labour Party's action backfired. I was already well established. Without exception, every institution on whose governing body I served as a representative of Manchester (including Salford Royal Technical College) re-instated me in my own right when they found my name removed. This put me in a strong position, beyond the vagaries of local authority elections. I remained as an independent with Salford through all its up-gradings for over thirty years, serving for about ten years as chairman of the council's finance committee and becoming a deputy chancellor.

Many years after the warning from Dame Mabel, I was told that Lady (Shena) Simon, who once slighted my parents as mere shopkeepers, and who was also a Labour Party co-opted member of the Manchester education committee and a colleague of Dame Mabel, wrote to the Permanent Secretary at the Ministry of Education saying that if ever they were looking for an elected local authority Conservative woman as a nominee to serve on a national committee, I was the one to approach.

Invitations to address conferences concerned with technical education and training multiplied, and I was more widely reported in the national and educational press than ever. I became a member of a number of national committees concerned with the development of education and training in science and technology, the Oxford DPhil in mathematics being an important asset. The background gained at home in Manchester as an elected member of a large urban local authority was invaluable practical experience when debating national policy decisions. I was almost always the only woman member – and I never doubted that my nomination was partly to make these committees what is now called 'politically correct', with the added advantage that I came from 'north of Watford' and yet was willing and able to travel to London as often as required.

The mechanism through which the leading technical and other colleges gained in stature and, in due course, either themselves or in combination with other colleges, acquired the status of full universities was the creation of the Council for National Academic Awards (CNAA), established in 1964. The CNAA, chaired after its initial first few months by the industrialist Sir Harold Roxbee-Cox, had the responsibility of validating degree courses in colleges that were not universities. I was appointed a member (for the first four years the only woman) on its foundation. I was twice re-appointed and remained an active member for ten years until 1974. Like its predecessor the National Council for Technological Awards, the CNAA was remarkable in that it had no Royal Charter and itself conducted no examinations or courses. It was a validating body, responding to applications by leading colleges. When a college submitted an application to set up a specific degree-giving course, once the academic content of the proposed course had been examined by the appropriate expert sub-committee, a group of about six or seven members made a formal visit. So-called 'sandwich courses' were encouraged in which one year within a four-year degree course was spent working within an industrial or commercial firm. These arrangements also had to be carefully scrutinised. Both the academic staff and library and other facilities had to meet stringent standards. Few applications succeeded on a first round. As the only woman member of the CNAA at the beginning, I was frequently invited to be one of a visiting team. It was found useful to have a woman in the group, as a woman is sometimes sensitive to shortcomings that many men would not notice. We did not all have to be experts in the particular academic subject proposed for a degree. Only when mathematics (or the lack of it) formed a part in a course had I any special knowledge.

It was through the work of the CNAA that leading local authority colleges, after many mergers and much new building, were gradually upgraded to become polytechnics and eventually to award their own degrees, becoming in due course and after much debate, universities in their own right.

The argument centred on whether higher education in the UK should be developed in a 'binary' system of polytechnics and universities or in a 'unitary' system with all higher education in universities. I confess that I favoured the binary system, probably because I had become so involved in science and technology and thought so highly of the Massachusetts Institute of Technology in Boston. The decision went the other way. Polytechnics didn't want to remain outside the university system, just as teachers did not want diplomas but wanted degrees. As Lord Robbins had said: 'There is everything in the name'. Twenty years later, in the Education Reform Act of 1988 introduced by the Conservatives (the first major

Education Act since the Butler Act of 1944), the issue was settled. In 1992 the polytechnics and several other leading colleges gained their independence as universities. They had passed through the second stage of development from private enterprise, via the care of local authorities, to government-funded (and thus only partial) independence – the loyalties to and affections for their parent local authorities remaining. Manchester Polytechnic became Manchester Metropolitan University (the Met). I had been awarded an Honorary Fellowship of Manchester Polytechnic in 1979 and was proud of its success. Now they were in a position to award full Honorary Doctorates of their own. The CNAA had by then finished the job it was set up to accomplish and voted itself out of existence in 1992. It had awarded me an Honorary Doctorate in 1976 during the time when I was Lord Mayor of Manchester, which was especially pleasing.

Every success story has its minor disasters. Before the establishment of Manchester Polytechnic, the constituent colleges had their own ceremonies and Honorary Fellowships. The College of Art and Design had a long history going back into the mid-1880s. Among its students had been Laurence Stephen Lowry. He was born in my own ward, Rusholme, in 1887 but was brought up and lived most of his life in Salford, the birthplace of many other men of talent. He was not a good student; the records show that he failed in his examinations. In 1967 when he had become the most famous of the college's alumni he was offered an Honorary Fellowship. He accepted the award and was duly robed in gown and mortar board. I found myself sitting next to him at the dinner that followed. He was thoroughly crotchety about the whole thing: 'What does an artist want with a gown and mortar board? I am only interested in painting'. Anxious to make the conversation easier, I remarked that some years earlier I had bought a painting of his entitled *The Lonely House*. He brightened. Like every artist, he had a felt-tip pen in his pocket. He reached for my menu card and on the back drew an outline sketch of his picture. The tragedy is that, although I hoarded signed menu cards over the years, this trophy I lost.

Some years later I spoke of this loss to Harold Riley, another famous Salford artist and a great admirer and friend of Lowry. We had become friends and when I was Lord Mayor he presented me with an etching of Notre Dame in Paris. At a dinner at Salford University, he sketched for me on my menu card (that I have not lost) my two little dogs looking at the stars through my telescope. Recently I told him about my lost Lowry menu card. He capped it with a story of his own. When he was a young student, he plucked up courage to visit Picasso. The great man was sitting in his garden, sketching. Harold showed him some of his own work. The outcome was that Picasso invited him to a garden party planned for the next weekend, the condition being that every guest must come disguised as an animal. Harold spent the rest of the week creating a papier-mâché goat's head and a suit to match. This was a success. Picasso approved. He picked up a piece of papier-mâché, scrumpled it in his hands and produced in a flash a small masterpiece of a goat. Harold put this priceless treasure in a box and brought it back to Salford where he lived with his parents. He showed it excitedly to his father. His mother was out and he put it on the mantelpiece for her to see as soon as she came home. When he came downstairs a little later his mother remarked, 'Oh, I saw that rubbish on the mantelpiece. As usual, you're only back in the house for five minutes and your untidy stuff is every-where. I threw it on the fire.'

During the process of rapid expansion we were, as mentioned, always having to make-do with inadequate buildings. The opportunity to build something impressive, such as the town hall or the university quad-rangle, never arose. The price of my insistence on having brick instead of concrete outside walls for the administrative block of the new polytechnic was that the inside ceilings are uncomfortably low. The choice was between building down to a price that government would sanction or having no new building at all. It is easy to criticise, but I was there at the time; the obstacles to progress were legion.

On balance, there was much to be pleased about. The City of Manches-ter's great traditions in education-for-all, in opportunity, in achieve-ments in science, medicine, engineering and technology, as well as in music and the arts, were sustained even in those bleak immediate post-war decades, and the foundations laid for a new surge forward in further and higher education in the new third millennium. The traditions of the three leading colleges that formed the core of Manchester Polytechnic were deep and strong, giving the new university a rock-solid start. Ironically, the process has seemed to have come full circle. With the merger between Manchester University and UMIST, the Met may wish to emphasise its roots as at one time the largest polytechnic in the UK, giving unique service and entry for its graduates into successful business and entrepreneurial employment, living up to its motto, given it by its first Director, Sir Alec Smith, 'Many arts, many skills'. I feel a great pride in having been so much a part of its initiation.

CHAPTER 16

Negotiating:
the local authority associations

The swing to the Conservatives in the May 1967 local elections was not confined to Manchester; it happened throughout all urban local authorities in England and Wales. This fundamentally altered the membership of their national representative bodies: the Association of Municipal Corporations, referred to as the AMC, and the County Councils Association (CCA). There are certain issues that are common to all local authorities and that cannot be decided unilaterally, for example teachers' salaries and conditions of employment. As these are heavily subsidised by government grant, there has to be a machinery for discussion and negotiation between the local authorities and the government of the day. The education committees of these two powerful bodies, together with the Inner London Education Authority as it then was, provided the link. At the first meeting of the post-election AMC, I was made a member of its education committee and subsequently elected its chairman. I retained this position for the four years until 1971, when, after the General Election that returned a Conservative government, Labour regained its control of the city and town councils and so of the AMC.

These four years were the only period of my life when there was no time for active mathematics, although I was always closely in touch with the work of the Institute of Mathematics and its Applications from its foundation in 1964. The local authority associations often angered Ministers of Education in that they told central government to keep out when it came to making policy decisions. Education was a local government service in the tradition of administering the poor law or dealing with rubbish disposal. Next to being made Minister of Pensions, to be Minister of Education was one of the least sought after or rewarding positions in the Cabinet. It is well known that when Edward Heath was leading the Conservative party and felt obliged to have at least one woman in his shadow cabinet and that woman could only be Margaret Thatcher, he gave her education as a means of keeping her quiet. She went on to be Secretary of State for Education and Science when he became Prime Minister. He underestimated her – the nickname Iron Lady was not earned by keeping quiet and away from conflict, but even she found the job frustrating at times.

I invited Margaret to Manchester to be the official opener of one of our new colleges near my home. She knew a lot about schools and universities, but had little first-hand knowledge of further education. She is an extremely fast learner. During supper I put her in the picture about our plans to build thirteen new colleges. The following afternoon she gave a first-class speech at the opening, from which both those present and the press could be convinced that she was expert in the field.

Work with the AMC brought me into close contact with the activities of the Ministry of Education. Along with the other employer representatives, we negotiated with various groups involved in education, particularly within the Burnham Committee which handled teachers' salaries. This brought my first experience of negotiating directly with trade unions – an unbelievably wearisome process. People whom one regarded as congenial and reasonable friends on a social level suddenly became intransigent opponents, unwilling to give a straight answer to any suggestion from us, the employers, without retiring to a private room for discussion. A meeting might in this way drag on long past the departure time of my last evening train back to Manchester and thus necessitate yet another sleeper journey.

In addition to meetings of the AMC itself and its education committee, I was also attending meetings of other national advisory committees to which I had been appointed. I resigned the chairmanship of the Association of Governing Bodies of Girls' Public Schools, as I found that the interests of the public (i.e. private sector) schools and state schools within the ambit of the AMC were too often in conflict, particularly on salaries.

Although the commitments in Manchester and in London took up my time almost exclusive of anything else, there were many rewards: I met successive Prime Ministers and Education Secretaries on several occasions and was invited to No. 10 Downing Street more than once.

Harold Wilson had an amazing memory for people and for names. He had opened John Dalton College in Manchester on a wet Saturday morning in December 1964, soon after he began his first stint as Prime Minister. About a year later I was walking up the platform at Euston station, having just come off the Manchester sleeper. I heard footsteps behind me and turned to see the Prime Minister, pulling at his first pipe of the morning, accompanied by his security guard, walking from the Liverpool night train that was standing on the adjacent platform. I turned to let them go ahead of me through the narrow exit. 'No, Dr Ollerenshaw, you go through first!' As, at that time, he had met me personally only once before, this was remarkable.

A political party in power at Westminster has not only its own party headquarters and research organisations to advise and guide on the issues of the day, but also expert and experienced top-rank civil servants, as well as any other academic expertise the Prime Minister and Cabinet colleagues may wish to consult. The Opposition, in contrast, has none of this. When a political party is first demoted to opposition, ex-cabinet ministers can find themselves adrift. When I became chairman of the education committee of the AMC in 1967, I was in a unique position to provide on-the-ground information and advice about education to Conservative MPs then in opposition. It was not unusual when the House was in session to receive an early-morning telephone call from the Parliamentary Private Secretary to the Shadow Minister for Education for the best current information on some issue to be brought up in Question Time that afternoon. One morning Robert came downstairs, his face covered in shaving soap. He had answered the telephone. 'Would I ring back within the hour to give the best up-to-date state of play about sex education in primary schools?' I hadn't a clue about sex education in schools, but I had my methods and I had friends. Every primary school head would already be at his or her school by 8.30 in the morning and relatively free until 9.00. I rang three heads and had their answers within fifteen minutes. There was no e-mail, no fax, no mobile. My reply had to be back in London before 10 a.m. at the latest, dictated over the telephone. The system never failed. In those days, House of Commons debates were available in full transcript in Hansard the following day. It was satisfying to read that my paragraphs had been delivered almost verbatim the previous afternoon. Robert was impressed.

My chairmanship of the AMC education committee and of the Manchester education committee both ended with a bump when, in the May 1971 local elections, there was a big swing back to Labour. But I had other more personal troubles to occupy my mind and every moment of my time.

In June 1970, our daughter Florence, by now a teacher at a school in London, had an emergency operation for appendicitis. I went to London to be near her, waiting with increasing anxiety when she was far longer than anticipated in the operating theatre. They had found cancer. This devastating news was confirmed after tests and conveyed to us a few days later – coinciding exactly with a confidential letter telling me that I was to be awarded a Dame Commander of the British Empire 'for services to education'. Two further major surgical operations followed over the next eighteen months (neither radium treatment nor chemotherapy at that time were suitable). Each operation gave Florence hope and bolstered her morale, but Robert and I both knew what was to come. City council colleagues showed the greatest kindness and tolerance when I attended a minimum of committee meetings. I was with her every possible moment of the time that was left to her. We played chess together and did large jigsaw puzzles at which she was very good, having a gift for matching colours and shapes. We went shopping and bought elegant clothes. Her illness made her slim and she liked this. She seemed to become all the more stunningly beautiful to our eyes as she became more frail. We managed to go on two holidays abroad and, with Charles, she accompanied me to Buckingham Palace in London for the DBE investiture. She died at home at the end of October 1972, aged 26.

CHAPTER 17

Lancaster: returning to teaching

In June 1972 I had a telephone call from the Vice-Chancellor of the new University of Lancaster, Charles Carter. I knew him as a past president of the Manchester Statistical Society of which I later held the presidency. He had been told about Florence's illness and had a proposal which he felt might help me when the end came. The big swing back to Labour in the local government elections of May 1971 meant that, after four years tenure, I lost the major committee chairmanships. I was keen to return to my mathematics activities. Nevertheless, it could be assumed that I might have time available for something new. He offered me a part-time senior research fellowship at Lancaster in their Department of Educational Research. The project proposed was to explore possibilities of attracting more married women trained teachers to return to teaching after an interval out of school bringing up their young children. I accepted immediately, with the proviso that I was not free to start work for some all-too-short time. Officially the project was to start in September, but I did the preliminary work from home. Florence, fighting to live, went with me to Lancaster twice, finding satisfaction in being able to help in a practical way, putting questionnaires into envelopes.

To help in getting the project off the ground for the new academic year, the application to the Department of Education and Science for a grant to cover the costs was prepared for me. When I saw the draft, I hit the roof. The request was for £10,000 for each of three years to finance a team of myself and two research assistants. This was then a *lot* of money. My thinking was strongly influenced by my American experience of 1965 (see Chapter 20). If a research project is to have any impact on national policy it must be concluded quickly. I preferred to ask for funding for one year only (although this became two years) and one assistant, a grant of £3,000 being adequate. When the Permanent Secretary at the Department of Education and Science, then Sir William Pile, heard about the application, I am told he exclaimed: 'Don't bother with the details. Give her the money. She always brings home the bacon.' I was found an excellent graduate assistant, Christine Flude, and in the event the main work was done within twelve months and a follow-up survey was completed the next year.

We concerned ourselves only with potential married women returners. There is a crucial moment in which to make a first approach to women who have left teaching to start a family. I knew it well: when the youngest child starts to go to school every morning. All the excitement and involvement with the infant, delivered for the first time into the care of teachers, the return to an empty, silent house, the abandoned breakfast table to clear. At that moment the young mother, with or without qualifications, feels a yawning gap. Skilled promoters of courses know the susceptibility during that fortnight in September when a new school year begins: a new adult education course, some new work for charity, or, maybe, a return to teaching if that had been the pre-child-bearing occupation. For a mother, who had previously had all or most of the responsibility, left at home alone to tackle only routine chores, this can be a deeply traumatic and often depressing time. The idea of undertaking a new venture can lift the spirit, but if not acted on at once, it wears off: November brings colder weather, Christmas looms. Suddenly we are into another year and another round of domestic problems. For the 'returning to teaching' project I knew that the first and second weeks in September were critical. How to get the initial 'guinea-pigs' to make a start? The answer was easy, even in those days before the internet. Christine and I drafted an attractive letter and sent it, in the first week of September 1972, to the national and educational press, local newspapers and women's journals. The BBC gave a radio broadcast on *Women's Weekend* and on *Woman's Hour*. We had the generous co-operation of a number of university departments of education and other college house journals and notice boards. None of this cost us more than the postage.

The response was immediate and astonishing. Within a couple of weeks we had over 4,000 replies with offers to collaborate in answering any questionnaire we might send or ask over the telephone. There was no need to go further. We were only interested in qualified teachers who showed some desire to return to teaching. We divided the replies into groups of a hundred as they came in. The number in each hundred who responded to certain aspects of returning was so uniform that to extend the sample to, say, 10,000 would have given little that was new and would have involved us in more expense, more work and more time for a return of very little improvement in the statistical validity of the conclusions. We sent out detailed questionnaires during October and by November almost all had been returned. We then began the telephone interviews, always by pre-arrangement.

It proceeded without a hitch. The great majority of respondents had first entered teaching at the age of 21 or 22, had taught for three to six years before leaving to raise a family and had been out of teaching for about fourteen or fifteen years. It was plain from the answers to the questionnaire that most of these qualified women teachers had a real sense of vocation. In answer to the question 'What was your reason for first leaving teaching?' only 1 per cent ticked the slot 'Dissatisfaction with particular teaching post'. Although many had left on marriage, the majority had not left teaching until the imminent birth of their first child. Fifteen years later the youngest child, probably the third, was just starting school. The average age for wanting to return was 35. A common feature of the replies was a lack of confidence: a doubt whether they could move to full-time employment without a trial period, and, more significantly, whether they would find themselves out-of-date in the classroom after so long away, unless they first attended a 'refresher' course. Just over a third of would-be returners said specifically that they were willing to return only part-time, and only 6.5 per cent said that they were willing to return full-time in the first instance. Nearly half (49 per cent) said that they wanted to return initially as part-timers and then gradually increase to full-time.

The schools were very willing to accept returners on a part-time basis, often arranging for two part-timers working in tandem. When the number of children of school age began to fall and the pressures eased, this eagerness to accept part-timers diminished. Time-tabling is simpler when staff are working full-time, but a school probably gets more from two part-timers than from one full-time teacher. Our respondents expressed resentment that they would have to pay their own fees (as much as £20 a session) for any refresher course – that is if they could find one conveniently near where they lived. One way round this was to register as a 'supply teacher'. To quote from a reply: 'My advice to anyone in my position would be to do supply teaching, because I learnt so much doing this. I went into so many different schools and saw different methods at work, always with the let-out that if I was really unable to cope I could say, "I can't come next week" and I wouldn't be letting them down any more than they were already. This was better than doing a course and I actually got paid for the experience!'

Interviewing was by arranged appointment over the telephone from my home, usually on a Saturday morning. It proved surprisingly successful. Women like to chat – and chat we did (at Saturday morning cheap telephone rates). Especially interesting were the views expressed in the supplementary survey after our initial respondents had found a teaching post and returned. They seem relevant today, despite so much that has changed. To quote from one conversation: 'It only took a month or so to settle in, apart from the difficulty with maths . . . It just seemed as natural as breathing that you sort of started again. It was very odd . . . I have asked about courses to bring me up to date at the local Teachers' Centre. There are none, simply because the demand is hidden . . . I did want a course very much, even now. I've got through this year, but I still feel that with maths particularly things have changed so much.' Time and again it was this early fundamental weakness in mathematics that was the root cause of the fear and lack of confidence. Mathematics at a level other than the most elementary is perhaps the one subject above all that a qualified teacher cannot readily keep up with when away from school education.

Our report was widely read, and acted on. Indeed, so many copies were sold that we made a profit on the grant we had received. This was almost unheard of and to simplify the accounts we spent the surplus on a new advanced calculating machine for the department. This machine needed a trolley to be moved from one room to another. It had four memories and we thought this a tremendous help.

I was not able to resist adding some strictly mathematical contributions. In November and December 1973 I published two papers in the

Bulletin of the Institute of Mathematics and its Applications, the first giving a method of calculating the potential number of qualified married women returners to teaching; the second giving an actual calculation. The formulae devised for this calculation depended on the data in the survey showing the current attitudes and patterns of behaviour of those who had left teaching earlier. The two papers were added as appendices to the final Report. Although attitudes and conditions change, those papers are still relevant to the present situation regarding the shortage of teachers.

The University Council and Court

While the returning to teaching project was still in progress, I was invited to serve on the council of the university, and later on the court as well. The first Vice-Chancellor, Sir Charles Carter, had retired and there were two successors before the appointment in 1985 of Harry Hanham, a historian of distinction who had spent fourteen years in Manchester University editing the definitive *History of the British Empire*. We became close friends and for several years when visiting Lancaster I stayed with him and his wife in the Vice-Chancellor's residence. We did indeed 'talk of many things', not only 'of shoes and ships and sealing wax', but also 'of cabbages and kings.' I never came away from Lancaster without feeling wiser and much better informed of the day's national and international affairs. Two successive chairmen of the council also became valued friends: Sir Alistair Pilkington, one time chairman of Pilkington Glass, and Sir Christopher Audland, whose home is just north of Lancaster and who had retired from a senior civil servant post in Brussels. They were both extremely skilled chairmen when meetings became difficult and I gained the greatest possible pleasure from witnessing this. From 1978 to 1981 I was a Deputy Pro-chancellor of the university. This entailed taking the chair at the Annual General Meeting of the court, as the Chancellor, HRH Princess Alexandra, could never be exposed to the risk of abusive debate led by protesters against cuts in student grants and other grumbles. I enjoyed myself when debates became tough. I was used to it within Manchester city council. I was stimulated by hassle and at my best – never being myself disturbed as I found it amusing rather than a threat to my chairmanship.

HRH Princess Alexandra was installed as Chancellor in the very beginning of 1964. After forty years of unremitting loyalty and attendance at innumerable events, she is to retire in November 2004 and will be succeeded by Sir Christian Bonnington, the internationally renowned mountaineer.

Lancaster University was in the forefront of expansion of the new 'green field' universities that followed the Robbins Report of 1963. Student numbers had unsurprisingly increased year by year and building programmes struggled to keep pace. Troubles about finance became serious for all universities in 1981. The University Grants Committee with its five-year rolling grants had been abolished and Government required the universities to look more stringently at their own resources. Student fees were introduced and there was much unrest. The huge expansion in the numbers of overseas students had brought hardship when they were required to meet the full costs of their courses without automatic support from their home country.

The biggest financial troubles came to Lancaster somewhat later. Lancaster was proud to be the first, in 1992, to become a public company and therefore to have large sums of money available through borrowing for capital building projects, including student residences. Unfortunately there was, almost immediately, another round of fierce government cuts in university grants towards annual expenditure, and the whole system was in jeopardy. Recruitment of both home and overseas graduate students fell dramatically and with it anticipated income. In many ways university management and the responsibilities of governing councils are today far more arduous and wearisome than in the heady 1950s to 1970s of unparalleled expansion when I held chairmanships.

My links with the two non-Manchester universities, Lancaster and Salford, were an important part of my life for over thirty years and the deep friendships made then remain.

CHAPTER 18

Music, music, music:
the Royal Northern College of Music

To many people Manchester means cotton mills, terraced houses, education, science, medicine, and football, especially football; but it also means music. Manchester was famous for its Gentlemen's Concerts that began in about 1775, for its music-hall stars, for Charles Hallé and the succession of renowned conductors of the orchestra that bears his name: all this a hundred years before 'pop' made Manchester a leader in the pop scene and brought new life and youthful exuberance in the 1980s and 1990s.

I was never a musician. I did not have the gifts and my poor hearing would have made it almost impossible to become one, but I always loved music, especially the rhythm. As a child I was taken by my parents to concerts in the Free Trade Hall. I don't remember much about the music – I couldn't hear properly anyway – but I watched with fascination as the conductor Hamilton Harty's starched dress-shirt collar became soggier and soggier until it hung like a rag round his neck. He came back after the interval in a fresh shirt and a new collar which, in turn, became a rag. Father Bob, after he was widowed in 1933, took me with him regularly to Thursday evening Hallé concerts in the Free Trade Hall. After the Hall was destroyed in the German air raids, the concerts continued wherever they could be held, including the King's Hall at Belle Vue zoo. When in 1952 I at last had an efficient hearing aid, everything changed for the better. A whole new life opened up, including a new enjoyment of music.

In 1958 while I was deputy chairman of the city council's further education sub-committee, I was particularly interested in our scheme to provide thirteen new further education colleges. The building which housed the Northern School of Music (NSM), founded by Hilda Collins in

1920, was threatened with demolition to make way for a new elevated highway. It occurred to me that it would be splendid if one of the new colleges of further education were built as a college specialising in music within which the NSM could be incorporated. The 'county college' idea seemed to appeal to Ida Carroll, Hilda Collins's successor as principal, and I was invited to become a member of the NSM's governing body; the conductor Charles Groves was a member. However, this would have left in limbo the Royal Manchester College of Music (RMCM) founded by Charles Hallé in 1893 and still making do in totally inadequate buildings within the University precinct. The Royal Manchester College did not look with favour at the prospect of a rival in new purpose-built premises. Percy Lord, Chief Education Officer for Lancashire and a leading member of the RMCM's governing body, advocated a joint venture. He suggested that a joint committee be formed by the four local authorities, Lancashire, Cheshire, Manchester and Salford, to establish jointly a music conservatoire to serve the whole of the North West of England and beyond.

A Joint Education Committee for this purpose was eventually formed and held its first meeting late in 1966. I was one of the four Manchester representatives (the other three, including the chairman Sir Maurice Pariser, being members of the Labour Party). A site for the new academy within the newly established Manchester higher education precinct was allocated, and, after much controversy, a London architect was engaged. Preparations went ahead. It was in the next local elections of May 1967 that the Conservatives had their huge gains and I became chairman of the Manchester education committee. In February 1968 Sir Maurice had a heart attack and died. I was elected chairman of the Joint Committee in his place. The Joint Committee became in due course the governing body of what was to become the new Royal Northern College of Music (RNCM) and I remained the chairman of the governing body, voted in each year as is required in local government, for eighteen years until 1986. Party political changes in the two shire counties and new representative governors then caused the vote to go against me. I never resented these changes; that is what democracy is about and it was an honourable way to go.

The first task was to erect the building. The capital cost would be met through shared budgets between the four local authorities in proportion to their population size, but the project had first to gain a place within the Government's annual further education building programme. The steering committee had envisaged a start in 1964, but this was wildly optimistic. The needs of technical education were considered paramount – music and other such luxuries were squeezed out. Design plans for the building were submitted, but found no place in the government programme for two successive years. Each year the plans were revised and estimated capital costs rose by some 30 per cent, putting the project even further out of reach. Then came a dramatic suggestion. Heating engineers advised the architect that the provision for boilers could be greatly reduced, cutting the costs down by as much as £300,000. Even then the 1968 submission failed, to our great disappointment and frustration. As so often, Lancashire County Council came to the rescue. Almost at the last possible moment, early in 1969, came a telephone call: Lancashire's building plans for one of their approved further education projects were in difficulty. If we could act immediately, it might be possible for the proposal for our college to be slotted in instead. This was done, approval was granted and all seemed well, but we had only a matter of weeks in hand.

The cut-off date for approved building programmes was 1 April. If a start was not made by then, there would have to be a new application which still might not find a place within the national allocations; a start by the last day in March was imperative. For some time there had been trouble in Manchester with tinkers. They took over unoccupied sites and, once established, there were no legal powers to evict them. Building work had been held up on some Manchester sites for several months. We heard that a band of tinkers already in the neighbourhood were planning to set up their caravans on our site that very weekend. There seemed only one thing to do: on the critical Sunday evening, I took my car and drove round and round the site continually from dusk until 4 o'clock in the morning, determined to call for police help if I saw a sign of a caravan. When daylight showed, I drove home satisfied – to be greeted by a very irate husband: 'Where the hell do you think you've been? I have been worried out of my mind.' It had worked. At 8 o'clock on the Monday morning our bulldozers arrived. The building had begun and the project was safe.

We later learnt that the heating engineers' advice had been wrong. We had been led to believe that air heated by one central boiler and channelled into the rooms would somehow find its way out through vents into the corridors, thus saving the cost of pumping. It was a total failure. There was no effective circulation of the warmed air. Within about a week of the college coming into use there were serious complaints. When the boiler was switched on sufficiently high, the concert hall was swelteringly hot (cellos were rumoured to be falling apart, not to mention audiences being overcome by the heat), but the tutorial rooms were freezing cold. Even the most loyal of teaching staff were threatening to go home in protest. This was ridiculous: apart from loss of face for all concerned, the waste in money would have been huge. Did not all the rooms have electricity power points? Yes. I took it upon myself to give instructions for the immediate purchase of fifty electrically-powered 'blow-heaters'. The long-term solution, for which we had to wait several years, was plain: the boilers had to be doubled in capacity and the system redesigned, which meant closing the college for at least the span of a summer vacation. Worse, the capital cost was beyond our means until, generous as ever, Lancashire county council came to our rescue by offering to meet the total capital cost of a new heating installation without calling on the other three local authorities to help. The City of Manchester has the good fortune to have the college within its boundaries, but it is to the county council of (old, pre-re-organisation) Lancashire to whom we owe the greatest debt.

The appointment of a principal was critical to the whole project. Frederic Cox had retired from the RMCM, and Ida Carroll of the NCM, although she had supporters and was a serious applicant, was not likely to be the first choice. I was out of my depth, but problems are sometimes solved in strange places. One evening, on my way home from some meeting in London, I bumped into Charles Groves at Euston station. The Manchester and the Liverpool trains used to leave within minutes of each other from adjacent platforms. As we both hurried down the slope to the platforms, I mentioned the issue that was so occupying my mind. 'Oh', said Charles, 'There is only one person, and he is not free to accept'. This was too much to leave unfinished. On the spur of the moment I followed him onto the Liverpool train and travelled with him as far as

Crewe. He, as always, had a bulky music score to peruse with some urgency, but he told me about John Manduell, who, after a glittering span with the BBC in London and in Birmingham, had recently been appointed first director of the music department at the new University of Lancaster. When I got home, I found that Simon Towneley, an influential member of the governing Joint Committee had been thinking on the same lines. How was this to be brought about? Simon arranged a dinner in London to which Dudley Fiske, our Manchester Chief Education Officer, myself and a few others were invited. It was agreed that John was the man to have, if free and if selected. Simon undertook to approach Sir Charles Carter, the Vice-Chancellor of Lancaster, to see if John could be released. With typical magnanimity, Carter agreed. At the bottom of his letter he wrote, in his own hand, 'Damn you'.

Through the usual procedures of advertising and interviewing applicants, John Manduell was chosen to be the principal. He took up post in 1971 and the college admitted its first students a year later, eighteen years after the first suggestion in 1954. When the RMCM ceased to exist as such, the Royal Charter also lapsed and the new college began as the 'Northern College of Music'. After much skilled negotiation in high places by Simon Towneley and John Manduell, the Queen approved the retention of the title 'Royal' inherited from the RMCM (which had not been at all certain). This brought the new college great kudos and benefit. (Salford University on whose governing council I also served, failed in roughly similar circumstance to retain the 'Royal' title it had inherited from the Salford Royal Technical College and suffered severely from this loss ten years later in 1981 when it narrowly missed extinction through government cuts). The presidency of the college was accepted by the Duchess of Kent, who has been an enthusiastic supporter and visitor all the years since. She opened the college officially on 28 June 1973

John Manduell proved an inspired principal. He wasn't interested in just being head of a college. He wanted to create a music academy of international standing. He succeeded in a remarkably short time, against all the odds, in doing precisely that. He is a genius in handling people – sensitive and caring for individuals, but ruthless when hard decisions are needed, as all too often they were, especially at the beginning. He had inherited two disparate institutions with their existing staffs and for the first two years he was obliged to have the existing students 'on roll' until they had finished their courses, while recruiting new students with both greater potential and higher minimum entry standards.

It had taken eighteen years of endeavour and frustration before the new college actually came into existence, but perhaps it was a blessing that plans didn't move more quickly. The potential conflict between the heads of the two combining institutions was so great that only the passage of time paved the way to greatness under the newly appointed principal. John rose above the worst of the conflicts, not having been a part of them himself. On 1 April 1971, exactly two years from the day the building work was started, a foundation stone was unveiled on an inside wall. Both Frederic Cox, the former principal of the RMCM, and Ida Carroll were there, their names on the stone. Inevitably, the occasion was somewhat strained. A press photographer asked them to kiss. They could hardly refuse. Michael Kennedy writes, succinctly, 'the kiss had the warmth that might be expected if Edward Heath were to kiss Margaret Thatcher'.

My job was to look after rules and regulations and protocol, seeing that they were not transgressed. The cream of inherited staff were there when professional support and advice was needed, and Charles Groves and Simon Towneley were never far away. The music community of the North West gradually woke up to the new miracle and responded, although London was slower. John insisted that all productions and performances had to be spot on, no excuses. Because he expected this, he got it. There were no first night blips, no orchestral disasters. The college's reputation grew – especially in Europe as, year after year, the RNCM-trained performers gained star roles in renowned opera companies.

In June 1971, as I have already related, Robert and I had the devastating news that our daughter Florence had terminal cancer. During the next fifteen months while, with unshakeable courage and hope, she underwent three major abdominal operations, she came with me many times as the college was being built, tramping in our wellies over the muddy footings. She was not to live long enough to see it finished. A choir from the college sang the anthem at the funeral service, probably one of their first engagements. Robert and I wanted to donate something in Florence's memory that would give pleasure to young people.

The stark new concrete building was almost complete, but it had no relieving architectural features. John Manduell suggested that we might like to provide a roof garden and we leapt at the idea. A garden was created in her memory – with a specially designed fountain because Florence loved fountains. Over the years the garden has been much used by students and by staff for relaxation, compensating somewhat for the bleak surroundings. In 2003, after thirty years, renovations had become urgent, some of the space was needed for other purposes and the garden itself was reconstructed.

The college had certain advantages over professional opera companies. First the principal could decide what operas to mount without too much regard for box-office returns. Second, there were no salaries to meet for solo singers, choirs and orchestral players – all were students in training. Third, there was time for rehearsals and special coaching, all part of the students' training courses. The supporting activities, such as stage management, the design and production of stage sets and in particular lighting, were undertaken by professional staff and contractors. Everything was to the highest standards. There were no excuses – ever. John Manduell insisted that a first night was as trouble-free and polished as subsequent performances. The students, young, hard-working and ambitious, were aiming to be professionals. This was a recipe for success.

There was one near disaster It came during a performance of *Billy Budd*. The fire alarms sounded just as Billy was to be hanged: there was a fire in the kitchens. Auditorium and stage were rapidly evacuated – a tribute to the college's professionalism and efficient precautions which, as far as I am aware, had never before been tested in reality. Fire engines extinguished the fire, the audience re-assembled, and the opera continued as though nothing untoward had occurred. The only problem for me was that Robert, who was with me that evening, was by then severely lame. There was no provision for the disabled – an omission now remedied.

In 1975 John took four operas to Sadler's Wells in London. Two were full length: Britten's *A Midsummer Night's Dream* and Stravinsky's *The Rake's Progress*, and there was also a double bill of two one-act operas. The reviews were ecstatic. After that the money ran out and no further expeditions to London were possible. This did not deter John from arranging an invitation to Copenhagen in 1976, where I was able to accompany them.

It was not only in the opera theatre that the college was successful. Notable concerts were presented in the concert hall: symphony orchestras, chamber music, jazz, with many visiting celebrities. I have vivid memories of Peter Donohoe on the timpani, still a student with a mop of red hair. He has returned many times as a distinguished pianist – without, alas, the mop of red hair. John Ogdon, a graduate of the Royal Manchester College, gave concerts. Joint-winner of the 1961 Tchaikovsky competition and famous in Russia and America, he had a phenomenal gift for reading and memorising difficult modern piano scores at sight. Twenty years on, in 1995, at the opening concert in the first of the biennial 'Glories of the Keyboard' festivals arranged by John's wife, the pianist Renna Kellaway who was head of keyboard studies at the college, the renowned pianist Shura Cherkassky gave a recital. A small neat figure with a characteristically short fast stride, he was in his eighties and I felt a special empathy with him. At the end of a brilliant performance he met thunderous applause, bowed and strode off – stage right into a tier of seats, his real exit being stage left. This absent-mindedness brought a further roar of applause. A few weeks later he died, his Manchester recital proving to be his last public appearance.

As soon as the college was up and running, the Joint Committee was superseded by a new governing structure: a court, of which I was elected chairman, whose main concern was the annual budget; and a council, chaired by Charles Groves, with responsibilities for the music side, courses, teaching staff and day-to-day affairs. My main responsibility, apart from finding the money and seeing that budgets were approved on time, was to keep an overall eye on general progress. As a member of the finance committee of the city council since 1956, I was well versed in the complexities of government grants and building programmes. Gaining approval for the annual budget was a major preoccupation. All four of the constituent local authorities had powers of veto. To have an annual budget approved by one local authority is bad enough – to secure the approval of four was a nightmare. I talked separately to representatives from each of the four authorities. Lancashire was always helpful and gave approval without demur. To my Manchester colleagues I emphasised how much we gained from having the college within the city and advised them to keep quiet and pay up. When Salford grumbled, I reminded them that they had asked to come in, that they could sever the link if they wished, but only if prepared to forego their share of the capital investment. Cheshire were the awkward partners; once, they held back approval until July before being forced to give in and contribute. Public relations were all important – that was the chairman's job. A bad press accusing us of extravagance, particularly over opera productions, could have wreaked havoc. The answer was for the college to watch expenditure like hawks and to give such unquestionably excellent performances and have such good reviews (as we almost invariably did) that the public began to value and praise what was in their midst, forgetting to ask awkward questions.

From the start we were short of accommodation. The opera theatre and concert hall had been priorities and there was space for snack meals, but all amenities had been skimped out of necessity. There was no lift other than a hoist and no student residential accommodation at all at first. Even tutorial spaces were overloaded and the work survived only by hiring rooms in nearby buildings, most of which were scheduled for demolition. During the summer of 1972 we managed to acquire a large building, Hartley Hall, that had been the home of the Methodist Theological College. For the next thirty years it provided ideal accommodation for our students. The drawback was that it was nearly two miles away and students were physically at risk after dark in the rough area. Now this building and its extensive grounds has been sold to developers and the money used to build a new residential block on a cleared site adjacent to the college. The residence, named after Sir Charles Groves who died in 1992, was opened in the summer of 2002.

As I have already related, in 1981 I lost my seat on the city council in a massive party political swing. Nevertheless, the majority Labour party still left me as a Manchester representative on the court of the college with a tacit agreement that I always kept the leader of the city council fully informed of what was happening at the college. My fellow Manchester representatives solved the problem of voting for someone of the wrong political party by sending apologies or arriving late at the first meeting of the municipal year. In this way they did not actually vote *for* me – and I retained the position without opposition through the support of the representative of the other three local authorities of the partnership. In 1986 this came to an end. A worthy candidate was put up, a member of the Labour party from Lancashire, County Councillor Stanley Henig, later Professor of Sociology at the new University of Central Lancashire. Knowledgeable about music, especially opera (his life-long hobby being collecting opera recordings), he gained the majority vote. I did not resent this any more than when, in the same way, I had been voted out of the chair of the Polytechnic on a party political vote some 15 years before. I had had a long innings and immeasurable pleasure. As I was no longer a city councillor my nomination to the court ceased, but not my close links with the college – after so long, they will never cease.

The court arranged a party to mark the end of my chairmanship and the date chosen was 6 December. This was brilliantly arranged by Christopher Yates, Dean of Postgraduate Studies and later Vice-Principal of the college. Robert had died in October and this party became a tribute to us both and thus had a special poignancy for me. I assumed that the party would be a formal dinner at Hartley Hall. The week before, I had attended a dinner at Goldsmiths' Hall in London to raise funds for Somerville College, Oxford, of which I had been an Honorary Fellow since 1977. Margaret Thatcher, also an Honorary Fellow of Somerville and at the time Prime Minister, was the chief guest. I had worn my best evening dress which had a wide full-length black skirt with a deep red velvet edging. I had not had the opportunity to hang it away in its special wrappings. It seemed a bit excessive for a dinner party, but, I thought why not? After all, this was to be a party for me – no harm in being somewhat overdressed. The registrar, Frank Mais, came to fetch me, together with my son Charles and his wife Margaret. Frank drove along Wilmslow Road and I protested 'a silly route to take to Hartley.' He replied 'No, decorators are busy at Hartley – we're going to the boring college'. When we arrived, there was no-one about – very strange! Frank led us through the empty entrance area and up to a small rest room. There, assembled and awaiting, in full evening dress, were Sir Charles Groves (as he by then was) and his wife Hilary, John and Renna

Manduell, and one or two others. 'Ah, a small select party', I thought. We were ushered through Florence's roof garden, along a narrow corridor with the portraits of honorary graduates, to the closed doors of the opera theatre. There was not a soul in sight. The doors were flung open. I stood dazed: down below, on the apron stage and in front of a glittering silver backdrop curtain, was a large assembly of over a hundred guests. It was so astonishing – so magnificent. Stunned and disbelieving, I stood for a moment stock still. Then, picking up the wide skirt of my dress, I walked down the steep theatre steps as though I were Greta Garbo herself. Drinks were served and then, dramatically, the silver curtain was slowly raised, and, lo, on the full stage setting of the final scene of *Don Giovanni*, chandeliers and all, were dinner tables.

Then each course of this dinner, prepared in our own kitchens, was brought in by a succession of singers in period costume and accompanied by music. Sir Charles presided. He made a speech that I have kept on tape ever since. My reply, totally unprepared, came from the heart – how could it be otherwise? There was never before such a party and I doubt if there ever can be again, whatever the occasion. Now I have all the pleasure and enjoyment of many generous privileges that the college can give without the worries and responsibilities. It is wonderful for me to have this splendid academy of music so near, to feel that I had some part in its creation, and to have the unstinting friendship of so many people connected with it.

There have been many changes since 1986. Sir Charles died in 1992 and his wife, Hilary, my close friend for over forty years, died in January 2003. The college moved from the control by local government into the general scheme of national higher education, funded from central taxation. There have been several changes of chairmanship. Sir John retired as principal in 1996 and was succeeded by Professor Edward Gregson, formerly Professor of Music at Goldsmith's College, University of London, but a *conservatoire* man through and through, having trained as a composer and pianist at the Royal Academy of Music in London in the 1960s.

Over the years, adjacent land was cleared of derelict properties and, after a spell of being used as car parks, it is now entirely taken up by new buildings, including a large extension to the college itself, almost doubling the space for teaching and administration, as well as the new student residential block. The concert hall, the opera theatre, the new classic theatre, lecture and recital rooms, and the reception areas are continually in use by not only the college, but are also let to outside organisations, ballet companies, pop groups, military bands and wedding parties. Standards of performance among students remain as high as ever and the College attracts an impressive number of postgraduate students already playing leading roles in music nationally and internationally.

In 2002 I was privileged to be allowed to celebrate my 90th birthday by sponsoring a concert given by the college symphony orchestra. The concert would have to be towards the end of the term, and I chose 6 December deliberately – in memory of Robert, and of Sir Charles Groves and other friends who were at the party in 1986 but no longer with us. The conductor was Elgar Howarth who, as a student at the RMCM forty years before, had been, along with John Ogdon and Peter Maxwell Davies, one of a group of musicians that came to be known as the *Manchester School*. There were over 200 guests within a capacity audience of 400 on an event which brought back memories of the great party exactly sixteen years before. Eddie Gregson composed a celebratory opening piece *Occasional Fanfares* incorporating in its sparkling ending the tune of *Happy Birthday*.

CHAPTER 19

USSR (1963)

Manchester, with its great tradition of industrial and commercial education, has many flourishing scientific and sociological societies. When, in 1954, I became a member of the education committee, I applied for membership of those that especially interested me. I was already a member of the Manchester Statistical Society, of which twenty years later in 1979 I was elected to the presidency for the two years that covered their 150th Anniversary. I also joined the Manchester Literary and Philosophical Society, which some thirty years later awarded me their Honorary Membership.

In particular I applied for membership of the British Association for Commercial and Industrial Education (BACIE), which was a national body with an active branch in Manchester. This soon found me in London attending their national conferences. I was elected to the BACIE governing council and in May 1963 was one of a delegation of five members to pay a three-week visit to the Soviet Union under the auspices of the Foreign Office. The objective was to learn about their post-school vocational education and training. Our itinerary took us first to Moscow, then to Leningrad (as St Petersburg was at that time called), then down to Tblisi and finally back to Moscow. We were treated as though we represented the British Government itself; with all the checks and obvious suspicions and monitoring typical of the Cold War years.

On our first morning in Moscow a group of officials went through the programme that had been arranged for us, and closely questioned us about our motives and attitudes. We were always accompanied by minders, except when we were the guests for luncheon at the British Embassy on the northern bank of the Moskva river, faced by the Kremlin on the opposite side. We were transported hither and thither in official cars with drivers chosen to take note of our every word and comment although they professed to knowing no English. Our hotel bedrooms were certainly bugged. One of our group was an electrical engineer, and detected where the microphones were. We were extremely careful throughout the whole visit in all we said to one another.

In the huge and impressive university library in Leningrad there was a special pleasure for me: in a rack of recent publications was the current edition of the *Oxford Quarterly Journal of Mathematics* in which was one of my own research papers on critical lattices. I was quick to turn to it and show off. This set me up greatly both with our Russian hosts and with my own colleagues.

We visited mainly leading technical colleges, but also some schools and two universities. The buildings were usually large and shoddy, crowded with students. There was never any need to ask where lavatories were – the stench made this plain on every corridor. Maintenance was poor, the edges of steps were chipped and dangerous, but there was no shortage of equipment in laboratories and classrooms.

Most striking was the ruthless insistence on merit lists of examination achievements and marks. Pupils' promotion in schools depended on placements in end-of-year tests, not on age. If the required standard was not attained, pupils were kept down for the following year, having to repeat the work with the younger up-coming pupils – a tyranny that had been abandoned in Great Britain for over sixty years. Teachers and lecturers were assessed on their pupils' and students' results. Without tenure, they faced dismissal or demotion if their classes did not achieve the statutory standards, or if too many of their pupils or students failed to make the required grade. Even the vice-chancellor of a university was subject to the same strictures. It was harsher than anything we had experienced at any time in the UK, either in schools or in colleges and universities. In addition there were differential salaries for teachers in shortage subjects, in particular for those with qualifications in mathematics. Our hosts regarded this as common sense and seemed mystified that our teachers' unions would find this unacceptable. We could, however, point out that in Great Britain where mathematics teachers were also in such short supply, they tended to achieve fast promotion and enhanced salaries.

Whereas our educational philosophy was first to estimate how many young people could benefit by higher education and then aim to provide for them, in the USSR it was the other way about: teachers' salaries and students' grants were adjusted according to the requirements of the Soviet manpower plans. They estimated the number of people needed in certain disciplines, provided the places and then filled them competitively using financial incentives and generous merit awards. These merit awards could add as much as 25 per cent to the basic grant. All students entering university and other forms of higher education were required to have had at least two years in industry or in the workplace, and they could gain additional grants if sponsored by their employers. Direction of labour, we were told, was no longer practised. A system of financial incentives had taken its place. Absolute discipline and punctuality prevailed. The slightest deviation or absenteeism and a student was 'out', with no redress and no rights of appeal.

We were never given the opportunity to see how anyone actually lived, as we stayed in government owned and controlled hotels where the food was reasonably good. On official visits it was fabulous: we were plied with caviar, enormous helpings of luscious fish dishes and vast quantities of wine. This was laid on to impress. Senior members of staff of the institutions we visited accompanied us, as did the clearly identifiable 'party member' silently noting everything we said: the merrier the proceedings became the better. We were honour bound to eat up and ask for second helpings so that our hosts could do so too. For them these feasts were clearly a special treat. As guests we were morally obliged to play our part; if we put on weight that was the price we had to pay. Only when down south in Tblisi could we relax a bit, their fine red wine flowing in abundance as we visited wineries and colleges devoted to this national export trade. We returned to Moscow in a crowded, rickety propeller-driven aircraft with no seat belts and passengers standing in the aisles, loaded with paper bags full of possessions.

The day before we left for home we were assembled before the same group of officials who had interviewed us on the first morning. Now there were no polite greetings and wishes for a pleasant journey – it was an interrogation with a vengeance. Comments that we had made at various stages were brought up and repeated to us for further explanation as to what exactly we had meant. The diligence of the party members was all too plain. We passed muster, but there was no escaping the slight feeling of threat. It had been a wonderful trip, but it felt good to be going home again.

CHAPTER 20

USA (1965)

In 1957 Russia launched Sputnik I – the first man-made object to escape earth's gravity and encircle the globe. Four years later on 12 April 1961 the first man, Yuri Gagarin, made his historic journey round the earth in space. The capsule in which he travelled had to be as small and as light as possible and he was chosen for his small stature as much as for his skills as a test pilot. I saw a replica of the capsule in the Museum of Science and Technology in Washington DC. It is so small that I doubt if I could have squeezed into it and I stand only 5' 3". A few weeks later Gagarin came to Manchester at the invitation of the Foundrymen's Union. I stood with Florence, then aged 15, at the end of our road to wave as he was driven past from Manchester airport to the town hall where he was entertained to lunch. Later I lined up with other city councillors to shake hands with him and his fellow visitors from the USSR. I remember being captivated by his smile. Provoked by these Russian achievements, President John F. Kennedy determined that America's answer should be to put the first man on the moon. The space race had begun in earnest.

The population of America is over five times that of the UK. They have always had enough extremely clever people and leaders to carry the nation intellectually, but for 'big science' to flourish a general ambience of support is needed. Not only is skilled manpower required but huge amounts of public money. Non-private schools in the USA are the responsibility of the individual States, the Federal Government having no direct powers over them, except willingness to provide grants for special purposes. It was a blow to their national pride to realise how low the general standards in mathematics really were. President Kennedy was alerted to the abysmally poor levels of attainment in schools throughout America. It also came as a great shock to have evidence that the USSR was significantly ahead in the technology related to space travel. Unlike a British government faced with issues of this magnitude, the President of the United States did not have to set up a ponderous advisory committee, representative of all relevant interests, and wait two to three years to know their findings. He simply chose the most respected educationalist in the country, Dr James B. Conant, president of Harvard, and gave him *carte blanche* to choose his own team of experts regardless of expense or their current commitments, recompensed by the Federal Government. Dr Conant was required to report back within six months. The report, with its recommendations for immediate action, was devastating. It was made available worldwide; those of us in the UK with a special interest in mathematics education eagerly read extracts from it. This was my particular interest. I was determined to get to America as soon as possible and see things for myself.

Luck was with me. Under the auspices of the British-American Association, an organisation housed at the English-speaking Union in London, there had been for several years a Winifred Cullis Lecture Fellowship that arranged 3-month exchange visits between the United Kingdom and the USA. One applicant was selected each year, an American citizen to lecture in the UK one year and a British citizen to visit the USA the next year. The main purpose was to enhance international understanding. Such exchanges had become commonplace in the aftermath of the war, but were mainly sponsored by universities and most were available only to men. The Winifred Cullis Fellowship, although not exclusively for women, was unique in giving women equal opportunities. There was no restriction on the content of the lectures and the selected fellow could choose broadly where to go. My application was accepted as the fellow for the year 1965. I specified from the start that my main interest was in mathematics education. Before I left home I arranged with the *Manchester Evening News* to send back fortnightly accounts of my experiences.

The links in the USA were with the Association of American University Women (AAUW) and with Rotary. I had to prepare four standard speaking scripts to be used during the tour as material for my hosts to select from and for the press, radio, television and other publicity. As speaking scripts they survived barely a week; they were continually modified and adapted. It was plain before I left home that, if I were to fulfil my personal aim of learning about mathematics in the USA, I would need to achieve this through my own initiative. Happily it aroused the interest of the then Permanent Secretary for Education, Sir Herbert Andrew. He sent ahead a letter of introduction to a few selected top administrators in the USA, including importantly the Massachusetts Commissioner for Education, Dr O. Kiernan, in Boston. I contacted him on my first day in Boston and was given a warm welcome. He offered to send letters of introduction to colleagues in other States and to presidents of universities and heads of other institutions on my itinerary. This meant that I was able to double the value of the tour, filling any gaps in the Fellowship schedule with privately arranged visits to meet leading educators.

For the official schedule, I found myself guest speaker at lunches once or twice each week addressing all-male audiences of Rotary. In the evenings I mainly addressed all-female audiences of married graduates. Rotary Club audiences differed greatly; they certainly did not want to hear about mathematics, but they seemed to be mesmerised by my English accent and it didn't really matter much what I talked about. The most popular title chosen from the four lectures I had prepared was *Teenage problems in Britain today.* I learned how to adjust the theme on each occasion to match the interests of those present.

The university women made very different audiences. Most of them had school-age children and they were passionately concerned about education. They wanted to hear about education in England and were especially interested in what we were doing about mathematics in our primary schools. Did we permit the use of the new calculators in schools? What did I think of the 'new math'? In general I was aghast at the staggering basic ignorance of any important political or economic issues beyond the borders of the United States. What was happening in Europe and in the Middle East seemed not to be relevant to the go-ahead American of 1965. It was all so far away and did not concern them.

This was the era of the introduction of what is referred to in the USA as 'the new math'. There was nothing wrong about the new math, merely an emphasis on logical arguments rather than on straight addition, subtraction, multiplication and division. In England we had already encountered the bewilderment of teachers who were not confident enough to absorb new methods in mathematics teaching, and the even greater bewilderment of parents who didn't understand what it was about. Americans can be hot on 'crazes'. Perhaps they were disappointed that I was only a lukewarm advocate. To say that it all depends on the calibre of the teacher is at best a useless statement. Even differential salaries in favour of mathematics teachers (unthinkable at the time outside a communist state) can achieve little if there are not enough good teachers of mathematics and not enough good mathematicians to meet a nation's overall needs. When abroad I make a habit of browsing in bookshops. A best-seller on US education shelves in 1965 was entitled *Hey kids! Do you dig the new math?*, with advertising blurb: 'Here's your guide to the space age. Don't wait for ol' teacher, or mom, or dad – this is an easy cram, make it and go to the head of the class.' There were other popular titles: *How to Outsell the Business Salesman*; *The Tyranny of Testing*; *Academic Freedom in the Age of the University*; *Don't wait to be below standard*; *How to teach your two-year-old to read*.

The main obligation of the tour was the pre-arranged Fellowship schedule. The personal introductions gave me, in addition, everything I could have wished for and more, and helped me to fulfil my original aim of learning something of what was happening in American education. I was intensely happy. I kept a journal, making entries every night. I visited sixteen States in the USA, and Ontario in Canada, staying in forty different places, was guest speaker on 66 occasions, gave fourteen television interviews, met staff and students at 16 universities (five public, 11 private), three Institutes of Technology, 12 Liberal Arts Colleges, five Junior Colleges, six High Schools, and seven nursery and elementary schools. This involved 34 long-haul flights, two long train journeys and 14 self-drive car journeys, mostly in California. Overall I covered a distance not far short of 10,000 miles.

There is no mention in my journal of ever having been off-colour; the food suited me and the hospitality was always considerate. I was almost always in bed in good time. The hearing aids never let me down. With them switched off there was the advantage of silence when required – on aircraft and at night. I slept like a log each night wherever I was and was never tired. As I was always the chief guest in any group, conversation was directed toward me. I never had the social problem of needing to hear others conversing between themselves, probably at a noise level below my effective threshold – and I was always in a position where the lip-reading assisted me without this being evident. I had to tell any host (and hotel receptions) that I would be virtually stone-deaf at night without my aids and, as had long been my practice at home, I did not hesitate to ask the chairman in advance at any lecture to, please, repeat any question asked me from the audience. This was a technique I had learnt long before. It has hidden advantages: the chairman has to pay good attention throughout; it gives an audience a second chance to hear what the question was; and (if I have in fact heard adequately) it gives me an extra moment to consider my answer. I did have some problems with television interviewing but managed to deal with them well enough to hide the handicap.

The tour started in earnest when I flew from New York to Boston. The first engagement, my meeting with Dr Kiernan, set the pattern of courtesy and welcome wherever I went throughout the tour. The introductions that Dr Kiernan initiated formed the centre of it all for me. The conversations and discussions I had with distinguished scholars and administrators, their generosity in giving me so much of their time, would each have been worth individual visits across the Atlantic.

The first meeting of note was at the Massachusetts Institute of Technology (MIT) where, on my second day in Boston, I had what I described in my journal as a 'marvellous hour' with Dr Julius Stratton, the chairman of MIT. We talked about sponsored research and the idea of a university. MIT, although famed for its contributions to science and technology, was particularly proud of its activities in developing its social science and liberal arts. Here I saw at first-hand some of their latest work in computer sciences, and the new software programs to match the advances in hardware. I was well versed in the pioneering work at home in Manchester and this made a great impression.

I had asked that throughout the tour I should be allowed to sit-in, incognito, in middle-of-the-road high school classes, preferably during a mathematics lesson. In Boston the class I attended was having a history lesson. The subject was the Boston Tea Party of December 1773. I had already made a tourist visit to the *Mayflower* and was *au fait* with the facts as I saw them. This had nothing in common with what was taught to these 14-year-olds, where the English were portrayed as the worst of rogues and enemies with no justification or reason whatsoever for acting as they did. The account was so fiercely anti-British I wondered how America had ever been persuaded to come to our aid in either of the two world wars.

From Boston I went to Toronto to visit relatives of Robert and to fulfil my desire to see Niagara. The Falls mesmerised me. Tourists can stand behind high railings where the huge river approaches them only a matter of a few yards from the edge, leaves floating on the surface as they flow inexorably with a kind of fated elegance toward the right-angled drop into chaos and oblivion. The emotional impact was so over-whelming that I was grateful when my hosts took me away to a nearby restaurant to recover my composure.

I then crossed the border again, to Cleveland. There I sat in during a mathematics class of 14-year-olds in a large high school. This was a doleful experience. They were struggling with long division with seem-ingly no firm background of multiplication tables. They knew no geom-etry and had never heard of Pythagoras. It was no surprise; I had seen this in too many of our own schools when visiting with the Newsom Committee.

From Cleveland I flew back to New York to meet Dr James Conant. This was a key meeting. He was by far the most eminent and important person in American education at the time. He had invited me to meet him at the Harvard Club on 44th Street. We exchanged gloomy views about mathematics in schools, but not much else. The prestige of having met him personally carried great weight with other educationists during the rest of my stay in America. Some twenty or more years later, I was sitting reading in the small garden of our holiday cottage Hodge Close, when a tall handsome grey-haired gentleman leaned over the gate and, in a strong American accent, asked directions. When I went to the gate, he was astonished to see Conant's book in my hand. I had borrowed it the day before from Professor Harvey Hanham the Vice-Chancellor of Lancaster University. The stranger was a distinguished

American civil servant who had known a lot about Conant. He and his wife had spent their honeymoon walking in the English Lake District and they were making a nostalgic re-visit on his retirement.

After my brief return to New York, I flew directly to Denver and then on to San Francisco, fulfilling what had by then become a customary busy schedule of lunch-time and evening speaking engagements. I was then driven to Sacramento, the capital city of California, where I had agreed to address students at Riverside Junior College. I hoped to repeat in California the welcomes and facilities for visiting schools and colleges independently of the lecture tour that I had enjoyed during the first month; to do this I needed authoritative introductions and permissions. I was given the name of the State Superintendent of Instruction, Mr Max Rafferty. I telephoned and asked if I could see him. The reply was that his diary was choc-a-bloc for the whole of the next day, but if I could come to his office at 8 a.m. he would be happy to give me break-fast. I did just that and achieved all I could wish for. This was another example of the extraordinary willingness of American leaders to make themselves available; there was never that routine 'brush-off' answer so often given in England: 'he is not in today' – or 'he is busy at a meeting'.

Armed with these introductions, I flew south from Sacramento to Santa Barbara where another aunt of Robert's made me welcome. I had, however, missed an opportunity in San Francisco when visiting Stanford University in Palo Alto. The principal of a college in Santa Barbara told me that at Stanford a research project was being set up to measure standards of attainment in mathematics in different countries. This was exactly what I was most interested in, so, with a day free from speaking commitments, I returned to San Francisco, hired a self-drive car and drove to Palo Alto and on to the university, finding my way somehow around the vast campus to the Institute of Behavioral Sciences. The project, still in its early stages, was fully explained to me. Of the major advanced countries only Russia had refused to co-operate or take any part in the research. This was the beginning of the first comprehensive tests of mathematical attainment worldwide. In America there was the dreaded Standard Achievement Test (SAT), just as before the war we in Great Britain had our School Certificate and later the GCE and then GCSE. The French had their Baccalaureate. These were for individuals, not measures of performance of schools, although used as such by the most successful schools. There had hitherto been no method of comparisons between different countries.

Four years later the first stage of the research was complete and a report published. Testing of attainments by individual schools and colleges is never popular. Apart from the additional work entailed, those with poor attainments will (with justification) plead special circumstances. It is nice to be top and nice for it to be acknowledged. So long as the tests are not the be-all and end-all, and results treated with a proper addition of salt, they can provide a challenge and an incentive to improvement. That was nearly forty years ago. Now, in 2004, for better or worse, measurements of attainment between schools and other institutions are the norm in Great Britain. Despite the massive resistance to tests, it does seem that now at last the effects are beginning to show and that attainment in mathematics in our primary schools is ahead of that in other advanced countries in the West, which in the immediate post-war years they certainly were not.

There was a heavy programme of speaking engagements but, after the first four or five weeks, I must have been thoroughly into my stride. I overheard a flattering comment after a High School visit, that pleased me so much I made a note of it: 'Oh, she was smashing – English intellectual and all that'.

One evening, when addressing a group of members of the AAUW, someone in the audience asked, with undisguised scorn, why we had girls' schools. I think I exploded, coming back with 'And you have women's universities!'. More dramatic was a question about hygiene. There had been a recent report in the British press about housing in Manchester, England stating that 10 per cent (or some such) houses still had no bathroom. This was given headlines in a much-distorted manner in the San Diego gossipy tabloids. A loud voice from the back row of the audience called out. 'Oh, you come from Manchester – that's the place where you never have a bath'.

Over the three months only one flight went wrong and that was to the Grand Canyon. The booking for the Friday evening had been made in London. What had not been known in the London booking office was that flights from Phoenix to Flagstaff, the airport used for the Grand Canyon, ceased for the winter on 1 November (four days before) and the plane I was booked on was to go direct to Las Vegas. With my bag already on the plane, I made a great fuss and the flight was held up while it was retrieved. I then found myself alone in the huge airport lounge, stranded. There was, however, always the credit card. I hired a car, asked for directions and, helped by a bright full moon, set off for Flagstaff 200 miles north of Phoenix. This was a hairy drive on a near-deserted free-way. Notice-boards warned of rock falls. About 20 miles from Flagstaff the worst happened: a great shower of stones fell onto the bonnet of the car, somehow releasing the catch so that it sprang open, completely blocking my view. The fan belt had snapped also. There was no alterna-tive but to wait and hope that someone reliable would come by. After about half an hour three young men in a van stopped to see what was amiss. They were fascinated by my English accent. With a pair of spare nylon stockings (!) from my overnight bag, they constructed a make-do fan belt, cleared the worst of the stone and gravel from the engine case, got the car started and then drove slowly ahead to Flagstaff, making sure that I was following safely. I was able to put up in a motel. In the morn-ing, with the car back in good order, I wended my way in thick mist to the hotel on the southern lip of the Grand Canyon. There I had 24 hours to drive around and marvel at the Grand Canyon from above. I eschewed the donkey ride down to the bottom: that would have been too much.

Next day, the Sunday, I drove back to Phoenix in daylight through the magnificent canyons that I had not been able to see in the dark on the Friday night. I stopped to take pictures and only just made it back to the airport in time to catch my flight on to Albuquerque for a whole new phase of the Fellowship tour, and then on to Santa Fe where my hosts regaled me until late each evening with marvellous stories of the native Indians, the Pony Express and the like.

I then turned south, spending time in Houston and in New Orleans, learning at close quarters about the appalling problems of trying to inte-grate the black and the white communities. After that it was northward all the way. I was looking forward to seeing Robert again when he was to join me in ten days time. Meanwhile there was Atlanta, in Georgia, where the temperature was down to a welcome 64 degrees. The high spot of my four-day stay there was an afternoon spent with the Vice-Chancellor of Atlanta University, Dr Rufus Clements, the first and I think at that time only black vice-chancellor of a major university in the States. He was such a mature and magnificent-minded man that all my inhibitions and fears of saying the wrong thing fell away. We spoke in depth of the problems that had been disturbing me so much, especially after reading the popular novel *Black Like Me* by John Howard Griffin. Indeed, I felt that it was because I had read this book and been so moved by it that he opened up in the way he did. In America, particularly in the American South, housing is very definitely not mixed. Schools had been built to serve neighbourhoods, especially elementary schools that should be within walking distance of home. Enforced integration meant bussing children from areas where they lived to alien neighbourhoods some distance away. It is not difficult to imagine the strength of the white protests.

At the highest levels, black scholars and statesmen were treated on their true merit. There were many outstandingly able black undergraduate students accepted at Atlanta University, but for the average black student opportunities were few, especially in the South. Dr Clements told me that over 65 per cent of blacks in Georgia were turned down for the draft each year for medical or physical reasons.

My penultimate stop was in Washington DC. Robert had come over to be with me. We toured the Capitol, saw the Lincoln Memorial and fulfilled my wish to visit the late President Kennedy's grave at Arlington National Cemetery. Like so many people, I have vivid memories of the precise moment when he died, on Friday 22 November 1963. I was the guest speaker at a school speech-day in our Free Trade Hall in Manchester. As I arrived the hall's manager told me that Kennedy had been shot and had been taken to hospital. I told him that I couldn't wait for two hours, incarcerated with an audience of some 2,000 people, not knowing what was happening. He agreed to give me a signal. We were well under way when a side door opened slightly. Only I could see the manager. His thumbs were down – and I knew, with shock, what this meant. What to do? The answer had to be nothing – carry on as though I did not know this dreadful news. I was glad to have the opportunity to visit the grave and pay my respects – almost exactly two years later.

On the next day I had meetings at the Office of Education with senior civil service staff and representatives from the British Embassy. They showed intense interest in accounts of the full tour, but this was no inquest as it had been in Russia two years before. There could hardly have been a greater contrast with the grilling our delegation had to go through in Moscow at the end of the visit to the USSR in 1963.

People asked: 'What did you think of America?', 'How did you like America?'. These are non-questions. America is so large that one can find everything – so it is a matter of choice and circumstance. I met people of such high intellectual quality that an hour in their company was worth a life-time of casual contacts elsewhere, and, in contrast, communities of such stultifying small-mindedness that the mind boggled. I was cared for with astonishing generosity and thoughtfulness – and accorded every possible kindness and consideration in what was almost always a refreshingly relaxed atmosphere. There seemed generally to be a real interest in all things British. It was easy to find oneself respected (and even admired) as something out of history – which, indeed, I probably was, even forty years ago. They never seemed able to hear enough of what I had to tell.

I was lucky with the weather. I did not have to suffer extremes of heat, or storm, or snow, ice, flood, drought or other uncomfortable hazards that almost all States in the US have to endure at some point in the year.

I have never been the victim of fads, such as excessive dieting or religious fervours, and only marginally aware of them. The level of deep prejudice against defined sections of society could be painfully obvious, but the conflict between black and white communities was to be expected. More shocking to me was the male/female divide and what I then considered the high divorce rates. To some extent this was a consequence of my Fellowship programme, almost exclusively based on all-male Rotary and all-female AAUW, but it came through in every newspaper article I read (and I scanned leading newspapers every day as an essential routine). This prejudice was evident in family attitudes (whereas with my Fellowship hosts, the woman was very much top dog) and in the universities, the professions, in industry and in politics where men ruled almost exclusively. When it came to sex discrimination, women's struggle in the UK had mainly been fought, and largely won, immediately before and during the First World War. In America, spared the worst impacts of two world wars, social integration seemed decades behind our own.

In 1965, young people in America seemed not to have a care in the world. The universe was theirs for the taking. If one job collapsed, there would be another tomorrow. Moving house, even to far-away States, was merely a way of life. Indeed, to remain always within the same neighbourhood (as I have done) was considered fuddy-duddy. Perhaps what filled me with the greatest horror of all was the accepted provision for elderly (and not-so-elderly but early retired) well-to-do people in huge condominiums, specially designed for what to me looked like a premature incarceration.

When I came back to New York, the tour almost at an end, I kept to the invitation I had three months earlier from Alistair Cooke on my first arrival in America. Renowned for his weekly *Letter from America* on BBC radio, our common interest was Manchester, England and his background as an erstwhile member of staff of the *Manchester Guardian*. He invited me to come for cocktails on my return in December, when I could meet members of his family and tell him of my experiences on the tour. This I did. I met his wife and a daughter on my last evening – our discussion mainly centred on the black/white problems in the education system. These were particularly acute in New York. White people with money solved them by sending their children away to boarding school or having their permanent home in, say, Long Island, and a city flat as a weekday base. The black population had to make do with what the City could provide.

On Friday 10 December Robert and I boarded the liner *Sylvania* for Liverpool and home. The one-time Winifred Cullis Fellow, who had greeted me at the airport three months before and had looked after me during my first two days, came aboard with champagne to make sure that I had a good send-off. There were thirteen large packages and parcels awaiting me in our cabin – the books and presents that had been given me and that I had posted back to New York during the tour. My journal records: 'perfect day, ever-memorable view of Manhattan as we move down the river past the Statue of Liberty'. And a final entry: 'Here ends a superb and infinitely rewarding tour'.

Astronomy

26 Members of The Manchester Astronomical Society in 1995 with guest, Sir Hermann Bondi (l to r): Kevin Kilburn, Michael Oates, Sir Hermann, Dame Kathleen, David Nicholson, Tony Cross

27 Full Moon from the small balcony of the house in Pine Road, Didsbury, 1990

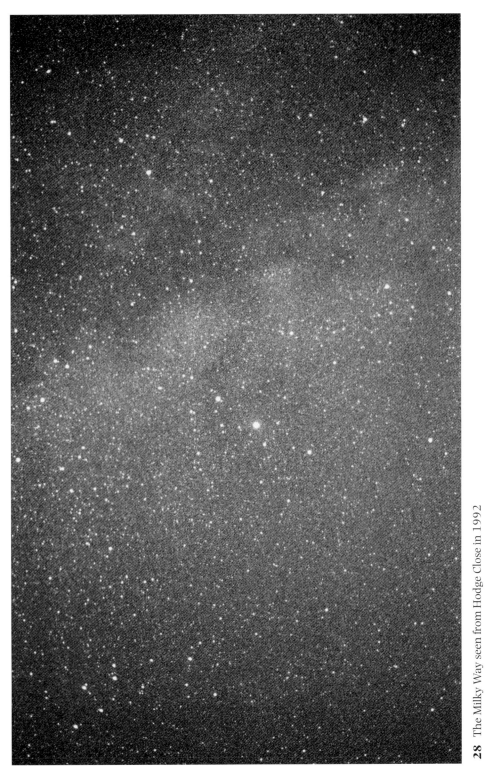

28 The Milky Way seen from Hodge Close in 1992

29 The M5 Galaxy (Globular Cluster) in the Constellation Serpens, taken by the author in 1994

30 Eclipse chasing in the south of France (with hat), 1994

31 Orion, an image formed by computer-stacking with the help of members of the M.A.S. taken at Hodge Close in January 2004

32 With Sir Patrick Moore at the Opening of the 'Dame Kathleen Ollerenshaw Observatory' at Lancaster University, May 2002

33 Michael Kennedy with Dame Kathleen at her 90th birthday party in 2002.
Copyright © James King-Holmes 2002

34 Dame Kathleen working at her laptop, February 2004 (picture by Ray Grover)

CHAPTER 21

Japan (1970)

I never had entrenched plans or ambitions, but responded to opportunities when they arose. In 1969 a report arrived on my desk giving the outcome of the research into international standards of achievement in mathematics that I had learned about at Stanford University in 1965. The results showed that children in Japan at each of the ages tested – 7, 11 and 14 – were far ahead of all the other ten or so participating countries. Neither Russia nor India had taken part. There was no doubt in my mind from my brief visit to Russia in 1963 that, if the Russians had done so, they would have come high on the list. If we take a scale of 1 to 100 and put Japan at 100, then Israel (also isolated in the list) stood at 75, the main European countries clustered together around the halfway mark of 50, with England the lowest of the bunch. The USA was lower still at about 40 and Turkey well down below 20. This superiority of Japan raised my curiosity to fever pitch. I felt that I had to go there and see if I could find the reason.

My first problem was how to get to Japan in some official capacity. I was in luck. Sir John Maud's report on local government in England and Wales had recently appeared. Any re-organisation of local government would affect me in Manchester and I had been closely following the evidence given to the commission. I devoured the report as soon as it appeared. The Japanese were also interested in the relationships between local and central government. They are great learners and wanted to know as much as possible about this report. It was the year of Expo '70 in Osaka. I approached the British Council and received their sponsorship to visit Japan and talk about local government, as well as giving lectures about mathematics education in England and Wales. This brought an opportunity to visit India, also under the auspices of the British Council, on the way home. Here was a chance of fulfilling a desire to see the Taj Mahal in moonlight. Full moon would be on 17 August. With this date in mind, I asked the British Council to arrange for me to travel to Tokyo on 31 July, spend a fortnight in Japan and then come home through Hong Kong and New Delhi.

I spent the time available before the visit reading everything I could lay my hands on about Japan and could hardly wait for the day of departure. My main personal interest was in the history and teaching of mathematics. History points us not to Japan but to China, where fantastic numerical discoveries were made centuries before Christ, and to India, famed for its mathematicians and the birthplace of Scrinivasa Ramanujan, born in 1887, self-taught, one of the greatest mathematics geniuses of all time.

My arrival in Tokyo was overshadowed by a great sadness. Sir John Barbirolli was due to conduct the New Philharmonia Orchestra in Osaka and Tokyo at the beginning of August. I was looking forward to this opportunity of attending one of his triumphant concerts abroad. We often met at home in Manchester and I knew that his health was deteriorating, but this didn't lessen the acute shock to hear on my arrival in Tokyo that he had suffered a sudden heart attack and died the night before in London. There was an invitation awaiting me from the British Ambassador, HE Sir John Pilcher, who had interrupted his summer holiday to return to the Embassy specially to entertain Sir John. As it was, I found myself the sole guest, dining in state alone with the Ambassador. Sir John Pilcher told me stories of the ancient traditions of the Japanese, their art and their customs, their attitudes to women, to education and music, to science and mathematics – above all (perhaps for my special benefit) of the high regard for talent in mathematics.

It was easy to see why the Japanese were so successful. They always seemed to act in concert, facing the same way – whether it was queuing for a streetcar or whatever. In industry when some new product was being considered, there were long and fierce discussions about design, marketing and other aspects, but once a consensus was reached all dissension was dropped. More perhaps than in other developed countries, disputes were put aside and everyone united to get on with the manufacture. The sheer force and weight of this unity then drove production forward. Employees were attached to a company for life and lived in the same complexes – succeeding or failing together. There was, I was given to understand, unremitting loyalty and commitment to one's company for better or worse. The snag about this unquestioning loyalty to a company was that if wrong decisions were made, or uncontrollable external factors changed in an adverse direction, then the situation could alter catastrophically. There was no quick way to adapt to the rapid changes of world markets and conditions, as was to happen in the 1990s.

This mass co-ordination was amazing to witness. For example, in a busy street in Tokyo huge numbers of people would arrange themselves in queues to cross the road and then, when the lights changed, make the crossing *en masse* in disciplined order. Although it was very hot in Tokyo in August, there were heavy showers of rain. In the doorways of large stores were racks of umbrellas. If it began to rain, people took an umbrella, leaving it in a similar rack in the doorway of the next store they were visiting.

At the meetings arranged by the British Council with government officials there was the traditional courtesy – and incessant formally served tea in tiny cups. My hosts were not used to having a woman as an official guest, but they got over this by treating me exactly as they would have behaved toward a male visitor, although I was offered a chair instead of a cushion on the floor as a concession to a European rather than as a woman. The Japanese establishment had wasted no time. The Maud Report had only recently been published, yet they already had a full translation into Japanese, along with all the appendices. They gave me a copy and on my return home I sent it to Sir John as a curiosity present. There was a standard technique at these meetings. I was allotted an interpreter. The leading questioner had his own interpreter. The questions were asked in Japanese; after interpretation, an instant answer was expected. It was clear that the questioner understood English, but this was not admitted. This gave him more time to consider the answer before proceeding to the next question. The whole process was painfully slow. I did not agree with all the Maud recommendations, but to disagree with an official government report would have been unheard of in Japan, or so it seemed to me. It was wiser and simpler to keep my points of disagreement to myself.

In the schools I visited it became plain why achievement was so high compared with that in other advanced countries. First and foremost, there was a passionate desire among parents that children should do well in school generally and in mathematics in particular. Mathematics was regarded as a key subject. For a child to be top of the class in mathematics was a matter of the greatest parental pride. Classes in the cities were not small, averaging over forty in a primary school. Discipline was absolute. In one school I visited, the children sat at individual desks arranged in tight rows at one side of the classroom facing the teacher and blackboard. On the other side of the room were trestle tables laden with the usual kinds of models and aids-to-learning that had by then become familiar in the West. The lesson I witnessed (for children aged about 8 or 9) started with drills in mental arithmetic – addition, subtraction, multiplication – and revision of what had been taught in the previous lesson. Not until a child had demonstrated that these lessons had been well learned was he or she permitted (as a reward) to move over to the table on the window side of the room and get busy with the practical toys. Admittedly there was a visitor present, but it was difficult to imagine that there was anything other than total attention in all such lessons. The pressure to do well may have been too great for comfort, but it would have been impolite and tactless to have enquired too deeply about that.

I went from Tokyo to Kyoto where I gave a lecture about mathematics. Despite having an interpreter, I felt rather despondent afterwards; it could not have been properly understood – the language difficulty was too great. I returned to Tokyo and the next day took the then new bullet train to Osaka, built especially for Expo '70. This afforded another experience of the herd instinct. The train was two-thirds empty, but the few passengers sat tightly together exactly as if it had been crowded. I spread my reading material around me, covering the space of five people. In Osaka I spent some hours at the Exhibition and did some serious sightseeing.

After three nights in Osaka, I flew to Hong Kong. Before leaving Japan I had stuffed my suitcase with everything I could spare (including cameras I had purchased for Robert) and sent it off direct to Manchester Airport, keeping with me only one light bag. This, as it turned out, was a great good fortune.

My flight from Hong Kong to New Delhi was delayed and did not touch down until after midnight. The airport was almost completely deserted. After a slightly anxious wait, a flustered young man from the British Council arrived and grabbed me by the hand, rushing me to his car. The city was in the midst of a riot about pay and conditions in government employment. He took me to the government hotel where a room had been reserved for me. There was one man at reception who directed me to the lifts, having given me the key to my room on the 24th floor. He did not accompany me. The room had not been cleaned. There was no water and no light. It was unbearably hot and past 2 a.m. There was no alternative but to lie down on the unmade bed – with my hearing aids in place and switched on. At daybreak there was the sound of gunfire. Far below on the ground groups of men were firing rifles. The telephone seemed dead. Then, to my surprise and relief, it rang. The same young man from the British Council was on the line. He told me to stay exactly where I was and he would try to get to me. Half-an-hour later he did. We went down all 24 floors by an outside fire-escape and got to his car. He drove me to the house of one of the British Council staff, depositing me there. I was glad to have only a light bag to bother with. However, my commitment to visit two education establishments still remained. One was to a teacher training college, but no-one made any useful comment when it came to training for teaching mathematics.

I was driven to the Taj Mahal on 21 August as planned. The road was long, straight, dusty with small settlements on each side, the sacred cows being much in evidence. The mausoleum itself is truly magical: my particular interest in tiling patterns added to the delight. I stayed overnight at a tourist hotel and saw the building in moonlight. The next day a hired car drove me back to New Delhi for the journey home. On an otherwise deserted stretch of road, a man's body lay inert. My driver swerved to avoid it and went on at the same speed, remarking almost casually that if he had stopped he would automatically have been accused of having knocked the man down. This would cause endless trouble and delay: 'Hadn't I an aeroplane to catch for England?' On the flight home, we set down at Beirut to refuel. The same flight twenty-four hours later was hijacked; the passengers were held hostage on the tarmac for four days before being released. This was the first of a series of Middle East kidnappings in the hope of high ransom payments. Had it occurred a day earlier, it would have made a sorry finish to a remarkable tour.

The emphasis in the United Kingdom was to reduce the size of classes in schools irrespective of standards of competence of mathematics teaching, whereas in Japan it was the achievement of pupils (and of teachers in ensuring this) that mattered. Back in England, I nagged on about this without much success. As related previously, my efforts to make competence in mathematics a requirement for entry into teaching eventually succeeded. It is distressing to see that because of the continuing shortage of teachers these requirements are again being relaxed – setting us back by thirty years.

All was well when I returned home. It felt very much 'mission accomplished'. I had satisfied my curiosity about the Japanese success in school mathematics. This did not help much with mathematics in the schools in the UK. It confirmed my experience that the attitude toward mathematics, of parents, teachers and the general populace, is of critical importance, and that (given good class discipline) the mathematical competence and enthusiasm of the teachers matters more than the size of classes. A good teacher of mathematics with a large class can achieve good results, whereas a teacher who dislikes the subject is no teacher at all. But this is true of any subject and the problem is to find the good teachers in a subject that so few have themselves enjoyed at school – a vicious circle that is hard to break.

CHAPTER 22

Greater Manchester

The Maud Report on the re-organisation of local government in England and Wales that had so interested the Japanese took effect in 1973. It made a fundamental difference to my position in Manchester. Re-organisation was long overdue. There were, for example, over 3,000 housing authorities in England and Wales and every 'county district' had its own separate police force. In the heavily built-up urban areas, apart from the redrawing of some local boundaries, the main idea was to create a two-tier system everywhere with neighbouring towns (boroughs) grouped together to form 'metropolitan counties'. The ten boroughs of which the City of Manchester formed the central pivot were linked to form a new 'Greater Manchester County', in some areas at the expense of the counties of Lancashire and Cheshire. 'Wards' remained substantially unchanged as the units for local elections, with four or five wards forming a parliamentary constituency. Local elections were changed to a four-year cycle instead of a three-year cycle. In each of three successive years a councillor for the lower-tier borough was elected, making three representatives in all. In the fourth year a 'county councillor' for the upper tier, the 'county', was elected.

The rank of alderman was abolished. I had become an alderman in 1970. It was very much a matter of 'dead man's shoes'. I was made alderman on the death of the incumbent for Rusholme ward because, after sixteen years, I had become the longest-serving councillor for the ward. Aldermen did not have to stand for election and could remain members of the city council for life. They had equal voting powers with elected councillors. As average longevity increased, this was beginning to be an embarrassment. A new rank of honorary alderman, in the gift of the council, was established. This gave the right to attend council meetings but without the power to speak in debates or vote.

Those of us who were already aldermen in 1972 had three choices: to throw in the towel, resign and accept the offer of becoming an honorary alderman; to seek adoption as a candidate for the new county council; or to make a bid to revert to being an elected lower-tier city councillor. A large number of the senior members of the city council of both the Labour and Conservative parties chose to call it a day and bow out. Another group of senior members saw membership of the new upper-tier county council as promotion and took that route. For me there was no hesitation. Education was to remain a city council function: I stayed with education. The changes meant that those of us who chose to remain at the lower (city) level and were successfully elected rose in seniority, so many others having departed. As a result my opportunity to become lord mayor occurred at least four years earlier than would otherwise have been the case. The average span between first becoming a Manchester city councillor and being elected lord mayor had been twenty-three to twenty-four years, whereas, because of re-organisation and the creation of a Greater Manchester county council, my turn came in 1975 after only nineteen years as a member of the city council.

The new structure of a Greater Manchester Council did not last. The division of functions between the county and the ten boroughs was cumbersome and expensive; and not understood by the electorate. Services such as Police and Fire could be equally well cared for by joint committees composed of elected members of the boroughs. At the review ten years later, required by statute, it was decided that the county council should be discontinued and in 1986 the government abolished it, the functions it had carried out being redistributed either to the boroughs or to new joint committees of representative or appointed local people.

Although administratively the county council did not survive, there was a residual spin-off: an enhanced sense of the inter-relationship and common interests of the ten boroughs that comprise what is still called Greater Manchester. In particular this was evident in the outstanding success of the Commonwealth Games held in July 2002 when all the boroughs contributed to the general enthusiasm and financial triumph. The Games were a success, financially, socially and administratively, bringing worldwide acclaim from athletes, sponsors, press and television. If, in the early planning stages, the local populace had sometimes been somewhat cynical about the prospects, when it came to the event itself, all joined in with tremendous enthusiasm and were swept along with the pleasure and pride in what Manchester can achieve. What was particularly impressive was the whole-hearted contribution of the 10,000 volunteer guides.

Whether this same sense of identity could be extended to the whole of the North West if plans for a regional assembly find favour in the future is another question. The experience of the defunct Greater Manchester County Council does not augur well for an elected regional council for the North West with administrative and rate-raising powers, although as the coordinating body for a recognised region fighting for fair treatment by central government it could have considerable merit.

The services that most directly affect local populations – education and housing – had remained throughout with the local borough councils. My work and involvement in education at all levels continued as before, although after the swing back to Labour control in the city of Manchester in 1971, I was no longer chairman of the education committee.

In 1973 I was re-elected a city councillor, again representing Rusholme Ward, relinquishing the title of alderman. In 1975 it was the Conservatives' turn to nominate the lord mayor and I was elected. In 1981 there was a further huge swing to Labour in local government elections and I lost my seat on the city council, along with several other Conservative colleagues. Ironically, the issue that most influenced the vote in my ward, where the largest concentration of university student residences are concentrated, was government plans to stop awarding automatic grants to overseas students, an issue not remotely linked with local government. Nonetheless, students poured out of their tower blocks, halls of residence and bedsitters to vote against me, the Conservative candidate, and thus brought to an end my twenty-seven years on the city council. As I had been an alderman before re-organisation in 1973 I was made an honorary alderman, an office that remains a life-time position. In 1984 I was awarded the highest honour the city can bestow: the Freedom of the City, a recognition that I treasure above all else.

One consequence of re-organisation of local government in the urban areas in 1973 had been a change in the structure of the lieutenancy, which has been in existence since the reign of Henry VIII. Historically the militia was organised under the lord lieutenant. Not until 1921 did the lord lieutenant finally lose the theoretical power to call on all able-bodied men of the county to fight in case of need. The fundamental principle concerning the office of lord lieutenant is that he (or she) is the Sovereign's representative in the county. The lord lieutenant of Greater Manchester, currently Col. Sir John Timmins, whose appointment is until the age of 75, has with him a high sheriff, also an honorary appointment made by the Sovereign but held for one year only. The high sheriff has usually, but not always, had experience in the armed services and accompanies the lord lieutenant on most formal and ceremonial occasions. The modern Greater Manchester lieutenancy was created in 1974 to comply with the re-organisation of local government. Robert was appointed the fifth high sheriff in 1978, the year after I had completed my year as lord mayor. After Robert died in 1986, I was appointed one of the hundred or so deputy lieutenants from all over the county.

Another link with the armed services came to me through nomination as a representative of the court of the University of Manchester on the Military Education Committee which oversees the activities of the Manchester and Salford Universities' Officers' Training Corps. I was no stranger to the OTC; indeed Robert and I had done much of our courting during the 1930s in the local army training barracks in Chorlton-cum-Hardy, a Manchester suburb. As a statistician I have always been interested in the logistics of recruitment.

Few people realised how dependent I was, despite the hearing aids, on lip-reading; by then the techniques I had developed to disguise the deafness had become a matter of habit. In 1977, the year after I had ceased to be lord mayor, I was invited to become Honorary Colonel of the OTC contingent for the usual three-year period (in the event extended to four years). This was an interesting and rewarding experience, but I remember one incident of abject shame. I drove myself to the annual camp, which took place in the 1977–78 year at Strensall Camp near York. Although the weather was generally poor, I took the annual passing-out parade in brilliant sunshine. I developed within a few minutes a viciously itching rash and, unwittingly, accepted two anti-histamine tablets to relieve it. I failed to take into account any side effects and fell sound asleep during the ensuing lecture by the visiting General, which hardly gave the best impression of my interest.

This involvement with the OTC in Greater Manchester has remained and I am still a member of the Military Education Committee.

When I was born in 1912 the population of Manchester was about three-quarters of a million. The mass unemployment and exodus from the city brought this total down in the next twenty years to under half a million and today, in 2004, despite the movement back into the city centre and new flats built in the suburbs, the population is still under 400,000. This would not begin to sustain the economy of the city as a whole were it not for the strength of the outer areas and the surrounding boroughs. It took us a long time to recover from the ravages of two world wars and industrial decline; other areas of the country seemed to be far ahead. However, the tide was turning and the shock of the devastating IRA bomb in 1996 seemed to galvanize both us citizens ourselves and outside investors into remarkable activity. Whereas not long ago Manchester was a desert after 5 o'clock on weekday evenings and at weekends, now people in their thousands pour into the city centre to shop and to seek entertainment. The cafés, cinemas, restaurants, bars and clubs are regularly crowded, the pop and café culture creates a vibrant community intent on enjoying city lights and celebrity events. This in its turn attracts tourists from both the UK and abroad. Manchester United football stadium is packed with 67,000 spectators at every home match, and now that Manchester City have taken up their new home in the stadium where the Commonwealth Games took place (in the once derelict area now being transformed into a virtual new town called Eastlands), there is space for another 48,000 people to enjoy football. We can also celebrate the replacement of the old Free Trade Hall with the award-winning Bridgewater Hall and the Manchester Museum of Science and Industry, of which I have recently been made a Patron, and which drew 450,000 visitors in 2002. The crowd-drawing Manchester Evening News Arena, the G-Mex exhibition centre and a new conference centre on the site of what was once Central Station all draw large numbers of people. There is the Velodrome, the entertainment complex called the Print Works (once the home of the *Daily Telegraph* and *Daily Mirror* newspapers), the new international-standard swimming baths and much else besides. These venues are attracting world entertainment celebrities almost every week. Manchester Airport, which the city stubbornly refused to give up all through the years of economic depression, is a gateway to the world. To me who lived through the dark days of the between-war decline and watched with despair as other parts of the country seemed to pick up ahead of us in the after-war years, it all seems a miracle.

CHAPTER 23

Finding the money:
the Layfield Committee

The re-organisation of local government highlighted the growing general
dissatisfaction with the rating system which was increasingly thought to
be unfair between one householder and another. The system had been
introduced in the reign of Queen Elizabeth the First to make provision for
vagrants: a property tax that had the merits of being inescapable and
quantifiable according to the assessed capital value of the buildings. The
rating system based on property values alone, irrespective of the number
and status of the occupiers, was perhaps not as unjust as it was thought
to be: successive governments had made concessions about income tax
for widows and other retired elderly people. The local rates covered only
about a quarter of total local government expenditure, the rest being met
by a variety of government direct grants. In particular, expenditure on
schools in the 1970s was subsidised by a 70 per cent grant, and 'further
education' outside the universities was met by all local authorities
together, subsidised by a 75 per cent grant, in a system known as 'pool-
ing'. The rating system had become somewhat chaotic and was not
understood by the general public. Revision was long overdue and had to
take place anyway to meet the new circumstances of having two-tier
local government for the first time in the urban areas. A committee
was set up in 1974 by the Labour Government to examine the whole
structure of local rates and report within two years. It was an 'all-party'
committee and I was invited to serve as one of two Conservative elected
members of an urban council. The committee was chaired by Sir Frank
Layfield QC and became known as the Layfield Committee.

Sir Frank was a brilliant chairman and attending the committee's
meetings was like taking part in a John Gielgud performance of a Shakespeare play. He had a way that was sheer genius of persuading witnesses

to keep to the point. Before each session the committee decided what questions needed to be answered, and the member in whose particular area the questions lay was invited to sit next to him. When the representatives of the National Union of Teachers were to give evidence, I was the one whose task it was to ask the questions. I did my best. I felt a gentle tap on my arm. Sir Frank intervened: 'Dame Kathleen, that was an excellent and important question. Could I phrase it another way so that it can perhaps be better understood?'

None of the three distinct possibilities for reform that we suggested was taken up: the government changed to Conservative control and Margaret Thatcher had been persuaded to institute a different alternative to anything suggested by Layfield: a 'flat-rate per capita council tax' unrelated to property values. I was bold enough to warn her that this would be unacceptable and would severely damage her chances of the Conservatives winning the next election (which it did). No prizes are won for predicting a doom that happens. The outcome of the furore against the proposed reform resulted in a much better formula emerging: a system by which property is allocated to one of eight 'bands' according to its market value and the tax charge rises through the bands. Although taxpayers will always grumble about 'waste in public spending' and about any rise in taxation, there do not now seem to be the same vociferous protests about the 'injustice' of the local tax as there were during those bitter discussions, although criticism is certainly growing.

My service on the Layfield Committee led to an unexpected visit to America. Much of our discussion had centred on the relationship between central and local government. This issue was also exercising the minds of political leaders in the United States. In 1979 the then President, Jimmy Carter, called a conference specifically to discuss such relationships and invited our government to send a representative. I received an invitation from Anthony Crosland, then Secretary of State for Local Government in the second Wilson Government, to attend on the Government's behalf. I was treated as though I were a member of the British Government itself; met at the airport in a limousine, entertained at the British Embassy as chief guest at a dinner arranged to greet me (Peter Jay was Ambassador at the time), and allotted a prominent seat in the conference hall that was within a stone's throw of the White House. President Carter addressed the assembled delegates and questions were invited. With great temerity I ventured a comment, telling of our experiences in the UK. Whether it was because I was the only woman in the hall or my English accent, the remarks were warmly applauded and quoted in the national press.

A high point of this, my second visit to the United States, was meeting again with HE Elliot Lee Richardson. He had stayed as our guest in the town hall in November 1975 when I was lord mayor and he was the American ambassador. He had perhaps the most remarkable intellect of anyone I met during the year. He had been appointed attorney general by President Nixon, but put his whole political career at risk by resigning when instructed by Nixon to sack his erstwhile Harvard professor and tutor, Archibald Cox, who had been appointed special prosecutor for matters concerning the Watergate affair. Richardson, despite all his loyalty to an elected president, avowed that had he agreed to do so he would 'never have been able to walk Harvard Yard again'. Nixon's successor, President Ford, appointed Richardson to the ambassador's post in London, but he was recalled within a year to serve as Secretary to the Department of Health, Welfare and Education. He was succeeded as ambassador in London by HE Anne Armstrong who also, with her husband, stayed with us overnight at the town hall. I fell totally for her husband – a very tall and immensely courteous man of irresistible charm. They were the owners of a huge ranch in Texas and extended to me an open invitation to visit them – which, unfortunately, I was never able to do. They did, however, invite me together with Margaret, my lady mayoress, to a reception at the ambassador's residence in Regent's Park in London. This we were able to accept, savouring the elegance of the mansion and its surroundings.

I kept in touch with Elliot Richardson after his recall to the States. We exchanged occasional letters and he always sent me one of his special Christmas cards. He was a talented cartoonist and amateur painter in oils and he had the cards produced each year from one of his own landscape pictures. President Ford's defeat in 1976 meant that

Richardson's post was quickly terminated, but in 1977 Jimmy Carter, the new President, made him his special representative to the Law of the Sea Conference – a job which he told me he found exceptionally frustrating as the jealousies between nations about their rights concerning the sea bed, beyond a limited area around their own coasts, were unresolvable.

When I was attending the Carter conference, Elliot Richardson invited me for supper. I met him in his government offices in Washington and he then drove me in his own car to his home in West Virginia. His wife Anne, an accomplished choral singer, was away at a concert. He raided the freezer and produced a fine meal which we ate at the kitchen table. I found it interesting that a man of such great distinction managed just as more ordinary mortals do. The next day I was going north to Boston which was his home city. He gave me an introduction to some of his Harvard friends. They invited me to dinner and treated me royally. My particular question was to ask if Elliot was likely ever to stand for president and if not, why not. The answer was blunt and, to me, shocking. His friends said that he had all the qualities to win such an election and become President – except one. He was, they explained, too honest. He would never sink to the essential 'bribery' of rewarding those who made massive donations to a campaign with promises of high appointments if and when successful, and without that no aspirant could ever hope to win. If anything makes me more of a supporter of a monarchy here in the UK, it is my horror of the presidential system (and elections) in America.

Anne Richardson died early in 1999. A few months later, Elliot had a major heart attack and died, in Boston, aged 79.

CHAPTER 24

Rescued by computer:
St. John Ambulance

A major consequence for me of the re-organisation of local government was an activity that became a new and continuing commitment. Robert, like many of his colleagues who remained active in the Territorial Royal Army Medical Corps after demobilisation in 1946, had been invited to serve as a county surgeon in the St. John Ambulance Brigade. Subsequently he became the national Surgeon-in-Chief. St. John units had traditionally been organised in England, Wales and Northern Ireland (Scotland had a separate organisation) in line with the structure of local government. Changes had to be made to the St. John structure in 1973 to match changes in local government. In particular a new Greater Manchester County St. John was created and I was invited to be its first chairman. I was not myself a member of St. John at the time, but I had long experience of its activities as Robert's wife. To create loyalty to a new county organisation from units which had operated for nearly a century without such a body was an extremely difficult task. However, reorganisation within St. John was long overdue. There were many old properties in urgent need of replacement: ancient legacies left for specified activities that had long since ceased, a perpetual shortage of money and a plethora of other problems. These had to be resolved by the new county organisation. We had no premises of our own and no staff. We made do with inadequate rented offices and staff seconded from local units. It was eight years before we bought a redundant post-war school building and could begin to build up strength on a sound basis, and it took another four years of unremitting effort to clear the capital debt.

All the work of the Brigade was voluntary and much of it needed modernising. When at last we were in our own building, we began to recruit a minimum of paid administrative staff. Details of membership, training, expenditure all had to be sent in annual returns to headquarters in London and all was done by hand. Our only source of income, other than subscriptions and donations, was the provision of first-aid courses for large firms obliged by law to have a trained first-aider on their premises during working hours. It became plain to me that, if we were to survive, we had to boost recruitment to these fee-paying courses.

It was also plain to me that we had to move to computers to cope with the heavy secretarial and administrative work. This was an innovation for St John. No other sector had experience of computers, but I had the advantage of having been an assistant lecturer in the Department of Mathematics at Manchester University where Alan Turing had recently joined the staff, and F.C. (Freddie) Willams and T. (Tommy) Kilburn were working just around the corner, on the first information-storing programmable computer in the world, which performed successfully on 21 June 1948. I had also been keenly involved as a city councillor and member of the council's finance committee when Manchester was one of the first four local authorities to invest in a computer – the famous Lyons Tea Shop 'Leo' (Lyons Electronic Office). I used my own money to acquire for the St. John work a Tandy desk-top computer and two large data-storing external hard-disk drives, and spent a year doing much of the clerical work and accounts at home before persuading the new Greater Manchester St. John Council (of which I was chairman) to duplicate this equipment at our Manchester headquarters. In due course the whole of the St. John organisation adopted computers, but we were some four or five years ahead and it had rescued us from possible oblivion through lack of funds.

When in 1981 we moved into our own building, St. John House, situated two miles south of the city centre, the North West was in the middle of a crippling economic recession; large manufacturing firms were closing their doors for ever. Lists of firms and addresses barely existed and telephone directories were seriously out of date, so approaches by post or normal advertising of our first-aid courses would be of no use. Personal visits seemed the only answer. It came to my notice one Thursday that there was a government enterprise scheme through which young people who had been unemployed for more than a year could be taken on for approved work. The deadline for receiving applications was the Friday. I reckoned that 'Friday' meant in practice first thing on Monday morning. I wrote the application overnight, and took it to our St. John county director, James Anderton, at the time the chief constable of Greater Manchester. He readily gave his approval and support. I drove into the city to deliver the application personally to the government office. Here I was thwarted. It was the period when fire-bombs were being planted by the IRA and all office and Royal Mail letter-boxes were sealed. Desperate, I hung around for a while and then had the good fortune to see a caretaker making his way into a back door and I entrusted my precious envelope to him. The outcome was that we received over £40,000 in grant aid to set up three teams of four young people each. One in each team was the designated leader and had the use of a car. We were fully operational within eight weeks.

The key to it all was my computer. I acquired the set of telephone directories that covered the whole of Greater Manchester with its two and a half million population. More importantly I acquired the post-code directories for the whole county. Postcodes are unequivocal and describe the position of a building down to the correct side of a road. My objective was to have a list of all establishments employing more than a hundred people. I knew that, by law, firms have to register with the Department of Health and Social Security, whose regional offices were in the centre of Manchester. I went there to ask for the list, which I found was in law available to any member of the public with a legitimate use for it. The director was on long leave. The acting director told me sor-rowfully that he had no authority to issue the list. It was essential to me. I don't take 'No' for an answer easily, not when I really care, so I risked the remark 'You are the acting director?'. 'Yes', he replied. In the sweet-est manner I could command, I came back with, 'Well, wouldn't it be a good idea to act?' He capitulated, called for his computer operator and asked him to produce the list for me for the next day. I duly returned the next day, to be greeted by the distraught young man. He had left the printer running all night. When he returned in the morning, the room was ceiling-high in continuous print-out paper. He had underestimated the length of the list, and the paper (which luckily did not run out) had failed to keep to its proper concertina folding.

By the afternoon I had my weighty pile of properly folded paper with the crucial list. From the start I reckoned that if a firm's name was not in the current telephone directory it had gone out of business. This eliminated a terrifying number of names. My second requirement was that the postcodes of firms that survived should be found and reliably recorded. This was where the computer came into its own. It was quite something in 1981 for a small system such as ours to be able to 'sort' automatically in any desired way. Using the postcodes we sorted the addresses so that there was no back-tracking by our visiting teams. Each firm that remained on our list was sent a letter telling them about the first-aid course St. John Ambulance could provide and warning them that a member of our team would call during the following week. Targeted firms were usually telephoned in advance to confirm the impending visit and there was nearly always a ready welcome. At the end of ten months we had established a base for recruitment to courses throughout the county on which our success then and in the future depended.

In addition to the invaluable help of a trusted friend, Pauline Ekersall, at St. John House, I had the indispensable near full-time labour of Robert at home. He had recently retired from his post at the Royal Infirmary and had time on his hands. He sat all day and almost every day at our kitchen table overlooking the garden, the radio on full blast, and went through the big list of qualifying firms, checking them one-by-one in the telephone directories. If they survived that first test, he looked up their postcode. To keep three teams of four people busy for five days for five hours a day every week meant having at least a hundred names ready for them each Monday morning. To do this I had to sit down at my computer every Friday evening and work like mad all through Saturday and Sunday. I did this relentlessly for ten months, with scarcely a break. Individual members of the team had their statutory holidays and leave. I had none. Although I had many other commitments that could not be neglected and meetings in London to attend, this project had to come first as there was no one else. It was infinitely worth the effort. I ended up with a bag in which were ten boxes each containing five computer disks. They contained valid bang-up-to-date information of almost 1,000 industrial and commercial firms actively operating in Greater

Manchester, firms moreover with co-operative managers willing to receive visitors like ourselves.

When John Ashworth, the then new Vice-Chancellor of Salford University, heard about this data his eyes lit up. This was exactly what he needed for his company 'Campus', created to help rescue the university from threatened closure by the government on grounds of economy. He offered me £10,000 for the use of the list, St. John Ambulance having the first and only other use. This was an astonishing amount of money for us at the time, and I accepted instantly. Later we heard that the Department of Trade and Industry had been so impressed by what could be achieved using the power and accuracy of the list that they awarded Salford University a grant worth several million pounds to support Campus.

My interest and activities with St. John Ambulance never slackened – even after Robert died in 1986. I became a member of Chapter General, attending meetings in London regularly. In 1987 I was made Dame Commander of the Order of St. John of Jerusalem (DStJ). In 1989 I relinquished the chairmanship of the council for the Order of St. John in Greater Manchester, after sixteen years: it was time for someone else to take over.

My exemplar, Alderman Dame Mary Kingsmill-Jones, who died aged 91 in 1968, was a great worker for the Red Cross, and in 1945 the first woman lord mayor in the country, once advised me: 'Always work closely for some charitable organisation. It makes a valuable antidote to being involved in party politics in government'. I know what she meant.

CHAPTER 25

Lord Mayor, 1975–76

In May 1975 I was elected Lord Mayor. For 366 days (1976 was a leap year) I would be the 'first citizen', representing the City of Manchester on formal and ceremonial occasions, living in the town hall. I was the first lord mayor to have been created a DBE or to have received a knighthood before becoming lord mayor (five years before and for 'services to education'), although several received such honour a year or so after for their public services.

I was also the first Lord Mayor of Manchester to wear a jabot when in full regalia. A jabot is an ornamental frill, usually white, used on a man's shirt front, especially by footmen and particularly when powdered white wigs were the fashion. Men by the 1970s usually wore dark suits and ties under their mayoral robes. It is convenient for a woman to wear whatever will be most appropriate when the robes are taken off – and this can make for an unsuitable neck-line. The jabot solved every problem. It has now been adopted almost everywhere for both men and women as part of the regalia. The only supplier I could find in a hurry was a theatrical costumier with premises in a back street. I also found that the three available tricorns, large, medium and small, were all intolerably heavy and impossible for me to wear with my essential hearing aids. I had an outwardly identical tricorn made, with a soft net base, that I could wear outdoors all day without even noticing it. This I bequeathed to the town hall for the use of future women lord mayors if they so desired. Each in turn (there have been six in the past 29 years) has sent me a grateful letter of thanks.

Extraordinary though it may seem, I had only the most sketchy notion of what the lord mayor actually did other than preside at city council meetings and civic functions. It is in fact a very personal job, each lord mayor in turn bringing to it his or her own style. Living in the town hall made it very special. Manchester was the only city or town in Great Britain where the first citizen lived in a working town hall in which all central administration was conducted – literally 'over the shop'. A suite of rooms overlooking Albert Square at the front of the building above the main reception rooms was described as the finest in the world and certainly I thought so. The large main bedroom at the corner of the building (now used as the lord mayor's office) I made comfortable with a television set for Robert to spend his evenings and spare time on his own in peace when he wanted. That our lord mayor lived in the town hall was the envy of Birmingham, of Newcastle, of Leeds and Liverpool, and it certainly brought its own special flavour to the year.

I came to love the town hall itself as a building, especially to live in, never too hot, never too cold, perfectly ventilated. Designed by Alfred Waterhouse, it was opened in 1877. It fits snugly into a difficult triangular site – every inch of space being used to best advantage. The arched main entrance leads through a hallway that supports the clock tower. In the tower are twenty-three bells weighing in total over 12 tonnes, thirteen of which can be played from a carillon similar to an old-time piano-player using punched paper rolls. On opposite sides of this entrance hall are statues of Manchester's most famous scientists: John Dalton (1766–1844) the chemist and James Joule (1818–89) the physicist. I make a habit of nodding my acknowledgement every time I pass through the entrance. Two staircases lead up to a central landing called The Bees that has a tiled mosaic floor depicting bees which symbolise our industrious history and are a part of the city's coat of arms. The mosaic design is bordered with intertwining strands of a stylised cotton plant. The main building is linked by two bridges to a large extension, opened in 1938 by King George VI, containing a modern council chamber. Alone with Robert in the town hall over the weekends I wandered around, finding hidden spiral staircases and corners; small features such as the builders' own faces carved on the stone capitals; the astonishing likeness of the marble bust of King Edward VII as a young man to our present Prince of Wales; the Ford Madox Brown murals in the Great Hall, especially that depicting William Crabtree of neighbouring Broughton in his weaver's loft observing the transit of

Venus in 1639. I cared for the fabric and the furniture and the historic artefacts. After any private dinner party (I gave fifteen of these), I took my guests on a conducted tour – a practice that culminated in an invitation to make this tour, live, for Granada Television.

I felt sad that there was no worthy portrait of the Queen in the town hall – as there was in Liverpool. I woke up early during my first week, remembering that in 1977 it would be the centenary of the opening of the building and that this would coincide with the celebration of the Queen's accession 25 years before. Would this create an opportunity to seek her consent to sit for a portrait for us? I took advice from the Rt. Hon. Charles Morris, PC, a local MP, and with his help acted quickly. Six leaders of industry in the city agreed to cover the cost anonymously. Negotiations with the Palace went ahead without a hitch. Michael Noakes was the artist. He was given six sittings. I sent him good wishes before every sitting and twice visited his house in London where he had his studios to watch the progress of the painting. It was completed during August 1975 and the Queen herself came to Manchester to unveil it the next July, by which time I was no longer lord mayor. The original site for the portrait was overlooking The Bees, but a few years later it was moved upstairs into the lord mayor's apartments for greater safety.

There is no hard and fast rule about who is elected lord mayor or how the choice is made. At one time the choice was given to the two main political parties in alternate years. When Labour began to have a large and persistent majority, a formula was adopted, each political party accumulating 'credit points' according to the numbers of councillors elected. Although this was manifestly fair and accepted, it was always slightly retrospective and did not reflect electoral swing immediately. After 1981 it was discarded, the controlling party taking absolute power to make the nomination for the lord mayoralty. It was through the workings of this formula that I was a Conservative lord mayor with the council controlled by a Labour majority. In a peculiar way it gave me more rather than less independence. I did what I felt was right and best for the city without consulting anyone, provided it did not involve spending public money. I did, however, pay meticulous regard to the system and, indeed, respect for the Labour leaders of the city council during my year in office. There was never to my knowledge the slightest conflict or criticism; if there was, then I did not hear it and no-one saw fit to tell me.

The position of lady mayoress is entirely a courtesy and has no statutory attributes. When, in bygone days, the lord mayor was almost always a man, he would normally invite his wife to be lady mayoress, or, if he was widowed, a daughter or other female relative A woman lord mayor also makes her own choice: a daughter, or relative, or a friend, or, increasingly often, her husband who is then referred to as her 'escort'. Our daughter Florence, had she lived, would have been my lady mayoress and I was extremely fortunate that our son Charles's wife, Margaret, was willing to take on the role. She was an enormous help to me. She supported me as hostess when we were entertaining and accompanied me on most official visits outside the town hall. She and Charles occupied one of the spare bedrooms in the apartments. Both Charles and Robert went about their own regular work during the day, Charles and Margaret usually spending their weekends in their own home in Knutsford. Although our house in Didsbury was only fifteen minutes from the town hall, I went home only once in the whole year, and that was to pick up a pair of gym shoes to meet the challenge of playing someone at squash.

The lord mayor is elected to represent the city, not to run it – that is the task of the leader of the city council and its members. For one year the lord mayor is (at least in theory) removed from party politics and, by convention, although in the chair at city council meetings, must never vote. Success is all to do with public relations, representing the city to outsiders, to the hundreds of visitors from all over the United Kingdom and abroad – and, equally important, leading the town hall and the administration of the city in service to its own citizens whatever their race, creed or status. I was lucky in that I had been doing this for years, particularly when chairman of the education committee. The records show that I received about 2,000 invitations and accepted and fulfilled between 1,600 and 1,700 engagements in the course of my year of office: that is an average of between four and five every day, including Saturdays and Sundays, which I accepted as the norm. This would certainly not have been possible had I not been living in the town hall.

I was one of the last lord mayors to live on the premises. Various party political and economic decisions brought to an end in 1984 this valuable feature of the Manchester lord mayoralty, changing the nature and public function of the position. It greatly influenced the way I set about this all-absorbing year. All my local authority committee work ceased for the year, although not my outside national interests. To a large extent I could organise my own public entertaining within the town hall. I chose to put first, above all other interests, the task of forming good relationships with the other nine boroughs that formed the still-new Greater Manchester County. I gave instructions that every invitation from any of the boroughs should be accepted if humanly possible. Early in my year I arranged for a special reception of all nine mayors and their mayoresses, so that I could get to know them personally from the start. Near the beginning of the year, in July, I arranged a bowls tournament at our large Heaton Park. Some bright spark produced an enormous cardboard challenge cup. After a supper of Lancastrian black puddings and real ale, we had a 'piggy' tournament, a traditional street game of the nineteenth century, played with the broken shafts of miners' picks as bats. A piece of wood about six inches long (the piggy) is laid across a wedge with one end on the ground. The player hits the other end of the piggy causing it to jump into the air, and then, as it falls, the player whacks it as far as possible with the pick-shaft. The winner is the player who whacks the piggy furthest. It is extremely difficult for a first-time player to make the piggy jump high enough and then strike it – all in one movement. The game has long been banned from streets because it was so dangerous to passers-by, for obvious reasons. Some of the mayors, particularly the Mayor of Wigan who won outright, were quite good at piggy. This was however sheer madness as we were in the glass-walled reception area of Heaton Hall and the risks of serious damage were huge. The Mayor of Bury and his team won the bowls tournament – we Mancunians were out-classed.

There was a large number of social commitments – visiting or opening schools and clubs; attending charity functions, calls on old people's homes; once topping-out a large new building for a bank. It used to be the custom for the lord mayor to call on every citizen who reached their hundredth birthday. In my year there were four. One somewhat confused lady was in a rage because she alleged that she had not received her telegram from the Queen. She had, but it was a card delivered with the mail. To satisfy her, we persuaded a young boy to dress up in a uniform and ride a bicycle to deliver a pretend telegram in a brown envelope, the message being typed on paper tape which was stuck in strips to an imitation telegram form. Nowadays, so many citizens reach their centenary that these visits are made only on request.

The lord mayor leads the city councillors in a number of formal annual ceremonies – in particular to the Cathedral on 'Lord Mayor's Sunday' at the beginning of the municipal year and to the Cenotaph on Remembrance Day in November. I went to the Cenotaph incognito on the previous day and practised laying a large dummy wreath, followed by the difficult manoeuvre of stepping backwards down the steps.

A great and special joy for me were the football matches – either City or United playing at home on alternating Saturdays during the season. I had the privilege of a seat in the Directors' box at both clubs – a great difference from the open terraces with my father when I could persuade him to take me as a schoolgirl. In 1976, City won the League Cup; United were beaten by Southampton at Wembley in the FA Cup final, but were top of the Second Division and gained promotion. Both teams were driven through the streets of Manchester into Albert Square on the top of an open bus. I stood on the podium, fully robed with chain of office and tricorn, to receive them. Over 35,000 enthusiasts crammed into the Square to celebrate on both occasions. That was twenty-eight years ago. Today the scenario is very different and Albert Square is not large enough to accommodate increasingly large crowds.

At most receptions it was the custom for the lord mayor and lady mayoress to shake hands with all the guests on arrival. I can have difficulty in catching names correctly. Margaret, standing beside me, was wonderful all through the year in knowing exactly when I really had heard and when I was merely pretending. Hearing names is much easier if one knows them in advance. Partly for this reason and partly because I wanted to know anyway, I insisted on having the full guest list with names, titles and special attributes given to me at least half an hour before any reception. Even when the guests were strangers, I was able to pick up the connection as the attendant announced them. It was a useful technique and effectively covered the weakness of poor hearing. In the office, when I was absolutely stuck and unable to hear what some guest calling on me was saying, I devised another method. I had available atlases and maps; it was a useful wheeze to produce a relevant map and ask visitors if they would point out precisely where they lived. Conversation could then flow more easily, even if I couldn't hear properly. The deafness was no serious handicap. I was used to it and the aids worked well enough all through the year. It was said in the town hall: 'It's no use moaning to the lord mayor. If she isn't interested in what you are saying, she can't hear, so you may as well save your breath to cool your porridge'.

Music was a priority. The grand piano in the apartments had not been tuned for years. I immediately had this seen to. It was a lovely instrument and, when we had guests, there always seemed to be someone who went straight to it and began play in the background for everyone's pleasure. In the Great Hall there is a fine Cavaille-Coll organ. One evening among my guests at dinner were Sir Edward Boyle (then Minister of Education), Charles and Hilary Groves, Sir Bernard Lovell (who, as well as being then Director of Jodrell Bank radio telescope observatory, is an organist of considerable distinction) and John and Renna Manduell. I took them on my usual conducted tour of the building. I had especially asked that the organ console be pulled into its playing position. Charles Groves sat at the organ console happily fingering the Bach D-minor Toccata and Fugue – in silence, because we couldn't find the switch to turn on the electricity. Sir Bernard found it and flicked it on unknown to Sir Charles. All the stops were out, and the tremendous blast of sound nearly blew the roof off.

There was then no pecuniary benefit from being lord mayor. Indeed, the opposite. For a whole year the lord mayor is removed from earning from a normal full-time occupation, although some who have been doctors or lawyers or in business have continued work as far as possible. Large firms and trade unions have usually agreed to meet normal pay on a one year paid-leave basis. There was, and still is, a lord mayor's allowance and I used this to meet the cost of living with my family in the town hall and for the private entertaining of VIP guests, which I regarded as part of the job.

Many very important people stayed as guests overnight with us at the town hall. Margaret Thatcher, then Shadow Minister of Education, spent a Friday night with us when fulfilling a local party political engagement to which I was deliberately not invited. The leader of the city council generously gave me permission to use the Great Hall on the Saturday morning to entertain 500 Conservative supporters to coffee to meet her. Harold Wilson, when Prime Minister, also came to the town hall, although only for tea and to brush up after a tiring engagement in the King's Hall at Belle Vue where I had been sitting next to him. He was an inveterate pipe-smoker and liked to drink a lot of water to keep his throat fit for speaking. Water used to be hard to come by at any formal function and a jug of water on the table unheard of. It is only in relatively recent years, with drink-driving laws so strictly enforced, that bottled water is available more or less automatically. I saw to it that the lord mayor's attendant who was there to look after me, brought him water, and more water, and again more water. The empty glasses accumulated. When press photographers swarmed around to get their pictures, I hastily swept these out of sight, for which the Prime Minister was duly grateful, the erroneous impression that he had been imbibing quantities of alcohol avoided.

In preparation for after-dinner speeches, a few days before the event I used to telephone whoever would be presiding, usually the regional or Manchester president of the organisation concerned, to ask what was the main point that I could usefully make. In this way my speech was almost written for me and a guaranteed success. Another ploy was to take note of the best joke made by the principal guest speaker at one dinner and then re-tell it (with acknowledgement) at the next dinner. It was bound to be up-to-date and fresh. Although some of the top-table guests may have been present on both occasions, it did not matter – if a joke is good and new enough, it will bear a second telling provided its source is acknowledged.

A stickler for protocol, I took immense care about guest lists and hospitality. On one occasion, when the guests were representatives of Manchester United Football Club, I found to my horror that white candles were being put into the candelabra. The town hall had run out of red candles. I dashed for my coat, asked the secretary to ring the nearest large store, Kendal Milne, which was just about to close for the day, ran as fast as I could and barged in at the door kept open for me, to be handed several boxes of red candles left for me on trust by the manager.

It was a tradition that only the lord mayor, maybe accompanied by the lady mayoress or a member of the Royal Family or some other special guest, could ride in N10, the lord mayor's car. On one occasion, however, I broke this rule. There was a big Roman Catholic celebration at the Free Trade Hall which is only about 200 yards from the town hall. Three archbishops and several bishops were taking part. When we emerged from the Hall it was teeming with rain and there was no transport arranged for them as it was expected that they would want to walk across to the reception. N10 was waiting at the door for me and the only courteous thing to do was to offer a lift. I don't know if any other lord mayor has ever had two archbishops, robed in all their glory, sitting on pull-down jump seats.

However late, I made sure before going to bed that I knew exactly what was arranged for the next day. In the morning I dressed accordingly, not needing to go up to the apartments again until changing for the evening. Always an early riser, I was up and dressed by 7 a.m. every day. My newspaper was delivered early and at 8 a.m. every weekday I was at the hairdresser in nearby King Street. Soon after 8.30 I was back in the town hall, the daily newspaper already scanned. Every night, however late back in my office, I wrote my letters of thanks for the day's invitations by hand, leaving them laid out on the floor for the envelopes to be addressed by the office typist (there was only one) in the morning.

For only the second time in my life I kept a journal (the first, in 1965, was during my tour in America). I dictated to a machine every night without fail, last thing before going upstairs to bed. The tape was typed up next day. I never read the typescript, always being too busy with the following day's programme. On my last day in May 1976 the typescript, with a carbon copy, was presented to me. There were 670 pages with 320 words per page, making about 750,000 words in all, probably a unique record of a lord mayor's year in office.

The week's diary was determined by the traditional duties, but also by spontaneous invitations from outside and the hospitality offered in return. I adopted the philosophy I had experienced in my 1965 America tour where people in positions of responsibility always seemed to make time for visitors, even if it meant inviting them to breakfast. I was asked if I would meet the current 'Miss World'. There wasn't a chink in the diary. I suggested 8.30 a.m. and guaranteed that the press would be present. Her manager said that she had never been out of bed before 9 a.m. in her life, but she came and so did the press photographers.

For a year I didn't have to do my own filing or worry about missing appointments; there was no shopping to do or preparation of meals. Time-keeping was the responsibility of others. This led to a blissfully trouble-free year. Our house in Didsbury was shut. There was no daily commuting, no getting stuck in traffic jams and tail-backs. All this led to an immense saving of that most valuable commodity – time. I never remember being tired, despite the long hours. I was doing what I liked doing and concentrating on the unique job allotted me without unwanted interruptions. I was very happy. Every event was a one-off: at the end of my allotted term, it would fall to someone else. This strongly influenced one's attitudes: never allow an opportunity to pass, never refuse an invitation; always make every effort to give maximum pleasure and care when entertaining. I never hesitated to ask for help when I needed it, but had no time for grumbles or gossip. It was said: 'If the lord mayor asks you to do something – like moving those chairs from here to there – do it immediately and get the kudos, saving yourself the trauma of seeing her do it herself.'

One day in September when, unusually, the secretary Bernard Lawson was away, I came back from a luncheon engagement to be told by the typist that she had taken a telephone call inviting me to make a courtesy flight in Concorde (not then fully in service) to Beirut and back. She had looked at my engagement diary and had seen that I had accepted an invitation from the Burgermeister of Amsterdam to the commemoration of the seventh century of their city. She had refused the invitation. I went berserk, subsequently writing in soap on the large mirror above the fireplace in the secretary's office: 'No-one, but no-one, is to refuse any invitation to the lord mayor without her knowledge and specific permission.' She had not made a note of the name or telephone number of the caller. Eventually I made contact. It was British Airways with a special promotion invitation to the two North-West lord mayors – of Manchester and of Liverpool. The date was a Thursday and the flight would be from Heathrow to Beirut and back. My engagement in Amsterdam covered two nights – for the civic ceremony in the morning and a dinner on the evening of the Wednesday. The town clerk was to accompany me and I was to be in full rig with the lord mayor's chain. Clearly I could not make the flight on Concorde to Beirut, but this was a chance of a lifetime. 'Could I, please, join the invitees on the flight home?' This was agreed. I fulfilled the official engagements in Amsterdam on the Wednesday and, after an interesting sightseeing stroll with the town clerk in Amsterdam's red-light district later that evening, got up very early on the Thursday morning (having left the precious lord mayor's chain and my evening dress in the care of the town clerk) and took an early morning flight via Rome to Beirut.

The arrangement was that I should await the arrival of Concorde, which had made a short promotional flight before returning to Beirut ready to take off for London at 2 p.m. I had no luggage, no foreign money, no ticket – only a handbag and my passport. There was no-one there to meet me. Had I made some stupid mistake? Which side of the barrier had it been arranged that I should be met? After a reasonable wait, I decided I had perhaps better go through the barrier. I went to a public telephone and rang the British Embassy. There was an immediate reaction. 'The Lord Mayor of Manchester? You are our special responsibility. Please stay exactly where you are, by the telephone you describe, and we will come for you.' Within about ten minutes, an alarmed-looking young man arrived and took me by the arm. He rushed me out into the street and around the outside of the building to get me back to the arrival/ departure lounge. It was the first day of serious riots in Beirut: bullets were flying everywhere and the noise of machine-gun fire drowned all else. We made it. I was delivered into the care of an anxious crew member of the Concorde which had now returned from its unscheduled promotional short flight. In record time we were safely airborne. I was beside myself with excitement as the speed mounted, when we went through Mach 1 and eventually, to cheers and champagne, reached Mach 2. In the cockpit was the famed pilot, Captain Brian Trubshaw. He invited me in and with my little tape-recorder I made a tape of our conversation. It was one of the highlights of my year.

In May, between the departure of a lord mayor and the arrival of the successor, there was no opportunity for cleaning the apartments. The tradition was that the lord mayor vacated the apartments completely for a fortnight during August so that a thorough cleaning could take place. For many years the city had owned a comfortable house in the Lake District, Dale Head, on the banks of Thirlmere that had been Manchester's main source of fresh water since a 100 mile pipeline was laid in 1894. The house was always made available for the lord mayor if required during August. There was a housekeeper and caretaker who lived there throughout the year and the house was a useful asset for waterworks personnel and for civic guests from abroad. Robert would have been happier to go to our own cottage, Hodge Close, above Coniston (with me doing all the housekeeping and cooking); but for me Dale Head meant a complete rest among my much-loved fells and mountains, and precious time to catch up on my general reading.

There were two other special attractions: the mere itself (to which public access was forbidden because it was Manchester's main source of fresh, unsterilised drinking water) and Helvellyn. In an old boathouse, approached through a large paddock waist-high in stinging nettles, was a rowing boat, but the oars were locked away. I asked if the nettles could be cut back and the oars un-padlocked. The answer from the caretaker was a stern 'No – that is not possible and no lord mayor had ever asked to use the rowing boat'. As it happened, at a dinner the week before, I had been sitting next to the chairman of the North-West Water Board. When one wants something done that is impossible, go to the highest authority one knows. I rang the chairman (it was a Sunday evening). On the Tuesday morning we were awakened by a strange noise: to our astonishment, a team of men with huge machines was mowing the paddock. An hour later they had departed. The view was improved out of recognition and there was a clear path to the boathouse. The next problem was access to the oars. That was rather more difficult, but the manager, located in Kendal, eventually agreed – only on condition that both Robert and I wore life jackets, which he provided for us. I had been rowing on Windermere since I was a child of six and Thirlmere has no dangerous currents as does Windermere but, for the sake of peace, we complied and had several pleasant afternoons on the lake.

Helvellyn was a different kind of challenge. Having been mountain mad during the interwar years, nothing would keep me from going up Helvellyn. Robert saw no virtue in going up mountains – he was lame by now and 'there is no beer at the top'. I went on my own. I planned to go four times, but once a bad storm threatened and I returned to Dale Head within the hour. Twice all was straightforward and I had two really good days. I arranged in advance where Robert should come in the car to meet me when I was down. The fourth and final time was more disconcerting. A heavy mist came down and enveloped the summit just as I was arriving. Many mountains in Great Britain have nondescript tops, rather flat and wide, the stone cairn being the only true indication of the highest point. Helvellyn is like that. The mist was so thick I could hardly see my hands, let alone determine which was my best route down. It was still midday and, after about half an hour, the mist began to clear slightly. The threatened crisis fortunately never materialised. I went down to Patterdale by the easiest though longest route, managed to contact Robert before he even became worried and he drove round by the main road to fetch me and take me back to Dale Head.

I was keen to bring schoolchildren into closer contact with the town hall. To attract the older pupils, an 'any questions' meeting and debate in the council chamber with a few senior officers present to answer questions was arranged. About 150 teenagers crowded into the chamber and I presided in my mayoral robes. For the younger children we ran a children's party in the Great Hall. We had games and a conjuror and children's dancing. Each of our 200 primary schools was invited to bring one boy and one girl aged 8 or 9, accompanied by one teacher – that made about 600 guests. I persuaded the town clerk to dress in his wig and gown. I wore my robes and the chain, but not the tricorn. The attendant and the mace bearer with the mace led us onto the platform for the children to see. At the end, as they left I stood with the lady mayoress on The Bees and had them all come by, shake hands and say 'Thank you very much for having me'. They were not used to this old-fashioned formality. One little boy was not having it. He stood stock still in front of me, his hands behind his back: 'I have shaken hands already. I'm not going to again'.

My links with Manchester University had always been close. In my last week as lord mayor I was honoured by being awarded an Honorary

Doctorate at the University's annual Founders' Day ceremony. It was pleasing to be invited to speak for the honorary graduands at the ensuing luncheon. This gave me the ideal opportunity to voice my firm belief in the importance of mutual co-operation between town and gown which had always been, and still is, a feature of Manchester life and a great source of strength. In the mid-1970s, when I was lord mayor, Manchester was still struggling to overcome the economic disasters caused by the decline of the cotton industry and from the growing competition from the Far East in both textile manufacture and engineering. To some extent we were whistling to keep up our courage. I was not to know then how dramatically the tide would turn; how commercial entrepreneurs with large sums of money to invest would see the potential in our derelict warehouses and the run-down remains of mills and dwellings which had once made Manchester the world's industrial leader. Nor was I to know that, with the help of the huge IRA bomb in June 1996 obliterating much of our commercial city centre (without even scratching my beloved town hall), we would emerge within the next few years, through sport, music, the arts, science and sheer energy, to be again one of the most successful cities in all Great Britain. One must not forget that the universities enhance the city's reputation and are a central tenet of its ethos and its strengths, taking pride in its achievements of the past and making them known as widely as possible.

Almost all lord mayors until recent times have been born in or near the city and have a bond of knowledge and understanding of local institutions and ways of thought. Both Robert and I had been born and brought up in Manchester. I knew the city well, originally through my parents' voluntary work in connection with the magistrates' court, particularly the poorer areas that needed the most help and encouragement – the down-and-out districts, the new housing estates with their social disruption, the old deserted streets of boarded-up terraced property, the disastrous post-war high-rise flats and the run-down erstwhile houses of the rich, converted into rooming accommodation. I had no inkling of what was to happen within less than twenty years – the astonishing rehabilitation of the centre of Manchester and the derelict area at the junction of two filthy rivers, the Irk and the Medlock. The higher education precinct now boasts one of the largest concentrations of full-time and part-time students and research workers in the United Kingdom and is still growing and developing. Election to the lord mayoralty gave me the chance to fill an ambassadorial role central to the growth and increased stability, and gave me the opportunity to be a full-time resident, even if only for a year, in the very heart of the city. It was sheer magic and I enjoyed every minute.

In Manchester each lord mayor's name is engraved on one of the glass panels that give light to The Bees. At the end of the municipal year, workmen with long ladders can be seen engraving the departing lord mayor's name on the next vacant panel. On my last day, returning with Gilbert, the attendant, to the town hall from some final luncheon, I saw the ladders as we were coming up the main staircase. 'Oh no, I cannot witness my name being engraved on my own tomb-stone.' I ran back down the main staircase and up by the spiral staircase in the far corner. When Gilbert caught up with me he said, 'It's all right, lord mayor, they've only got to "O ell"'.

The year was over, Robert and I went to Malta for a fortnight's holiday. It was there that I wrote my illustrated book for children *The Lord Mayor's Party*.

CHAPTER 26

Bubbles and bees:
the Institute of Mathematics and its
Applications, 1964–

In 1964 an important new influence came into my life – the Institute of Mathematics and its Applications (IMA). After the end of the Second World War, increasing numbers of qualified mathematicians were required for work in industry, commerce and government departments. The associations that catered for teachers of mathematics, whether in schools or colleges or for those working in research institutes, did not adequately meet the needs of people working professionally outside the academic and teaching world. A group of leading mathematicians decided to form a new professional institute, the IMA, to meet this need and persuaded Sir James Lighthill FRS, the distinguished mathematician and world-leader in theoretical fluid mechanics, to be the first President. I was invited to be a Foundation Fellow. This brought me into regular contact with mathematicians of the first rank working in a variety of fields. For me, the Institute helped to fill the invaluable role that a university department or research institute post would normally have played in a life in which mathematics played a central role, but which, by chance and because of the inherited deafness, became almost wholly taken up in voluntary public service, mainly to education.

In 1970 I became a member of the Institute's governing council. This brought me into contact with mathematicians of the first rank working in a variety of fields. Professor Bryan Thwaites, who first introduced 'new maths' into our schools, succeeded Sir James as president and was followed by Professor George Barnard, a statistician of distinction who had an authoritative influence on the form of the national Census. Sir Hermann Bondi FRS, was president for the two years 1975–77. He was succeeded as president by Prince Philip, Duke of Edinburgh, who held the office for a year and whom I knew well in several guises: through

Salford University where he was Chancellor for fifteen years, and through the several national committees of which I was a member and he was president. Prince Philip has a keen interest in science and technology and he seemed to enjoy the contacts with mathematicians actively linked to top-level scientific research and development. He is a great learner and likes factual information. If he asks how many members there are, one doesn't reply: 'Er . . . I think it is about 7,000', but with an unhesitating: 'Six thousand, eight hundred and seventy-two graduate members and four hundred and fifty-six licentiates.' Coming off the top of the head it might be wrong, but at least it is precise. The moral is always to have done one's homework.

During Prince Philip's year as president of the IMA our council meetings were held at Buckingham Palace. There were no obvious special security precautions or routines, just the friendly and confident atmosphere of any great house with perfect, unobtrusive service. After the Annual General Meeting he invited us to lunch in the dining room overlooking the Palace gardens.

I succeeded Prince Philip as president in 1979. During Sir Hermann's time as president and that of Prince Philip a great bond of friendship was established between Sir Hermann and myself. He was born in Vienna in November 1919 and as a child did not have good health. When absent from school he picked up much esoteric mathematics from books he came across that had contents far beyond the normal school curriculum. His mathematical talents were recognised early, but Vienna offered no mathematical academic future and he set his heart on coming to Cambridge. In September 1938 just before his 18th birthday, Hermann was accepted as an undergraduate at Trinity College. He was interned on 12 May 1940 (two days after Hitler's offensive had started) and was held as an 'enemy alien', first in the Isle of Man and afterwards in Canada. Without text books or books of reference, he taught fellow internees the principles and practicalities of relativity, developing a compelling style of lecturing totally without notes or complicated illustration. One comes away from a public lecture given by Sir Hermann on the general theory of relativity feeling elated that for the first time one really understands it. Whether it can be retold at breakfast next morning when Hermann's personal magnetism has worn off is another matter. Sir Hermann's best-known public monument is perhaps his report on the need for the Thames Barrier which led to its construction. In operation since 1982 it is successfully controlling the North Sea flood tides that might otherwise swamp the centre of London. It was my good fortune, through the IMA, to interest Hermann in some of my own pure mathematics and have the pleasure of his collaboration.

One of the obligations of the presidency of the IMA is to give a presidential address – not only to a general meeting of members and guests in London, but in as many as possible of the regions of the United Kingdom. From earliest childhood I had played with patterns and fitting things together – and I loved symmetry. In 1978, I was at a reception of the Institute of Physics where guests were entertained by a demonstration of soap film and bubbles. This fascinated me – it was all geometry and in my field, soap film having the property of finding stability in shortest paths and minimum surfaces. I decided to make soap film the basis of my presidential address. In the two years from September 1978 to the summer of 1980 this address was delivered, mainly in universities, to twenty-four regional branches of the IMA, including Northern Ireland and the Isle of Man.

Soap film and soap bubbles are beautiful. When suffused with light they take up ever-changing rainbow colours and delight people of all ages. All children should be encouraged to blow bubbles, even if it does make a mess (and it does) other than when in a bath (baths are good for mathematics in more ways than one).

Soap film can be used in a cunning way to find the shortest paths linking specified points on a map. Suppose we wish to find the most economical plan for a motorway network that links any four towns. Take two flat pieces of transparent perspex and link them together with four 'pegs' at positions corresponding to the four towns (see illustration on next page). If we immerse the whole into a bucket of soap solution and gently withdraw it, allowing the surplus water to drain back into the bucket, the soap film trapped between the two pieces of perspex takes up the shortest path between the four pegs. It is not difficult to prove mathematically that this linkage is the minimum length.

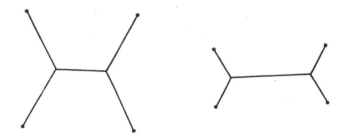

More spectacular still is when bubbles are trapped within a frame. For example, when a cube frame has been dipped in soap solution and then withdrawn a little central 'lamina' is formed as illustrated. If it is then carefully dipped for a second time and again withdrawn, a beautiful sight meets the eye. There is a suspended bubble in the centre replacing the (planar) lamina. The bubble is a cube with gently curved sides, as seen in the illustration. Under a spotlight it glows with rainbow colourings. A soap-wetted drinking-straw can be inserted into the bubble without breaking it. Sucking extracts air and causes the bubble to shrink: gentle blowing increases the size of the captured bubble without altering its shape.

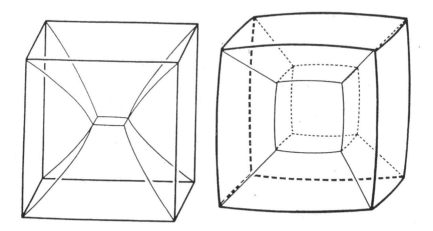

My particular interest is in three-dimensional 'solid' geometry and here soap bubbles have extraordinary similarities. We all know that if bricks or any other rectangular (including square) blocks are stacked correctly in rows then they can form a solid wall. In contrast, oranges (or solid spheres) canot be stacked without leaving air gaps between

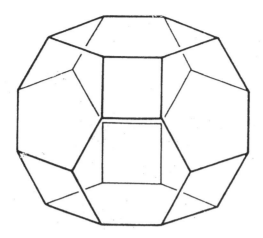

them. A cube (of which a 'special case' is the common brick) is the simplest example of a 'convex polyhedron' with the property described as 'space-filling': when identical cubes are 'similarly orientated' they fill space without gaps. There are five and only five such regular convex solids.* They were known to Archimedes (287–212 BC). Of these the fifth, the 14-sided tetrakeidecahedron (illustrated above) has the least surface area for a fixed unit volume.

A cluster of bubbles blown with a bubble-pipe gives a spectacular illustration of the 'closest packing' of pliable solid objects. The bubbles in the centre of a cluster (or 'froth') take up shapes that fill the space available without extraneous air gaps and give minimum surface area for the volume of air which they contain. This creates a structure exactly analogous to that of the 14-sided tetrakeidecahedra when stacked together. A cluster is never completely regular but if it were, these shapes could be modelled as these 14-sided semi-regular polyhedra.

* The five solids are: (i) the cube; (ii) the hexagonal prism; (iii) the elongation dodecahedron; (iv) the rhombic dodecahedron; and (v) the 14-sided tetrakeidecahedron illustrations and descriptions of which can be found in an article entitled *Form and Pattern,* by Dame Kathleen Ollerenshaw, Proceedings of the Royal Institution of Great Britain, Volume 53, 1981, pp.1–24. Science Review Ltd. ISBN 0 90 5927.

I used soap film to demonstrate the structure of the bees' honeycomb. Bees build their combs in the same way whether in the wild or in the frames provided for them in hives. They start their combs at the top, attaching the nascent comb with their wax to some suitable horizontal surface such as the branch of a tree or the top of an artificial comb in a hive. They build downward, creating as they proceed the central vertical 'interface', working head-to-head simultaneously on the two opposing sides. The interface (all wax) thus extends through the centre of the completed comb, the cells on either side slightly slanted to contain the liquid honey. The hive-building bees spew out wax that has been brought them by the worker bees, their crowded bodies making the wax warm and pliable, The wax behaves like soap film: it takes up a configuration that permits no empty space between the cells, while providing maximum storage space for the honey with a minimum amount of wax. These conditions explain the structure. If a honeycomb is sliced through, parallel to its interface, the cut surfaces are seen as a network of regular hexagons, reminiscent of a football goal net woven to cover a required area with a minimum of twine.

The structure of the honeycomb's central interface can also be explained in strictly mathematical terms. I made a model with straws and knobs and, on dipping it into my bucket of soap-solution, displayed for the few moments it could be made to survive, a soap-film bees' honeycomb.

Bees are happy to build in hives and to use old honeycomb 'frames' provided for them. These wood frames contain man-made 'interfaces' of beeswax forming precise replicas of the interfaces the bees would themselves construct and they are thus saved the labour. When a comb is damaged they even set about repairing it to become the comb they would have made themselves from scratch.

To the mathematician the most interesting feature of a bees' comb is the geometry of the central interface. Opposing cells meet in the only configuration that conforms to the geometry of hexagonal cylinders squashed together – in the 'blunt apicies' of the space-filling solid rhombic decahedra. I made a model of plastic straws and knobs (used by chemists demonstrating crystallography) and, dipping this into my bucket of soap solution, displayed for the few moments it could be made to survive, a soap-film representation of the bees' honeycomb.

Wasps build in a different way. They reconstitute paper and other fibrous tissue, not wax, to make the inner cell walls of their nests. They build in layers and the cells cannot be re-used for breeding although the nests can be extended year by year with new layers of cells. We often have wasps' nests at Hodge Close under the slates of the old roofs. They can grow huge and the wasps become a serious menace, difficult to get rid of. By chance, just as I was preparing my IMA presidential address, we arrived at the cottage for our summer break to find a perfectly formed wasps' nest suspended from the over-hanging ledge of our living-room window. With great care, using a thin carving knife, Robert helped me to slice it free. Its shape can be likened to a suspended cluster of soap bubbles. This nest travelled with me in a box as a valuable exhibit, along with several bees' honeycombs in the various stages of being re-built. I still treasure these exhibits.

With all this accumulated gear, travelling from one venue to another became difficult. Almost all the journeys were made by train. I had so many lightweight but bulky boxes, I could have been a film star or pop celebrity. I was usually accompanied by the IMA Secretary and Registrar, Norman Clarke, and the extremely efficient Assistant Secretary, Catherine Richards. They started from the IMA head office in Southend-on-Sea. I usually started from home in Manchester. There was, however, one memorable occasion when, *en route* for Aberdeen, we met up at Kings Cross station in London – the three of us, with ordinary suitcases but also a trolley loaded high with boxes. Other passengers seemed convinced we were heading for some film-making engagement or a TV show and were curious.

I was always grateful for help and being accompanied relieved me of a great deal of strain. Norman and Catherine had the IMA regional affairs to look after and helped with the publicity which ensured large audiences (the lectures were open to local teachers of mathematics and to sixth-formers). There was the added advantage of knowing that Norman could always tell if I was really hearing or only guessing when questions were asked and, if necessary, could help me by repeating questions – and people's names.

There were many moments of near panic. We always warned our hosts in advance that we needed a large bucket, water and washing-up fluid as well as the normal equipment of slide and overhead projectors. A bucket of water and washing-up fluid are not usual requirements for a mathematics dissertation, and sometimes things were not just as we had requested. On one occasion our hosts, proud of a lush lecture theatre in a new social science building, forgot all about the water. When we arrived, not only was there no water, there was no tap. In desperation Catherine and I had to go to the ladies' room and, with the only available vessel, a drinking tumbler, fill the bucket. This took a long time. On another occasion, in contrast, there was water in plenty, but it was filthy. The water has to be clear if the soap film demonstrations are to work well. There was only one answer: we went to the bar and spent a fortune on bottles of still mineral water. There was another dreadful occasion when we were not able to get into the lecture theatre until after 4 o'clock. There was not enough time for the soap solution to settle and be tested before the lecture. We arrived back in the lecture theatre after a reception for guests to find the audience already assembled. Quickly I dipped one of my frames into the bucket and withdrew it in the usual way to test the soap solution. Nothing! I tried again . . . nothing. The complicated presentation, all visual, depended completely on this soap solution – and I had nothing. I grabbed the half-empty bottle of washing-up fluid: some cheap brand the university used and it had sunk to the bottom of the bucket so that the mix was useless. I tipped the whole of what remained in the bottle into the bucket and hoped for the best. It worked, but only just. I was praying that it would last the length of the lecture. It ruined my evening and my nerve. From then on I took my own bottle of washing-up liquid with me, never again trusting my hosts.

The fun and the fear of delivering a public lecture is when the audience is invited to ask questions. There is usually some bright spark who has been harbouring an awkward question from the start. When one hasn't a clue about an answer the best response is: 'That is such a good question that it requires a whole lecture to itself, so perhaps it is best left to another occasion.' At one presentation, I commented that it did not matter in which way a cube-frame was withdrawn from the soap solution, the little lamina of film in the centre would always be of the same size. A bright sixth-former in the audience called out, 'Why?' Weakly I replied: 'Why not, and anyway you can see that it is the same size if I do it the other way round.' But they were not the same size. Sir Hermann Bondi, who was taking the chair, later suggested to me that perhaps the frame was not an exact cube. My frames were anything but accurate – they had been made from old wire coat-hangers. This question led to a whole new line of research in which I investigated 'critical heights' of cylindrical frames which caused trapped bubbles to change their configurations.

All football-gazers are familiar with the two different lattice formations of the association football goal nets: the rectangular lattice nets and the (six-sided) hexagonal nets. These are the only two possible practical patterns. Equally familiar today is the modern association football. It is manufactured from 32 tough plastic patches sewn together in a prescribed manner to form a hard, light-weight round ball. There are 12 near-planar (five-sided) regular pentagons and 20 near-planar (six-sided) regular hexagons. The ball in mathematical parlance is a 'semi-regular convex polyhedron' with 32 'faces', which meet in pairs in 90 'edges', the edges meeting in threes at 60 'vertices'. There is no need to have a real football to check this: the toy balls with painted patches serve as substitutes for counting. When Sir Alex Ferguson, the manager of Manchester United was awarded the Freedom of the City of Manchester after the triple crown victory in 2001, he autographed for me a real football.

The presidential address to IMA members and guests at the beginning of September 1978 was given in the Royal Institution in Albermarle Street in London. Its success gave rise to an invitation from Sir George Porter, the Director of the Institute, to deliver an RI Discourse the following May, 1979. This was a testing experience. Over nearly two centuries since its foundation in 1799 only one other woman, Jaquetta Hawkes, had delivered a Discourse before. The tradition is to be an overnight guest at the Institute itself and to attend a formal dinner, members of the Institute (nearly all men) in evening dress, before a start at precisely 8 p.m. The lecture had to end exactly as the clock reached 9.00, not a minute before, not a minute after. A common discipline, no doubt, for today's television presenters, but not easy for the first-time, one-off amateur. This would have been simple enough had it been an ordinary illustrated lecture, but my presentation was full of live demonstrations with unpredictable soap-film, bubble-blowing, and over-head projection co-ordinated with slides. I worked too hard in preparation, trying to leave nothing to chance, whereas everything depended on chance. I did not allow myself enough flexibility. Anxious that I should not overrun the hour, I cut out too much. Despite the rehearsal during the after-noon, I found myself coming to the prepared spectacular end at about six minutes to nine. I was able to fill in, but it is far easier to stop short in the middle of a sentence than to re-insert sentences that have been cut out and I was rather depressed by what I felt was failure.

Catherine Richards succeeded Norman as Secretary and Registrar of the IMA on his retirement, but died tragically of a virulent cancer at the age of 52. By then the Institute had moved from its cramped rented premises in an office block into a terraced house in the centre of Southend's legal community. This house was given Catherine's name in her memory. Norman lived with his family nearby in Leigh-on-Sea and we kept in touch, meeting from time to time in London. He came up to Manchester with Hilda, his wife, to the party I gave in the garden of my home in Didsbury to celebrate the publication (by the IMA) of the Magic Squares book. Sadly I did not see Norman again. He died at his home, in November 2002, aged 86, shortly before the concert I sponsored for my 90th birthday at which he was to be an honoured guest.

CHAPTER 27

Robert

Robert and I had a wonderful married life. We had known each other for so long and were so grateful to have survived the war, it would have been ridiculous to have had the slightest quarrel. There were no differences of opinion about anything that mattered – money, where we lived, children, holidays. When the two children were young I was engrossed, at home or at the university in my mathematics research. By the time I became involved in public life, Florence was already nearly 9 years old and Charles at boarding school. Although Robert did not at first take easily to this, he eventually got used to it and as initially it centred mostly in Manchester, it fitted in perfectly with his activities.

Robert was an accomplished craftsman, working in wood or metal; skills that all pupils at Oundle were encouraged to acquire. He bought himself a lathe for use at Broome House as soon as he left school, and established a well-equipped workshop in a room in a third-floor wing and made a working dark-room next to it for his photography. While he was away on active service during the war, German bombs dropped on the nearby golf course (where dummy replicas of the Metro Vickers engineering works were erected to deceive attackers) shook the house and dislodged the lathe. On his demobilisation when we were at last able to set up house together, he moved the lathe across Didsbury to the cellar at 11 Elm Road. It was a bitter, damp November and he had only recently returned from a hot Middle East. He drove to and fro between the houses with bits of equipment sticking through the open sliding roof of his 'mini' – and contracted pneumonia. He was the doctor; I was a mere wife. He insisted that it was delayed malaria. Not until my mother called in and recognised instantly how seriously ill he was did we send for the urgent medical help required. He had an 'old-fashioned' pneumonia crisis that night – without today's modern drugs – and he was closer to losing his life than he had been from Hitler's (and Rommel's) fiercest efforts. When we moved to the smaller house in Pine Road, we built a workshop behind the garage, making special provision for the lathe so that long strips of metal or wood could stretch through the opened doors unimpeded. There he repaired and constructed items of equipment needed in his Department in the Royal Infirmary and made gadgets to help in research; there he created the 'frames' I used for my presidential address for the IMA. This absorbing hobby was brought to an abrupt end. An injury to his ankle, sustained in a roller-skating accident at prep school, deteriorated into a severe rheumatic handicap and he became dependent on a walking stick. One evening when we were guests at a Christmas party someone knocked his stick from under him. He fell heavily and had an impacted fracture of his right wrist which could not be reduced. When he realised that he would never be able to use his lathe again, he gave it to a close colleague. It was an act of great generosity and courage that brought me to tears. I still, nearly twenty years on, never go into the workshop without imagining him there, bending over his lathe – creating something.

Apart from his intense involvement in his work at the Infirmary and the help he gave to consultant colleagues in preparing their major con-ference addresses and publications, Robert was always deeply occupied with the Territorial Army and with St. John Ambulance. Every Tuesday evening without fail, many weekends and every Whit Week he was totally committed to his Territorial Unit. He was a good and popular commanding officer – always fair, good at delegating and totally com-mitted. This came first – far beyond any thought of family convenience or holidays. The main activity as I witnessed it was the incessant up-dating and re-drafting of the all-important 'Mob-plan'. Reserve forces as well as regulars have to be ready to gather together all personnel and equipment within a matter of forty-eight hours in emergency. The gen-eral public saw evidence of this when the Royal Navy set sail from their British naval bases for the Falkland Islands in 1982. The logistics can be horrific, even for a single Field Ambulance. I remember returning from London one evening after two tough days of negotiating with trade unions about teachers' pay. I expected at least a civil hello as I walked into the house. All I got was the clatter of a typewriter and a gruff 'Don't interrupt me – this has to be ready for tomorrow.'

Robert's work with St. John Ambulance was also demanding, but in a different way. At the beginning when he returned from the war this mostly meant only monthly visits to Preston as the 'county surgeon' in the old Lancashire District St. John Ambulance Brigade. There were several rather grand social occasions which I attended with him, including regular visits of HRH The Princess Margaret. When Robert became Surgeon-in-Chief, he had to make frequent visits to London and he found this something of a strain as, by then, his ankle was causing him serious pain. He is best known in this context in doing the spade work for the provision of first aid courses in schools – something in which I was in a position to help. With others, he wrote the definitive course instructions and regulations. He resigned from the position of Surgeon-in-Chief when travelling to London became too arduous and was appointed Commander in Greater Manchester. This was great for me, appointed in 1973, as related, to the chairmanship of the council of the newly created Greater Manchester St. John. I was able to exploit his long experience and have his advice on the many complicated details at any time without even leaving the house.

Robert always had a passionate interest in military history and amassed a significant collection of military badges. While I was bashing away on my noisy typewriter and (in the early days) hand-cranked calculating machine, writing statistical and other articles in our shared study, Robert, if not out on duty somewhere or in his workshop or dark room, would be in his armchair, sunk in some heavy tome, with a steady flow of classical music from the radio or his extensive collection of records. It was all very satisfactory and satisfying. We did little or no entertaining at home – we were both too busy. We went regularly to concerts and theatre, but less frequently after his father died and as the years went by. There was a constant stream of evening engagements connected with our public lives and we attended these together. I made a good, almost professional, RAMC 'army wife' and a 'St. John Ambulance wife' long before I became involved in either of these activities in my own right.

Robert was not one for any physical recreation even before he became too lame – he could see no point in scrambling up a mountain if there was no photographic opportunity (or beer) at the top. When we were at Hodge Close, I did the fell-walking – alone – running my mathematics in my head and as happy as could be – while Robert stayed at the cottage building a wall or mending a roof, having supper ready on my return. His injured ankle deteriorated and gradually he was forced to submit to a wheelchair, which he hated, and a chair-lift in the house which made an upstairs/downstairs life possible. He developed diabetes and, after his retirement, I never left him alone for more than a few hours. My great regret is that we did not think of acquiring a dog which could have been a companion for him.

Being together was the greatest help to us both after Florence had died. If he had a fit of depression, I prepared a special treat meal so that he could recover. If it was I who became distressed, he became deliberately tough and forced me to get back on track.

A series of small strokes brought the end when we were 74. As I held his hand, I said that I would join him, but I had work to do first. It could never have occurred to me then that I would be able to continue for so long. We missed our 50th wedding anniversary by only three years, but we had been blessed with over seventy years, almost always together apart from his service in the war. When Charles died, twelve years later, I felt almost relieved that Robert did not have to know.

CHAPTER 28

Stars

Back in 1920, when my father lifted me up, aged 7, to look at an early-morning moon through the penny-in-a-slot telescope on the promenade at Hunstanton, I saw that the moon was not just a flat shining disc, but a landscape of mountains and seas, as my father explained. Over the years I came to recognise some of the constellations (Orion, the Plough, and a few others) and learnt how to find the North Star, but not much more. In 1927, when I was at school in St Andrews, a ship was chartered to take us on the North Sea to witness the total eclipse of the sun. We saw nothing because of cloud. Ironically the best view was from Southport, only 50 miles from home in Manchester. Mother and father and my sister Betty saw it all while we saw nothing. More than sixty years went by before my next opportunity to see a total eclipse of the sun.

Late one midsummer evening in 1990 I was driving home from Hodge Close. Above was a remarkably clear star-studded sky. Suddenly it occurred to me that I could, if I wished, satisfy a long-held desire to own a telescope. In the morning I began enquiring about telescopes and was surprised that one couldn't just pop into town and buy one – there are not all that many knowledgeable suppliers. I rang the only number related to astronomy that I had in my address book, Jodrell Bank, the home of Manchester University's radio telescope that had tracked Yuri Gagarin's circuit of the globe in 1961. Sir Bernard Lovell, the creator of the telescope and the first director at Jodrell had retired. A voice said: 'Smith here' and I realised that I was speaking to Sir Bernard's successor, Sir Francis Graham-Smith, then Astronomer Royal. He suggested an 8-inch Celestron Schmidt-Cassigrain – anything but a beginner's instrument. There was a suitable dealer in Liverpool. By 4 o'clock I was there looking at a range of telescopes. The particular Celestron was on loan to Patrick Moore for a lecture that evening. I did not hesitate: that was the one I wanted. A few days later, the supplier arrived at my home in Manchester with the telescope and a sturdy tripod in his Mini. He set it up on the balcony that overlooks the garden. It was a fine June evening. My first view was of a spider building his web on a nearby chimney stack.

Next day I contacted the Manchester Astronomical Society (MAS), founded in 1903. This brought immediate (and lasting) friendships within a splendid group of enthusiasts. With the guidance of Kevin Kilburn, who was serving his first term as president of the society, I fulfilled my desire to see Saturn and its rings through my own telescope and, a few months later, Venus and Mars when they were well placed in the winter skies. I was thrilled to be able to check each evening the changing phases of Venus. I had not realised before that it behaves like the moon, showing, as an inner planet, its full face or a waning or waxing crescent according to its position in relation to the sun. My most exciting early achievement was a photograph Kevin helped me take of the full moon. As it was a somewhat misty night with the sky washed by recent rain, there was no glare. The enlarged picture has decorated my bathroom wall ever since.

I had not been into astronomy for more than a fortnight before I booked a place with a group travelling to Helsinki for the July 1990 total eclipse of the sun. The weather was good for several days before the event but, as the critical moment of totality approached, it began to deteriorate. The sun was playing hide-and-seek behind thickening clouds and we saw nothing. After this disappointment, we went by coach up to the North Cape to see the Northern Lights. It was a long drive through endless reindeer forests. On the way we were treated to a rainbow encircling the sun, a rare and wonderful sight, but of the Northern Lights we saw not a glimmer. I have a snapshot of the others in the group standing on the viewing platform, gazing at absolutely nothing but thick all-enveloping icy fog.

I first met Patrick Moore at a star-weekend in Liverpool. He was one of the invited experts on the 1990 eclipse tour. He has been a prolific writer on astronomy since he was a young man and has a phenomenal memory for dates, names and other details. Amateur astronomers owe

Patrick a great debt. He, above all others, has paved the way for them to contribute to the serious research of the professionals, who nowadays are fully occupied in deep space research with their high-tech modern equipment. Amateurs can help with the donkey-work of ordinary observing, keeping watch on the sky and analysing the paths of strange or unidentified objects.

I had not aimed to have a telescope at home on the edge of a large brightly lit city and within a few miles of an international airport, but rather at Hodge Close where there are no intrusive lights. There, the abandoned earth closet gave promise of a working observatory. I replaced the heavy slate roof with a sliding top and fed in electricity from the cottage. An official opening was clearly needed. I knew that Sir Francis Graham-Smith enjoyed the Lake District and invited him. To my delight he answered by return, saying that he would make a special day trip from Cheshire to be with us. A date was fixed: 25 August, a Bank Holiday Saturday. There were several close friends who were regular visitors to Lakeland. With Charles and Margaret to help me, we were set to have a riotous party, provided the gods were kind about the weather. The invitation was from 12 noon to 12 midnight: an informal lunch, an observatory-opening ceremony at 3 p.m. and, after supper, a chance to view the stars through the telescope. During the morning one of the local quarry men turned up with a surprise gift, their own spontaneous idea: a green-slate plaque, engraved *Lovell II – 25.8.90*. The telescope at Jodrell Bank is named *Lovell*, after Sir Bernard, whose permission I asked to name this primitive observatory thus – all part of the fun. The weather had been atrocious all week, but on that Saturday morning we awoke to clear skies and sunshine. It was a fabulous day. In the evening, a thin layer of cloud spared me the embarrassment of having to demonstrate the telescope and show how much of a beginner I was when it came to finding and identifying stars

Lovell II turned out to be something of a disappointment. A barn roof interfered with the best views of the sky. I soon took to humping the heavy tripod and telescope out of its confines of the erstwhile earth closet into the small enclosed garden from which almost the whole of the sky above could be observed. On good nights there are magnificent views of the Milky Way. Kevin Kilburn encouraged me to make a panoramic set of slides. Ten-minute exposures (that must be guided to compensate for the movement of the earth) with fast colour slide film gave good pictures. I then spent hours at home with a large sky atlas, identifying the stars on my slides. When I exhibited these, friends were amazed how prolific and colourful the stars above our heads are. By taking my own pictures and then using a map for identification, I had an ideal method for teaching myself to recognise the constellations, and learn the names and characteristics of the stars within them. Only occasionally did I have the luxury of the company of experts by my side at the telescope. Working mostly alone made no demands on my hearing and my two little dogs were excellent guards.

A direct way of aligning the telescope precisely in relation to the (North) Pole Star every time it was set up in the garden outside the makeshift *Lovell II* observatory became imperative. I arranged for a deep hole to be dug in the garden and a permanent post on which to mount the telescope was fixed in two feet of concrete. This meant that the telescope would always be in correct alignment, although I still had to carry it to and from *Lovell II*. After about a year, I decided to have something better and had constructed for me a purpose-built observatory around the fixed post. With two years of experience I knew exactly what I wanted and, within a few weeks of drawing the design, I had a new working observatory: a wooden structure, not a dome, that blends into the surroundings, with a sliding roof operated by an old car starting handle and a long bicycle chain. There was no party to celebrate the opening of the new observatory, but Hermann Bondi and his wife Christine came up from Cambridge and we fixed a plaque, *Sir John Herschel, b.1792* in celebration of the great astronomer's birth exactly two hundred years before.

I began to arrange a regular visit to Hodge Close between Christmas Day and New Year's Day by a group of friends who were members of the Manchester Astronomical Society, led by Kevin Kilburn. They were joined by Dr Allan Chapman, a distinguished senior lecturer in the history of astronomy at Wadham College, Oxford, author and broadcaster, who is a valued friend. It was when he was with us at Hodge Close, that Kevin focused my telescope on our nearest galaxy, Andromeda. I was so thrilled to see this beautiful object for the first time for myself through my own telescope that I rushed indoors and brought out a bottle of champagne to celebrate. From then on, however late I was closing down after a viewing session, I never failed to turn to Andromeda and say a fond goodnight.

Allan is a remarkable scholar and raconteur – with a non-stop stream of accurate names and dates pouring from his fertile mind, enthralling all around him. I never doubted that it was the prospect of having his company in a car for the double journey from Manchester to Hodge Close that was the main attraction of these Christmas visits rather than the chance of clear winter skies and views through my telescope.

The routine had to come to an end – as with so many good things in life. An eye accident made it impossible for Kevin to make the two-way drive at night; the weather was too often prohibitively bad and the approach road too icy for safety. Others acquired their own computer-based guided telescopes. But the visits remain marvellous memories, and we see and listen to Allan on his regular visits to the Manchester and other Astronomical Societies in the North West.

Until 1994 I was still humping the Celestron 8" telescope to and fro, between home and Hodge Close. There was no long-term future in this. The telescope was about as much as I could lift by myself. Plainly I needed two telescopes – one for each location – and this gave me the excuse to justify an upgrading. I settled on a Celestron 11" that has magnificent optics. Ambitions grew. Now that I had a proper observatory, I could indulge in greater use of electronics. In particular, I wanted a telescope that would move to any objects in the sky that I commanded merely by entering their celestial coordinates in a control panel. My new Celestron 11" did not have this facility. Happily I learned that Lancaster University was in need of a good telescope: I was delighted to arrange for the 11" to go to them. With a clear conscience, I bought the telescope that I should have bought earlier: a Meade 10" (also American) that gave me everything I wanted. This made possible a progression to what is called a CCD (charged coupled device) electronic system, and I moved with excitement into this fast-developing field. By then I had a laptop computer and I could carry this out from the cottage to the observatory. At first I might be out until after 3 a.m. struggling with centring and focusing an image and deciding exposure times but, once the techniques were mastered, the process became almost routine and I acquired a range of images of distant galaxies, nebulae, globular clusters and other objects in the sky that a few years earlier would have been impossible for an amateur.

Soon after I had acquired my first telescope in 1990, I attended a British Astronomy Association (BAA) annual exhibition in London. Among the exhibits was a panel of pictures of comets taken by Denis Buczinski, the son of a Polish refugee who came to Great Britain in the 1930s. He had been attracted to astronomy when he saw Patrick Moore on TV talking about the 1985 visit of Halley's Comet to our skies. Denis had built his own observatory at Conder Brow on the southern edge of Lancaster.

In due course, Denis had built three domed observatories in his garden. The largest, now abandoned, had as its dome the top of a farmer's disused silo. Here, with a large brass telescope loaned from the BAA, he set about recording and photographing sky objects, with a particular interest in comets. He became recognised internationally as an expert and was invited to form one of the network of amateurs covering the whole of the earth's surface who receive and vet claims made for new discoveries. Time differences across the world mean that this has to be done immediately within the twenty-four hours of the earth's rotation. One night, just after he had packed in and gone to bed at 4 a.m., a telephone call came through from America giving him the co-ordinates of a new comet which had just been reported. There was very little time; it would shortly be dawn. He pulled on trousers and shoes and his little woollen bonnet, ran down his slippery path, turned his large telescope to match the stated co-ordinates, took his quarter-plate picture, rushed to his dark room, developed the plate, and there was the newly found comet. This was a triumph for Denis as well as for the comet-finder: the reward of never being caught unprepared or with the camera unloaded. Now everything is done by mobile telephone, e-mail and electronic controls. Without Denis's ready assistance I would never have moved so early into CCD imaging.

Denis was awarded an Honorary Master's Degree at Lancaster University. At the award ceremony they made a dreadful mistake: he was given in error a soft cap worn by women, instead of the hard mortar-board that he should have had. A man has to doff his head-dress to the Chancellor. When a soft cap is taken off it cannot be easily put back, at least not without using two hands, but in one hand Denis was holding the scroll he had just been given. The assembled degree-receiving students and their parents dissolved in fits of sympathetic laughter at his attempts to put the cap back on his head, until the vice-chancellor Professor Harry Hanham, sitting just behind, stepped forward and took it from him. Denis made his speech of acceptance. He told a simple tale that won the assembly's hearts. He is a butcher by trade, and one day a customer said 'Oh, I recognise you. I saw you on the tele. You are the man who stays out until three in the morning looking at stars?' 'Yes', said Denis. 'Well' came the reply, 'you ought to have more sense.'

To witness a total eclipse of the sun is probably one of the most awe-inspiring experiences one can have. However much we have read in advance, however careful the preparation, however often one has been lucky enough to have seen an eclipse, the first moment of totality is stunning. Having been unlucky in 1927 when at school and in 1990 in Finland, there was a great compulsion to persist. I arranged to go to Hawaii in July 1991 for the 'Big One' that had the almost maximum possible duration of nearly eight minutes. I invited Charles and Margaret to come with me.

A total eclipse is so short-lived and enthralling that everyone around at a view-point is completely absorbed in watching – or taking pictures. There is the shock as the moon suddenly covers the whole disc of the sun, then the prominences at the edges of the jet-black disc of the moon (red and orange flares that spring out into the atmosphere); then, with luck, a diamond ring where the sun's beams shine through a nick where a moon-crater exactly coincides with the edge of the moon's disc; finally, wonder of wonders, the corona, a brilliant halo of the sun's burning white light surrounding the black disc of the moon. The whole process is then repeated in reverse as the moon gradually completes its transit. Enthusiasts stay with cameras clicking through to the end an hour or so later, but most amateur observers are emotionally exhausted before the full return to normality, and prefer to stand around celebrating. The professionals (that is, the scientists, mathematical physicists, the astro-physicists, cosmologists and others) use eclipses to do important research. There are objects in the sky that lie too closely in line with the sun to be seen and studied at other times. The amateur and the general public are usually sufficiently engrossed to be satisfied with witnessing the eclipse itself.

The UK group in 1991 spent two nights in Los Angeles where we were taken up to the Mount Wilson Observatory – and next day on a visit to the movie-makers' Mecca, the brash United Studios, which could hardly have been a more contrasting experience. Mount Wilson is famous for its 100-inch reflector telescope constructed in 1917 and for thirty years the largest telescope in the world. Patrick Moore and Kevin Kilburn were with us, but we went in different directions after Los Angeles: Patrick and Kevin were with those who went to Mexico where totality occurred at midday, while we others flew west to Hawaii.

The eclipse was to begin in Hawaii just after 7 a.m.; the weather forecasts were not good. The British contingent was split into two groups. Those with the most influence went to the far western side of the 'Big Island' where it was thought the conditions would be best. We were allocated the eastern side and drove in rather rickety yellow American school buses up toward the telescopes on the top of Mauna Kea, an extinct volcano with a height of 14,000 ft. It was raining solidly. To our annoyance we were stopped for undisclosed reasons at a barrier at a mere 3,000 ft. As the time of the first phase of the eclipse approached, our buses parked along the road, I had a fixation that I must get as high as possible. I grabbed my tripod and camera and clambered up a steep bracken-covered slope until at last I came to a level spot and set up my gear. None of the others followed, preferring to stay (perhaps more sensibly) on the tarmac. I watched with growing gloom as a watery and sometimes almost non-existent sun revealed its presence dimly through what had turned from heavy rain to thick drizzle. Then, lo, there appeared a patch of pale blue sky. There was a great shout. At the crucial moment of the onset of totality the clear patch coincided with the sun and moon. The few of us on the hillside witnessed it all, whereas those below saw it only partially. I did not forget to remove the filter. I took my pictures. The moment I got home to Manchester a few days later, I rushed to have the film processed. I was so pleased with the results that I posted a copy of the best straight to Patrick who had already returned from Mexico. On the Sunday evening, I switched on TV to watch his *Sky at Night* programme. To my astonishment, I heard my name and saw my own eclipse picture. That was one of the several occasions when my two little dogs, Max and Min, and I danced a jig.

Halley's Comet in 1985 could not be seen well in the UK, but I joined a group of enthusiasts on a special flight from Manchester, which travelled high over the Irish Sea to facilitate a clearer view. Astronomers in Great Britain were extraordinarily fortunate in having in two successive years the spectacles of great comets in our skies for several weeks. In September 1996 Comet Hyakutake, the first comet of any size I had seen, was well placed in skies above Hodge Close for several successive nights. I had only one good opportunity to get a picture. This occurred at 3 a.m., lying on my back in the road outside the cottage at Hodge Close, the two dogs keeping guard. I then drove back to Manchester, had my film processed during the afternoon, mounted the slides myself and proudly took the best to show to colleagues at a concert that evening. One guest looked at it admiringly and then remarked: 'You are always so lucky – in the right place at the right time'! I nearly collapsed. It had required over a year of intensive practice and preparation. I had made two journeys to Hodge Close and back, only to be thwarted by last-minute onslaughts of rain. Few people who have not tried this sort of activity for themselves (bird-watching for example), really appreciate what is involved.

The following year we had the wondrous Hale-Bopp. It was the greatest and most spectacular comet in our skies in our generation. We had months of opportunity for good pictures and failure was inexcusable. It was a miracle to be able to look from my kitchen window in Manchester and see this marvellous object in the night sky for several evenings in succession. The phenomenon was so exceptional and lasted for so many months that it came even as a relief to return to ordinary sky observing again.

In February 2002 I received an astonishing letter. Lancaster University had kept the Celestron 11" telescope in store until they had funds to re-build their original observatory that had fallen into disrepair. At last, in 2001, funds had become available. A working group which included Denis Buczinski and his friend Glynn Marsh, a nuclear physicist and engineer, also a keen amateur astronomer, had master-minded the construction of a new observatory on a flat roof overlooked by a top-floor laboratory of the university's physics department. The Celestron was housed within it and the proposed name was the *Dame Kathleen Ollerenshaw Observatory*. To put it mildly, I was over the moon at the suggestion. An opening was arranged for 20 May 2002 with Patrick Moore officiating. The telescope can be controlled almost entirely by computer from the comfort of the adjacent laboratory. Already post-graduate students have made significant contributions to astronomical research and the observatory has been upgraded.

Now I am planning to take a step back again and try to finish the map-ping of the stars of the Milky Way as seen when at Hodge Close – a project I never finished when diverted by the attractions of deep sky photography with the then new CCD electronic cameras. There is no need, as there was thirteen years ago when I first took up astronomy, to depend on very long exposures and meticulous guiding. Computer tech-nique and programmes can produce spectacular results by 'stacking' short exposures and I am eager to try my luck with my old trusty Minolta still camera. In all this I shall be dependent, as I have been from the beginning, on the help and advice of my astronomy friends.

There is an affinity between mathematics and astronomy: the two activities have been linked throughout the ages. At a personal level, mathematics and astronomy have brought me great friendships and unending interest. Perhaps it is because half the joy is in sharing expe-riences and learning from one another to an extent that is not common to all social activities, or even to all the sciences. There is always some-thing new to experience and to try to achieve for one's own satisfaction. There is so much to absorb and learn from others – so much shared anticipation – so much discovery. This can take one's mind off some of the worst events in our earth-bound world. Most satisfyingly, there is the possibility of making discoveries for oneself. Buying a telescope was one of the best decisions I ever made.

CHAPTER 29

The magic square saga

The Institute of Mathematics and its Applications was of great importance to me in providing a publication outlet for short papers in their monthly Bulletin, now a quarterly journal *Mathematics Today*. When in 1980 the Rubik cube first appeared and flooded and fascinated the country, I was the first to find (and publish in the Bulletin) a general method of restoring the cube, however it was mixed up, to its original state with each of its six faces showing only one colour. Shorter solutions were found and published later on, but by following my instructions anyone with sufficient patience could solve it.

I damaged the ball of my left thumb with too much turning the cube. This was serious enough to lead to a surgical operation. It was reported in the American *Readers' Digest* as the first known case of 'mathematician's thumb.' There were other mathematical problems that became fashionable crazes and for which I found and published solutions.

There are many traditional mathematical conundra, some deep, some trivial, that re-appear every so often and are given great publicity for a short time. It is wise for anyone known to be a mathematician to be acquainted with them and prepared to answer them with aplomb when challenged. An example is: how many people have to be in a room for there to be a fifty-fifty chance that at least two have their birthday on the same day of the year? The answer is 23, which usually comes as a surprise as most people would guess a much larger number. Another is to identify a bad penny among twelve pennies that look alike, using only three weighings on a simple balance; and to say whether the false penny is too light or too heavy (see Appendix). This surfaced in 1944, brought across the Atlantic by American troops preparing for the Normandy Landing, but it is known to have been posed in the eighteenth century. I was in Oxford in the Spring of 1944 and was presented with the problem for the first time, expected to find the solution within fifteen minutes. On my mettle, I did, but it needed the lines of thought of an experienced puzzle-solver. The problem hit the British press again early in 2003, after a gap of nearly sixty years, bringing the same torrent of newspaper correspondence.

My interest in magic squares did not arise by chance. The damaged thumb caused by too much twisting of the Rübik Cube turned me to its two-dimensional predecessor, the age-old Chinese '15's Puzzle'. This led me to the equally famous 'Face Cards Puzzle' (see Appendix) whereby one places the 16 face cards from a pack of playing cards (Aces, Kings, Queens, Jacks), in four rows of four cards in each row so that no two cards of the same face value or of the same suit appear in any row, in any column or in either of the two principal diagonals. This is a special case of a 'magic square' and led me directly to considering magic squares in greater depth.

A magic square is an array of whole numbers in which the numbers in each row, in each column and in the two principal diagonals add to the same total, called the 'magic constant'. A 4 × 4 square is said to be 'of order 4', a 5 × 5 square 'of order 5' and so on. The interest is when the numbers are consecutive: the square is then called 'normal'. In a normal square of order 4 the numbers can be taken as 1 to 16 with the magic constant then 34, or sometimes more conveniently as 0 to 15 with the magic constant then 30. A classic example of a 4 × 4 magic square is that shown in Albrecht Dürer's famous painting *Melancholia I* (see Appendix) in the British Museum where the date, 1514, appears in the bottom row.

16	3	2	13
5	10	11	8
9	6	7	12
4	15	14	1

Over 300 years ago, a French civil servant and amateur mathematician, Bernard Frénicle de Bessey (1602–76) established that there are 880 and only 880 'essentially different' normal 4 × 4 magic squares.

(Squares are 'essentially different' if they cannot be transformed into one another by any combination of reflections in the vertical or horizontal axes or in either of the principal diagonals.) By considering general conditions for the 4×4 magic square and excluding those arrangements that cannot comply with the conditions, he progressively arrived at all essentially different solutions.

I was curious about this total of 880. A better guess might have been 864 which is 32×27 or $2^5 \times 3^3$ and so can be tidily expressed in powers of 2 and 3. Where did the 'extra' 16 squares come from to give a total of 880? I was doodling with this during some meeting of the IMA, as was my habit when a meeting became boring or when I couldn't hear properly what was being said. My scribbles caught the attention of Sir Hermann Bondi who was sitting next to me. The outcome was that we collaborated in devising the first (and still the only) *analytical* proof of Frénicle's counting, which he had arrived at by considering all possibilities, a method known as 'exhaustion', not by logic alone.

I usually have some mathematical problem in my mind that will fill an idle moment. On one occasion I moaned to Sir Hermann about having had a bad night on the sleeper: 'I couldn't be sure whether I had to multiply by two, doubling the chances, or divide by two, halving them.' Hermann is a cosmologist and cosmologists think in multi-billions. He replied: 'Oh, don't worry about a little thing like that. I remember coming into the Cavendish Laboratory at Cambridge one morning and a colleague saying "does that mean that we multiply by 10^{10} or divide by 10^{10}?"' The number 10 multiplied by itself 10 times is astronomically huge, whereas 2^{10} is the relatively tiny number 1,024.

Both Sir Hermann and I regarded long journeys as ideal opportunities for uninterrupted mathematics. We were both travelling a lot, so we made tremendous progress when collaborating. Like much in mathematics (as in other sciences), the proof for the enumeration of all 4×4 magic squares required a succession of linked arguments. Without sustained effort and the ability to hold in the head what has gone before, there can be no success. There were hitches and set-backs along the route, as there almost always are when developing new methods, but our compatibility was absolute and the experience of working with someone with such a clear and precise mind was a joy all its own. Our proof was published in the *Philosophical Transactions of the Royal Society* in 1984.

About a year later, Sir Hermann received a letter from an electrical engineer on the teaching staff of the University of Bremen, Dr Ph.W. Besslich. He wrote from hospital and he died before any of the consequences of his letter had materialised. In essence, he had found that he could use a certain type of magic square called *pandiagonal* of order 8 in a process known as *dither printing* sometimes used for fast production of pictures in newspapers. He wanted to know how to construct pandiagonal magic squares of order 16 as this would then give a finer mesh for the dither process and better results. He sought our help. This was a challenge I could not resist. Very little was known about magic squares of even order greater than four. I went to the John Rylands University Library of Manchester and searched the relevant literature.

Pandiagonal magic squares, in addition to being magic, have the property that the numbers in the 'broken diagonals' (as well as those in the rows, columns and two principal diagonals) add to the same magic constant. A broken diagonal wraps around from one edge of the square to the opposite edge. An inscription from the twelfth century showing the 4 × 4 pandiagonal magic square shown below, was reported in 1904 as having been found in Khajurado, India.

7	12	1	14
2	13	8	11
16	3	10	5
9	6	15	4

Broken diagonals here are, for example, 12 8 5 9, 1 11 16 6, 14 2 3 15. It is difficult to find essentially different 4 × 4 magic squares, or even just one such square, if no guiding rules are known. Let alone those that are pandiagonal.

In the *American Journal of Mathematics* of 1896, I found an article on pandiagonal magic squares by a professor of mathematics at Toronto University, Eamon McClintock. To make construction easier, he limited his discussion of squares of even order to those that are multiples of four, that is to those of order 4, 8, 12, 16, 20 . . . and imposed two further special properties, namely that *the numbers in the diagonals occur in 'complementary pairs' half way along each of the diagonals.* (A *complementary pair* of numbers in a 4×4 square add to the fixed sum that is half the magic constant. For example, in a 4×4 magic square consisting of the numbers 0 to 15 (for which the magic constant is 30), the numbers 0, 15; 1, 14; and so on to 7, 8 – form complementary pairs.) When the square is extended by repetition horizontally and vertically, then all numbers in any 2×2 block of four add to the same total. (In the 4×4 square this total is the magic constant). He gave a method of construction of these squares, which he described as most perfect; I adapted the name to *most-perfect* as a generic description. McClintock made no attempt to enumerate them. It is, however, easy to check from Frénicle's list of the 4×4 magic squares that there are 48 pandiagonal magic squares of order four and these are all most-perfect squares. In the 12×12 most-perfect pandiagonal magic square shown overleaf, four randomly chosen blocks of four numbers are seen to have the same total sum. McClintock had devised a method of constructing these most-perfect squares.

I worked for over eight years on most-perfect magic squares, on and off and mostly when alone at Hodge Close, after Robert died in 1986. They have an extraordinary fascination and bit-by-bit I worked out not only how to construct them but how to enumerate the totals that could be constructed, firstly for when they are of a size that is any power of 2, namely 4, 8, 16, 32 . . . to infinity, then for squares of all sizes that are multiples of powers of 2, for example 12, 20, 24, 36, 72, . . . and so on; finally, a formula for the total number of all most-perfect magic squares of any order which is a multiple of four. This was the first time in all the thousands of years during which magic squares have fascinated mathematicians and laymen alike, that a method of construction had been found for a whole class.

Throughout the years of involvement with the magic squares I received invaluable support from friends. At no time did I have the slightest inkling of where it would end up; my objectives were always limited, new targets presenting themselves only as each was, in turn, achieved. I followed many false trails, but every time I came up against the buffers and could get no further, an alternative route opened up and I started, sometimes from scratch, all over again. Sometimes my mind

64	92	81	94	48	77	67	63	50	61	83	78
31	99	14	97	47	114	28	128	45	130	12	113
24	132	41	134	8	117	27	103	10	101	43	118
23	107	6	105	39	122	20	136	37	138	4	121
16	140	33	142	0	125	19	111	2	109	35	126
75	55	58	53	91	70	72	84	89	86	56	69
76	80	93	82	60	65	79	51	62	49	95	66
115	15	98	13	131	30	112	44	129	46	96	29
116	40	133	42	100	25	119	11	102	9	135	26
123	7	106	5	139	22	120	36	137	38	104	21
124	32	141	34	108	17	127	3	110	1	143	18
71	59	54	57	87	74	68	88	85	90	52	73

In this 12×12 pandiagonal magic square, (i) all pairs of numbers distant six apart along any diagonal add to 143, which is half the magic constant; and (ii) the numbers in every 2×2 block add to the same sum, 286. It thus fulfils the conditions of being most-perfect.

leapt ahead and I envisaged more general results, but usually there was work to be done in finalising the step on which I was then engaged and I pushed further ideas to the back of my head without concerning myself with them.

I had several stalwart supporters who understood what I was doing. Sir Hermann Bondi had shared the early work when we found the analytic proof for enumerating the 4×4 magic squares. It was Hermann who had started me chasing answers for larger squares. When I found the answer for all most-perfect squares of a size that were powers of two and sent this to him on a postcard, I had an immediate reply: 'How about other multiples of 4, for example 12?'. This started a completely new train of thought and it took me the better part of two years to come up with a formula. After Robert died I made a habit of spending most of my time when alone at Hodge Close working on these squares. It kept me happy and occupied. When stuck (as I often was) I took the two little dogs, Max and Min, that I had acquired for company, for a run on the fells. Almost always some idea occurred to me which got me over a particular hump – and I was on course again.

I was often at Lancaster University for meetings of their council and the house-guest overnight of the vice-chancellor, Professor Harry Hanham and his wife, Ruth. He is an historian, with a real understanding of the way researchers work. I never left their house without feeling uplifted and with an enhanced sense of purpose in my mathematical efforts. Lancaster is almost exactly half way between my home in Manchester and the cottage at Hodge Close. Whenever I was driving between one and the other I called in on my erstwhile research assistant (on the 'Returning to Teaching' project) Christine Flude. Her husband, Ron, was a lecturer in the University's Department of Computer Studies. He had shown an interest in the magic squares and, when I called in, I discussed with him excitedly my latest ideas. Although not a mathematician, he was an experienced research-student supervisor and an ideal critic and friend. There was never a time when I was back on the motorway, continuing my journey to or from Hodge Close after a stop-off in Lancaster, without some significant progress.

Before an academic research paper, article or book is submitted for publication it is wise, even imperative, to have had the benefit of comments by someone who is willing and competent to make judgements on the content. Leaving aside actual mistakes or gaps in the argument, it is almost impossible in a long mathematical treatise not to have left some logical argument insufficiently clearly stated. Even the great mathematicians have usually had assistants or students to act as critics. The father of a friend who owns a cottage near ours at Hodge Close was a retired professor of mathematics, whom I had hoped to persuade to read the draft of my proposed book about these most-perfect squares. To my dismay and huge sorrow, I was told one day that he had developed a terminal cancer. On my return home, I was putting my car in the garage at the same time as the tenant who occupied the downstairs part of my house in Manchester – converted into a flat after Robert died. Almost in tears, I told him of this sadness and said that I did not know whom I could now approach for the help I sought. He replied with a remark that, between us now, has become historic: 'I'll read it if you like.' Professor David Brée, head of Artificial Intelligence in the Department of Computer Science in the University of Manchester, became my collaborator. We embarked on enumerating all most-perfect squares, the first enumeration of any defined infinite class of magic squares. Without him, it is unlikely that I would ever have succeeded, certainly I did not have the computer skills to express our result in its present form. Near the end he had an idea that greatly simplified our initial efforts. G.H. Hardy, in his 'Apology' wrote that the significance of a mathematical discovery lies in its generality. It is this generality that gives our magic square result its importance.

The book was expertly type-set by Bruce Goatly, an erstwhile assistant editor at the Royal Society whom I had met there some years before. His skills in presenting complex mathematical formulae were invaluable. He has since established a reputation for excellence working on his own. The IMA had from the beginning agreed to publish the book, which contains the proof of the construction and the formula giving the enumeration. *Most-Perfect Pandiagonal Magic Squares* was published in June 1998 and received international acclaim in leading scientific and mathematical journals, in particular in *Nature* and the *Scientific American*. There was a full-page article in the *Amsterdam Zaterdag* on 12 September and a television team travelled from Japan to make a recorded video interview with me which was broadcast on Tokyo Television on New Year's Eve 1998.

CHAPTER 30

Reflections on problem-solving

Mathematics is a way of thinking. It requires no tools or instruments or laboratories. It may be convenient to have pen and paper, a ruler and a compass, but it is not essential: Archimedes managed very well with a stretch of smooth sand and a stick for his magnificent discoveries in geometry. When Sir Hermann Bondi, as a noted cosmologist, gives a public lecture on relativity, he draws a wild circle with chalk on a blackboard to represent the universe – and this probably conveys the idea of immensity better than any sophisticated computer image. A professional mathematician does not, typically, have a good visual memory for the written word, yet many can give the value of π or the square root of 2 to an incredible number of decimal places – a useless but impressive exercise. I didn't have this gift, but I never forget a mathematical logic proof when once I have understood it – not over decades – and in this way experience accumulates. I never aspired to being a professional mathematician, or to being a professional anything for that matter. If you are deaf, you are glad to 'get by', to keep up with others in an ordinary classroom and not to be condemned as being lazy, inattentive or merely 'slow'. I worked carefully and accurately, getting answers right first time, and so became very fast. I always had time to spare for checking what I had written in mathematics tests or examinations and, for this reason, would do well. Mathematics is the one school subject not dependent on hearing. I was lucky with my teachers, but I was also to a large extent self-taught; reading books about the great mathematicians, solving problems set in magazines. I spent time solving (or devising) mathematical teasers, a habit that has continued through the years.

When I told a teenage friend that I was doing mathematical research, her reply was: 'Why do that? We have enough mathematics to cope with already – we don't want any more.' The renowned mathematician, G.H. Hardy (1877–1947) wrote in his *A Mathematician's Apology* in 1944, that the value of a mathematical discovery is measured not only by its originality, but by its generality and its usefulness in furthering new advances in understanding and knowledge.

In general, mathematicians do not invent problems, but they may find it necessary to invent new methods to tackle old ones. New problems tend to 'turn up', often by chance. We notice some phenomenon and this triggers the question – why? There is the example from my own experience: when a soap bubble falls onto a flat surface it forms a hemisphere that intersects the surface in a circle. When a froth of bubbles falls onto the surface they intersect the surface in random overlapping circles. To show this, I drew overlapping circles of different sizes on a piece of paper. I noticed that if straight lines were drawn through the points of intersection of these circles, then these lines (or 'chords') met in threes at a common point (see illustration).

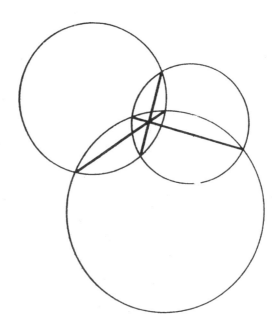

Something like this doesn't happen by chance; the challenge to prove mathematically that they 'must' intersect in this way was irresistible. There is a very pretty proof (given in some standard text books) that could have been learnt at school, although I had never come across it. I enjoyed the challenge of finding a proof for myself.

How are problems solved? Sometimes directly, but usually by having 'bright ideas' and experimenting to see if they fill the bill. We rarely work smoothly through to the end, but tend to jump about. We establish an hypothesis, a tentative objective or guessed answer, often working backwards for a certain distance: 'if that is so, then what would have been the immediate preceding stage in the proof that led up to it?' This narrows the gap between what we have deduced from the data and what we have conjectured. Intuition and experience sometimes then cause the spark that fills the gap and clinches the proof. This is a standard procedure and it has frequently worked for me, especially in examinations where we know that there is an answer, often given as the objective to be established. In original research there is often the difficulty that one does not know if there is an answer, let alone what it may be; targets are often raw guesses. Genius lies in perceiving and correctly annunciating the conjecture in the first place. This has to be supported by proof, that may again require genius, perhaps also the invention of new methods and, then, new notations with which to convey the methods to others. Publication of a new result, after verification by one's peers, is essential. Unless a result is available to be read, it does not exist; it is only a figment of the mind.

An interesting feature of much mathematical research is that the moment when the critical idea that leads to a solution flashes into the consciousness is almost always absolutely specific and can be recalled at will. We carry some problems in our heads all the time – sometimes even for months or years while dealing with other problems or coping with the daily grind. There is no predicting when (or if) this critical moment may occur. Once it happened to me disconcertingly when stepping onto a bus. On another occasion, after spending two days at a boring conference and making an equally boring long drive home alone, I was turning the key to our front door when the answer to a problem I had been pondering suddenly appeared. I ran into the house, saying to my husband, Robert: 'Sorry, darling, I'm on heat with an idea. Please get something to eat yourself. I must go and write it down before it slips away'. Sometimes there is no need to hurry: a sudden revelation can be so crystal clear that it is 'for ever', indelibly etched into the mind. Once I had been struggling for weeks with an n-dimensional geometrical problem. I was sitting on our settee at home darning Robert's socks. He was reading in his armchair on the opposite side of the fireplace. In this relaxed comfort, doing a routine job, I suddenly saw the solution to the problem. The answer that I had been seeking in vain for so long appeared so vividly that I stopped darning, the long needle in one hand, the wooden mushroom on which the heel of the sock was stretched in the other, and remarked calmly to Robert that I had 'got it'. I didn't leap up and jump for joy as I sometimes did, or dash to my desk to write it down; I knew absolutely that this was 'it' and that it would never escape me. An idea like that may take six months or more to develop, explain and prepare for publication – but, once a solution is made known and acknowledged by the mathematical community, time need not matter. This small triumph was of sufficient significance to appear later in standard European text books as *Ollerenshaw's result*.

For most people perhaps the stumbling block lies in the unavoidable use of symbols and the specialised language of mathematics. Artists, musicians, scientists of all kinds have their own ways of working. The artist sees in the sky not only varieties of white and grey and blue, but yellow and green and reds that ordinary observers do not notice – this expertise making all the difference in a notable work of art. The light and shade in a velvet skirt are reproduced to give a three-dimensional effect, impossible for the non-expert. The chemist needs a laboratory and substantiates ideas by actual observations – a contact with reality – in order to make progress and reach conclusions. This is a restriction that has no role for a pure mathematician, although the applied mathematician, designing a bridge or machinery, does need practical evidence of successful reasoning. Mozart's mind could have exuded limitless great music, but if he had no musical notation by which to convey this to others there would have been no public performances then and no concerts for us now. Even abstract art needs its language of communication: materials and paint. Today effects can be produced through the use of computer programs, enhancing colour, wiping out defects – but however technologically brilliant the process, the operator has to make the judgements to produce the artistic image that will satisfy the viewer.

Mathematics is a living activity with a living language, always developing to convey new concepts and new techniques for solving problems. This language can be a barrier to general understanding, putting people off, sometimes for life. It requires a gifted teacher to explain mathematics to the uninitiated in terms that he or she can understand from personal experience. I was fortunate. I was never taught mathematics other than by someone who was qualified to teach it and who loved it; and I have been fortunate in adult life to have met and made friends with mathematicians of distinction. The deafness was (and is) a hindrance to be battled with, but also a spur to effort; the mathematics has been the icing on the cake. I was also blessed from the start in having a passion for numbers. Numbers are fun and contain an infinity of mysteries.

An example (for optional reading)

The section that follows is written for readers who have some acquaintance with mathematics to A-level – and for the curiosity of any non-mathematician who may like to witness mathematics in action at a modest level. It is not part of the story and the reader should feel free to drop out at any stage and move straight to the Epilogue.

This is an example of a problem for which I knew no answer. It occurred to me while reading about the solution of Fermat's Last Theorem so famously arrived at by Andrew Wiles in 1994. After a bit of thought, I resolved the problem in my head while at a concert. A modicum of elementary algebra should be sufficient to understand the notation – otherwise it is only logic.

One mathematical definition is required: that of prime numbers, the basic building blocks of all number theory. *A prime number is a whole number larger than 1 that is divisible only by 1 and itself.* Thus 2, 3, 5, 7, . . . 101, . . . 1093, . . . and so on, are all primes. Euclid (c.300–250 BC) proved that there is an infinity of primes. He also enunciated what is known as the 'fundamental theorem of arithmetic', namely that *'every natural number other than 1 can be uniquely expressed as a product of primes.'* For example: $18 = 2 \times 3 \times 3$, and $819 = 3 \times 3 \times 13 \times 17$.

If for simplicity the numbers are all taken as positive, this statement is self-evident: it is however a deep and important truth.

We all know Pythagoras's theorem that *'in any right-angled triangle, the square on the hypotenuse is equal to the sum of the squares on the other two sides'*. Namely, if the two shortest sides of a right-angled triangle are of length x and y, and if z is the length of the long side opposite to the right-angle, then $x^2 + y^2 = z^2$. The numbers x, y, z that satisfy this equation are called *Pythagorean triads*.

Pythagorean triads

Define as a Pythagorean triad any set of three different positive whole numbers, x, y, z with no common factor other than 1 and such that $x^2 + y^2 = z^2$. Euclid, who was born in about 300 BC, some two centuries after Pythagoras, proved that there is an infinity of Pythagorean triads. To do this he showed that for any odd number 'x' (and there is an infinite number of odd numbers) there exists at least one triad satisfying the equation $x^2 + y^2 = z^2$. Here I give a method of construction for all Pythagorean triads and establish how many different triads there are for any particular finite value of x, where x is odd and, without loss of generality, we can assume that $x < y < z$.

Construction

A prime number is defined as a positive whole number greater than 1 that has no factors other than itself and 1. Notice that if x, y, z are the elements of a Pythagorean triad, then they have by definition no common factor; furthermore, two of them must be odd and one must be even (since odd + odd = even, and odd + even = odd, but even + even = even, giving the common factor 2, which does not satisfy the conditions). There is no loss of generality in taking x and z ($> y$) as odd and y then as even.

Use simple algebra to write the equation $x^2 + y^2 = z^2$ as

$$x^2 = z^2 - y^2 = (z - y)(z + y),$$

where $(z - y)$ and $(z + y)$ are, by definition, both positive whole numbers. A triad can then be arrived at by putting $z - y = 1$, so that $z + y = x^2$. For example, when $(x, y, z) = (3, 4, 5)$, then

$$x^2 \, (= 3^2) = (z - y)(z + y) = 9.$$

Put $z - y = 1$ and $z + y = 9$, to get

$$2z = 10, \text{ giving } z = 5, \text{ and}$$
$$y = z - 1 = 4,$$

giving the completed triad $x = 3$, $y = 4$, $z = 5$, and similarly for all odd values of $x > 1$.

For quick reference this method leads to the Pythagorean triads given by

$$3^2 = 5^2 - 4^2$$
$$5^2 = 13^2 - 12^2$$
$$7^2 = 25^2 - 24^2$$
$$9^2 = 41^2 - 40^2$$
$$11^2 = 61^2 - 60^2$$
$$13^2 = 85^2 - 84^2$$
$$15^2 = 113^2 - 112^2 \, (= 17^2 - 8^2)$$
$$17^2 = 145^2 - 144^2$$

and so on.

Enumeration

For each of the odd values of $x < 15$, there is one and only one Pythagorean triad, but when $x = 15$ which has two prime number factors: 3 and 5, i.e. $15 = 3 \times 5$, there are two different triads as shown. The second can be obtained from the relationship

$$x^2 = (z - y)(z + y)$$

by putting $z - y = 3^2 = 9$, $z + y = 5^2 = 25$, giving $z = 17$, $y = 8$ and hence the triad shown above. (Notice that, although $9 = 3^2$ is not prime, it is the square of a prime and fails to contribute a 'second' triad, because the procedure would mean that the three numbers x, y, z would have a common factor that could be divided out, leaving the triads 3, 4, 5, and 5, 12, 13, giving nothing new.)

What then are the working criteria for multiple Pythagorean triads? Consider again the equation $x^2 = z^2 - y^2 = (z - y)(z + y)$. With $x = 15 = 3 \times 5$, so that $x^2 = 225$, we can have, as shown, a triad given by $z - y = 1$ and $z + y = 225$, giving $z = 113$, $y = 112$, i.e. a first triad: 15, 112, 113; or, alternatively, $z - y = 9$, $z + y = 25$, giving $z = 17$, $y = 8$ and a second triad 15, 8, 17. There are no other possibilities.

As another example, consider $x = 3 \times 5 \times 7 = 105$, the product of three different primes, say $p_1 = 3$, $p_2 = 5$, $p_3 = 7$. The 'first triad' is given as before by

(i) $(z - y)(z + y) = 1 \times (105)^2 = 11025$, giving $z - y = 1$, $z + y = 11025$ and so $z = 5513$, $y = 5512$, i.e. $(105)^2 = (5513)^2 - (5512)^2$, which is correct.

The other three are given by

(ii) $z - y = (1 \times 3)^2 = 9$, $z + y = (5 \times 7)^2 = 1225$, giving $z = 617$, $y = 608$; $105^2 = 617^2 - 608^2$, which is correct, and

(iii) $z - y = (1 \times 5)^2 = 25$, $z + y = (3 \times 7)^2 = 441$, giving $z = 233$, $y = 208$, $105^2 = 233^2 - 208^2$, which is correct, and

(iv) $z - y = (1 \times 7)^2 = 49$, $z + y = (3 \times 5)^2 = 225$, giving $z = 137$, $y = 88$, $(105)^2 = (137)^2 - (88)^2$, which is correct. There are no other possibilities.

In general we know from Euclid's fundamental theorem of arithmetic that *every positive odd whole number is either itself prime or is the product of different prime numbers any of which can be raised to any power.* For example, $45 = 5 \times 9 = 3^2 \times 5$, and $405 = 3 \times 5 \times 27 = 3^4 \times 5$, both of which involve only two different prime numbers. We can therefore write the odd number x as

$$x = p_1 \cdot p_2 \cdot p_3 \cdot p_4 \cdot p_5 \cdots p_r \cdots p_n$$

where the dots represent multiplication and the 'p_r' are different primes each of which may have been raised to any positive whole-number power.

Note also that if the factors of x^2 when divided into the two factors $(z - y)$ and $(z + y)$ in such a way that $(z - y)$ and $(z + y)$ have a common factor, then all three of x, y, z have a common factor which can be cancelled, leaving no new triad. For example, if $x = 5 \times 9 = 3^2 \times 5$, so that $x^2 = 3^4 \times 5^2$ and we put $z - y = 3$ and $z + y = 3^3 \times 5^2$, then $2z = 3(1 + 27 \times 25)$, $2y = 3(27 \times 25 - 1)$, and all three of x, y, z have the common factor 3 which can be divided out to give the triad already obtained with $x = 15$, namely $15^2 = 113^2 - 112^2$.

It follows that the number of triads corresponding to each odd number x, which is not itself a prime but the product of n different prime factors raised to any powers, is given by *the number of different ways in which these different primes p_r can be divided into exactly two 'subsets', say A and B*. The first prime, say p_1, is either in the subset A or it is not (and then in B), so there are two possibilities. Likewise the second prime, say p_2, is either in group A or it is not, giving 2 multiplied by $2 = 2^2 =$ four possibilities. By continuing in this way, it follows that the number of possibilities when all the n different primes are taken into account is 2^n. But A and its complementary subset B generate the same 'partitions' and these are the only ways in which the total number of different prime factors can be divided into two different groups. Since A and its complement B are always distinct, every partition is counted twice. Hence the number of different options for the factors $(z - y)$ and $(z + y)$ is half of 2^n, namely 2^{n-1}. This then is the enumeration sought.

To check the examples above: when $x = 3$, or 5, or 7, or any one prime number raised to any power, e.g $x = 3^2 = 9$, so that $n = 1$, then the number of different triads is $2^{(1-1)} = 2^0 = 1$, and there is just one triad. When $x = 15 = 3 \times 5$, so that $n = 2$, then $2^{n-1} = 2^1$ and there are two different triads. When $x = 105 = 3 \times 5 \times 7$, so that $n = 3$, then $2^{n-1} = 2^2 = 4$ different triads as shown. This confirms the result.

There is another way of thinking about the different possibilities using an analogy that may be more familiar to the general reader and so easier to grasp. If we have one electric light there are two possibilities, either it is 'On' or it is 'Off'. If we have two lights, each of which can be switched On or Off independently, then they are 2 multiplied by 2, that is four, possibilities: they can both be Off; the first can be Off and the second On; the first can be On and the second Off; or they can both be On. If there are three lights, all with independent switches, for each of the four states when only two lights are involved, there are two possibilities created by the third switch being On or Off, making $2 \times 2 \times 2$ possibilities in all . . . and so on, until with n independent switches there are 2^n possibilities. Since the two groups formed by those with switches that are On and those that are Off are 'complementary', the total number of different arrangements is half of 2^n, namely 2^{n-1}. The pure mathematician will express these in a 'binary notation', with 0 standing for Off (or Out) and 1 standing for On (or In). Every whole number can be expressed in the binary scale by a combination of the symbols (digits) 0 and 1 put in specific order. On and Off switching has been the basis of computer systems from their very beginning.

Euclid's proof that there is an infinity of primes is one of the most beautiful classic mathematics proofs of all time and he proved that there is an infinity of Pythagorean triads. As far as I know, he did not give a method of construction for these triads or show how many different triads there are for any particular finite odd number 'x'. The answer is here shown to depend on the number of *different* prime factors (divisors) of 'x' and the number of different ways in which these can be placed in two distinct groups. This must almost certainly have long been known, but coming across this problem by chance for the first time when over the age of 90 and hitting on such a simple and elegant proof of the enumeration, even if it is only 're-discovering the wheel', brought me considerable satisfaction.

Pythagoras lived and established his famous School in the 6th Century BC. Euclid was born in about 300 BC and lived for about 40 years, his 'Elements' laying the foundations of number theory. Despite their prolific output and fame, little has survived that tells us of their lives. The third of these great Greek mathematicians, Archimedes of Syracuse, who lived between about 287 and 212 BC, may have studied under one of Euclid's pupils and would be well versed in contemporary number theory. His genius is usually recognised by his inventions in the applications of mathematics -- the lever, ships, engineering and the design of (potential) flying machines. Archimedes was killed by a Roman soldier in his home city Syracuse at the age of 85 in about 212 BC. He was so intent on a geometrical figure he had drawn in the sand he did not respond to answer a soldier's challenge. Or perhaps he was by then too hard of hearing.

Epilogue

I have lived a life of privilege, loved and cherished by my parents, never enduring poverty or hardship, and benefiting from the advantages of being educated within the private sector. There was an accepted code of strict honesty and a Protestant ethic of hard work and social obligation, of service to others less fortunate than oneself. It is not surprising that, when aged 40 I first had hearing aids and a little later found myself in public life, everything gradually became centred on the endeavour to help others as far as possible, to let them have the same opportunities as myself. This had been the keynote of my upbringing and that of most of my generation and background. According to my training and beliefs, it was the basis on which any final judgement of one's achievement would be made.

The passion for numbers and mathematics came to be regarded by the family merely as a hobby – which indeed it had become. It had however been the base from which everything had developed. All other serious occupations were a consequence of this, as I never had visions of some fine future, just the desire to do as well as I could at any task that confronted me, not to be defeated by circumstances and not to let people down. I knew that I would always need the help of others: it was therefore essential that I myself should help others whenever occasion arose.

The family and my relatives had never, at any time, been interested in the actual mathematics in which I indulged. They accepted and were glad that I was busily occupied and happy doing my 'sums', as Charles had called them when he was a little child. The success of the book which appeared in July 1998 giving the enumeration of the *most-perfect squares* and the glowing reviews came as a surprise, particularly to Charles who had probably viewed my preoccupation with magic squares as purely 'recreational'. We arranged a garden party at home in Manchester as celebration in October. Charles took a great interest and designed for the entertainment of guests a computer demonstration of the method of proof of the results. He was an inventor and a gifted electronic engineer, with long experience in computers, both hardware and software. He had spent several months between school and Oxford University with Philips in Eindhoven in the early days of computer development. He was working as a website master and he devised for my use a computer-generated presentation which demonstrates the method by which we enumerated the most-perfect magic squares. This is still in operation.

Charles and Margaret came to spend a few days with me at Hodge Close as usual between Christmas and New Year. It was plain that he was low in spirit, but we did not realise how low. I did not see him again. In the first week of January 1999 he died, aged 57.

In the summer of 1999 I was diagnosed as having 'age-related macular degeneration'. This was a major blow because it meant that I could no longer drive my car. I had been driving since my seventeenth birthday, averaging about 12,000 miles every year apart from the war years, mostly in long journeys and, in later years, in travelling to and from the Lake District. This blow greatly changed the way I organised my daily life, but it scarcely affected the work in mathematics, except that reading has gradually become more difficult. I cannot focus on a television screen, but I can still use my computer. I took up Braille as a precaution and quickly learnt the rules and the abbreviations which make reading and writing Grade II Braille possible. However, it would be almost useless in any meaningful way for reading or communicating advanced mathematics. If and when the time comes, when I really cannot see to read, I may make the effort to take Braille further, but meanwhile it is better for me to manage as well as I can. Unfortunately, even with improved technology, I find it harder now I am into my nineties to hear, as well as to see, but there is so much that is enjoyable still to be done that I can still do that I don't allow myself to indulge in worry. Now, as during all my life, it is the mathematical interest and the methods developed over the years to use this to overcome sadness or disappointment that keeps me in continual good heart.

About a year ago, sitting in a chair with my two dogs on my lap, I was astonished to see their coats seemingly covered in a thick white mesh of hexagonal lattices. I tried to wipe this away with my hand and realised that it was not real, merely some optical illusion; startling nonetheless. I went outdoors and looked down at the green grass of the lawn. It, too, was covered with a mesh of hexagons, in black, to the depth of about two feet, each hexagon about one tenth of an inch across. It was the same if I looked up at the clouds in the sky, at a flowering bush or any other object, with either the left or right eye alone, or with both eyes together. This persisted at all hours of the day whenever I had my eyes open, but was not there when my eyes were closed – in all conditions for exactly fourteen days. I made regular notes in my diary each day, until suddenly it had ceased; it had disappeared completely. By no effort of will or imagination could I bring it back, although the memory is vivid and precise. I was extremely busy. I told my doctor and reported it to my ophthalmologist, but could not afford the time at that moment to do anything about it, except to make the notes.

It transpires that this is a phenomenon first noticed and reported in the year 1670, that is over 300 years ago, by a Swiss doctor, Charles Bonnet, and the disease (CBS or Charles Bonnet Syndrome) is called after him. The illusions occur among elderly people who have had some eye damage. It is harmless and temporary, but can be alarming when first experienced, because the hallucinations are completely realistic and can seem to be actual solid objects or living beasts or people. Probably because of the increase in the number of people living into old age, this has recently become a subject for new research. The only rational explanation is that a hitherto active (or even over-active) brain has become starved of its erstwhile customary stimulation and compensates for this by re-activating images stored, perhaps many years before, somewhere within the cranium. An instance has been reported of a lady who from time to time saw Napoleon standing in front of her dressed in full uniform with all his medals. She cannot have seen this unless she had studied many pictures of Napoleon and was recalling them. Similarly it seems unlikely that I would have seen near-solid layers of hexagonal cylinders, sufficiently dense to black out my vision of the steps of a staircase which I needed to descend, unless I had been familiar through my mathematics with symmetrical images and models of patterns of this kind. I probably cannot help usefully in any research into this fascinating (if troublesome) phenomenon, unless the problem returns and investigations can be made by modern methods of what part of the brain is being thus activated.

One secret of finding a happy life, I would aver, is that talent shown when young, however esoteric, should be nurtured and never wholly neglected. We need luck, good luck, and we hope for as little bad luck and misfortune as possible, but it is inevitable that some things go wrong; and that, if we live beyond the average life expectancy, we lose some of the friends and relatives we treasure most. In times of trouble we need all the resources we can muster to fall back on.

Long developed interests have to be worked on, nurtured and constantly refreshed during the good times. A passionate interest in spiders or butterflies or dinosaurs; in spacecraft or satellites or the moon; in classical music or pop or poetry . . . or football. The subject needs to be taken seriously, read about, learnt about; the knowledge accumulating over the years into an expertise, even if one is not in actuality a practitioner. There may be long periods when the interest lapses or is interrupted, but the original knowledge is still there to be picked up again and updated when the opportunity presents itself. There is then something to turn to when the need for escape arises, as at some time it is sure to do. If that interest is not dependent on physical prowess, mobility, fitness or health, or even on good sight or hearing, then so much the better. My great good fortune was that I had this mathematics. With no high aspirations or ambition, I have been able to turn to it repeatedly when events have gone against me. Everything else has seemed, in retrospect, to have been ephemeral in comparison. Most of us have our bad moments. For me, when I have needed solace and I have had to depend on my own resources, the mathematics has been there. I am grateful.

My sister, Betty, died in July 2003 aged 94. Her husband, Roger Wood, had died in 1992 and gradually Betty lost her mobility and had to be cared for in a Home. When writing the early chapters of this book I spent time with her discussing our childhood and the twenty-one years we had been together under our parents' roof before her marriage in 1933. Although her short-term memory was failing, she could recall the names of our early childhood and school mistresses even more accurately than I could and we had many good laughs together. In particular, she remembered in detail the summer when it first became apparent that I was deaf and how distressed she was about it. When I was little she was very much my 'big sister'.

Towards the end she began not to recognise me and normal communication became almost impossible. But, with her lovely hair and smooth clear skin, she looked her serene and happy self, greeting those around her with her characteristic beatific smile. She died peacefully in her sleep. She was my only sibling; we never had a cross word or any differences. Although her death was expected, I was more desolate than I had imagined I could be. We had shared so much in childhood.

April 2004

Appendix:
three parlour tricks

Parlour trick 1: the False Penny Puzzle

There are twelve pennies all looking exactly alike, one of which is false but it is not known whether it is too light or too heavy. We have only a simple balance. The problem is to identify the false penny and say whether it is too light or too heavy in just three weighings. There are a variety of ways of solving this problem, but the main principles under-lie them all. From the variety of possibilities, this version has been chosen for its near symmetry of method.

Name the pennies 1, 2, 3, 4, 5, 6, 7, 8, 9, 10, 11, 12. The key to all the solutions is to divide the pennies into three equal groups, say, 1 2 3 4; 5 6 7 8; 9 10 11 12, and then to keep them in groups of three as illustrated below.

Step 1. Weigh two groups against one another, say, 1 2 3 4 versus 5 6 7 8. If

$$1\ 2\ 3\ 4 = 5\ 6\ 7\ 8$$

then all must be good pennies and the false penny must be one of the third group 9 10 11 12. In this case, 'borrow' three of the good pennies, say 1 2 3, and weigh

$$9\ 10\ 11\ \text{versus}\ 1\ 2\ 3.$$

(i) If 9 10 11 = 1 2 3, then these are all good and the false penny has to be the remaining penny, 12. Weigh this against any other (good) penny to determine whether it is too light or too heavy.

(ii) If 9 10 11 < 1 2 3, then the false penny must be among them and so 12 is good and one of 9 10 11 is light. Weigh 9 versus 10. If they balance then 11 is the false (light) penny. If they do not balance, then the lighter of the two is the false (light) penny.

(iii) Similarly, if 9 10 11 > 1 2 3, then one of 9 10 11 is heavy. Weigh 9 versus 10. If they balance, then 11 is the false (heavy) penny. If they do not balance, then the heavier of the two is the false (heavy) penny.

Step 2. If the two groups 1 2 3 4, 5 6 7 8 do not balance, then the false penny must be among them and the four pennies 9 10 11 12 are all good. Suppose, without loss of generality, that

$$1\ 2\ 3\ 4 < 5\ 6\ 7\ 8$$

'Borrow' three of the good pennies, interchange the positions of the pennies 4 and 5, and weigh

$$1\ 2\ 3\ 5 \text{ versus } 4\ 9\ 10\ 11.$$

(i) If 1 2 3 5 = 4 9 10 11, then these must all be good and so the false penny must be one of 6, 7, 8 and must be heavy. Weigh 6 versus 7. If they balance, then the false (heavy) penny must be 8. If they do not balance, then the false (heavy) penny is the heavier of the two.

(ii) If 1 2 3 5 < 4 9 10 11, then the false penny must be among them. As the pennies 4 and 5 have 'changed sides' (compared with 1 2 3 4 < 5 6 7 8 assumed at Step 2), without affecting the balance, they must both be good. Hence one of 1 2 3 has to be the false (light) penny. Weigh 1 versus 2. If they balance, then 3 is the false (light) penny. If they are unequal, then the lighter is false.

(iii) Similarly if 1 2 3 5 > 4 9 10 11, then either 4 is light or 5 is heavy. Weigh 4 against any good penny. If it is light then it is the false penny. If it balances, then 5 is the false (heavy) penny.

This covers all possibilities and solves the puzzle.

Parlour trick 2: the Magic Card Square

Arrange the 16 court cards from a pack (the Ace, King, Queen and Jack of Spades, Hearts, Diamonds and Clubs) in a four-by-four array, in such a manner that no row, no column and neither of the two diagonals contain more than one card of each rank or more than one card of each suit.

From these conditions it follows that there is one and only one card of each rank, and one and only one card of each suit in each row, in each column and in each of the two diagonals.

Denote the suits by S, H, D, C respectively and the ranks by A, K, Q, J respectively. Label the positions in the square as

	0	1	2	3
0	00	01	02	03
1	10	11	12	13
2	20	21	22	23
3	30	31	32	33

Start by considering the possible positions of cards of the same rank.

Step 1. Place any card, say, the Ace of Spades (AS) in the top left corner (00). *(Sixteen choices.)*

Step 2. Choose any one of the remaining three aces, say, the Ace of Hearts (AH) *(three choices)* and place it in the second row. It cannot be at position 10 or 11, so must be at 12 or 13. Choose 12 *(two choices)*.

Step 3. Choose one of the remaining two aces, say the Ace of Diamonds (AD) *(two choices)* and place in the third row. This now has to be at 23. The remaining ace (AC) must then be at 31.

The aces are now placed as shown below.

```
AS   ..   ..   ..
..   ..   AH   ..
..   ..   ..   AD
..   AC   ..   ..
```

This has been arrived at, thus far, by exercising

$$16 \times 3 \times 2 \times 2 \text{ random choices.}$$

Note the pattern formed by the aces. This pattern, with its reflections in the vertical, and horizontal axes and in the diagonals, must prevail for all cards of the same suit or of the same rank.

All four suits now have one member in each row/column/diagonal. The positions of all 16 cards of the four suits are thus determined and can be written in as shown.

```
AS  .H  .D  .C
.C  .D  AH  .S
.H  .S  .C  AD
.D  AC  .S  .H
```

It remains only to choose which ranks of cards are needed to fill the gaps while still adhering to the pattern for each rank. Choose the King (of Hearts) to fill the position at 01 (*three choices*), and then the Queen (of Diamonds) to fill the position at 02 (*two choices*). This leaves the Jack (of Clubs) to fill the position 03 (*no choices*), giving the solution below.

```
AS  KH  QD  JC
JC  QD  AH  KS
QH  JS  KC  AD
KD  AC  JS  QH
```

The number of choices has been:

$$16 \times 3 \times 2 \times 2 \times 3 \times 2 = 16 \times 9 \times 8 = 144 \times 8.$$

This total includes the eight permissible flections. The number of 'essentially different' solutions that exclude reflections and rotations, is therefore 144.

Parlour trick 3: Dürer's Magic Square

Ask someone to construct a 4×4 magic square using the first sixteen numbers – 1 to 16 – and there may be hesitation. It is useful to have one in the mind that can be produced at will. The easiest to remember permanently is perhaps the square that appears in the famous picture *Melancholia* by Albrecht Dürer (1471–1528), namely:

$$
\begin{array}{cccc}
16 & 3 & 2 & 13 \\
5 & 10 & 11 & 8 \\
9 & 6 & 7 & 12 \\
4 & \mathbf{15} & \mathbf{14} & 1
\end{array}
$$

The square appears in the top-right corner of the picture. The numbers of the square, in the rows, columns and the two diagonals all add up to 34. It is 'symmetrical', that is, all pairs of numbers that are reflections in the centre are 'complementary' adding to 17. The date 1514, when the picture was painted, appears in the two middle cells of the bottom row. If it is also remembered that the number 16 is in the top left corner of the square (so that the number 1 is in the bottom right corner) and that the principal diagonal is 16, 10 (7) (1), then the other numbers can be filled in at sight.

Honours and appointments

1954 Appointed a co-opted member of Manchester Education Committee

1954 Member of Council of St Leonards School, St Andrews
   1980–2003 President

1954–86 Member of governing body of Salford Royal Technical College, later University of Salford
   1976   Hon DSc.
   1983–89 Pro-Chancellor

1956–81 Elected member of Manchester City Council
   1956–67 Deputy Chairman, then Chairman, Further Education Sub-committee
   1967–71 Chairman, Education Committee
   1968–71 Deputy Chairman, Finance Committee
   1975–76 Lord Mayor
   1981–   Hon Alderman
   1984–   Hon Freeman of the City

1958–67 Chairman, Association of Governing Bodies of Girls' Public Schools

1960 Hon Fellow, College of Preceptors (now the College of Teachers)

1960–63 Member of Central Advisory Council for Education (England)

1960–73 Member of Education Committee, City and Guilds of London Institute
   1980   Hon Fellow

1960–74 Founder Governor, Further Education Staff College, Blagdon

1963   Member of British Association for Commercial and
          Industrial Education delegation to USSR

1964   Foundation Fellow, Institute of Mathematics and its
          Applications
          1978–79   President
          1986   Hon Fellow (Chartered Mathematician)

1964–74 Member of Council for National Academic Awards
          1975   Hon DSc

1965   Winifred Cullis Visiting Fellow to USA

1966–72 General Advisory Committee, BBC

1967–71 Chairman of Education Committee, Association of
          Municipal Corporations

1967–71 Management Panel, Burnham Committee on Teachers'
          Salaries

1967–71 First Chairman, Manchester Polytechnic, later Manchester
          Metropolitan University
          1972   Hon Fellow

1968–73 Chairman, Joint Education Committee for creation of
          Northern College of Music, later the Royal Northern College
          of Music
          1973–86   First Chairman of Court of Royal Northern
                     College of Music
          1976   Companion

1971   Dame Commander of the Order of the British Empire (DBE)

1971–74 Member of Social Science Research Council and of
          Technical Education Council

1972–74 Part-time research fellow, Department of Educational
          Research, University of Lancaster
          1975–91   Member of Council and Court

1986–92   Deputy Pro-Chancellor
1992   Hon LlD

1972–83 Foundation Director, Manchester Independent Radio
(Piccadilly Radio)

1973–91 First Chairman, Council for the Order of St. John of
Jerusalem, Greater Manchester
       1980–94   Member of Chapter General, Order of St. John
       1983   Dame Commander of the Order of St. John
               (DStJ)

1974–76 Member of Layfield Committee on Financing of Local
Government

1976   Hon LlD   Victoria University of Manchester
           1964–99   Member of Court
           1978–   Member of Military Education Committee
           1999–2003 Hon Research Fellow, Department of Computer
               Science

1976   *Mancunian of the Year* award (Junior Chamber of Commerce)

1977–81 Hon Colonel, Manchester and Salford Universities Officer
Training Corps

1978–   Hon Fellow, Somerville College, Oxford

1979   President, Manchester Technology Association

1979   Government representative at President Jimmy Carter's
Conference on Central/Local Government Relations,
Washington DC

1979–80 President, Manchester Statistical Society

1980–   Hon Member, Manchester Literary and Philosophical
Society

1983–86 Vice President, University of Manchester Institute of
Science and Technology
       1987   Hon Fellow

1985–87 Representative for North-West England on TSB Foundation for England and Wales

1987– Deputy Lieutenant, Greater Manchester County

1994 Hon LlD, Liverpool University

1996– Hon Member, Manchester Astronomical Society

2003– Patron, Museum of Science and Industry, Manchester

Index

Abbott, Edwin (1808–82, author of *Flatland*), 19
alderman, office of, 167–8
Alexander, William (1905–93, Baron Alexander of Potterhill, Secretary to the Association of Education Committees 1945–77), 86
Alexandra, HRH Princess (Chancellor of Lancaster University 1964–2004), 131–2
American Journal of Mathematics, 224
Amsterdam, 191–2
Amsterdam Zaterdag, 228
Anderton, James (Kt 1971, Chief Constable of Greater Manchester Police 1976–91 and Commander of St. John Ambulance for Greater Manchester 1989–96), 179
Andrew, Sir Herbert (1910–85, Permanent Secretary, Department of Education and Science 1963–70), 151
apprenticeship system, 115
Archimedes, 201, 229, 238
Archimedes' screw, 3
Armstrong, Anne (US Ambassador to the UK 1976–77), 175
Ashworth, John (Vice-Chancellor of Salford University 1981–90,

Director of London School of Economics 1990–96), 181
Association of American University Women (AAUW), 150, 159
Association of Education Committees, 86
Association of Governing Bodies of Girls' Public Schools, 87–8, 124
Association of Municipal Corporations (AMC), 108, 123–6
Auchterlonie, Laurie (Open Golf Champion 1893), 26
Audland, Sir Christopher (former diplomat, Pro-Chancellor of Lancaster University 1990–97), 131

Barbirolli, John (1899–1970, Kt 1949, CH 1969, celebrated conductor, resident with the Hallé 1943–68), 47–8, 162
Barnard, George (professor of mathematics, adviser to the government on census design, President of IMA 1968–70), 197
Baum, Vera (*née* Stops, aunt, 1899–2004), 86
Bayreuth, 49

Index compiled by Martin Hargreaves, member of the Society of Indexers, under the direction of the author